PHILOSOPHY FOR A2

Philosophy for A2 is an engaging textbook for the new AQA A2 Philosophy syllabus. Structured closely around the AQA specification this textbook covers the two units, Ethics and Philosophy of Mind, in a comprehensive and student-friendly way. All of the anthology texts are explained and commented on and woven into the discussion of the syllabus. With chapters on 'How to Do Philosophy' an⸝ provides students with the philosophic⸝

Each chapter includes:

- explanation and commentary of the⸝
- comprehension questions to test u⸝
- discussion questions to generate e⸝
- 'going further' sections for advance⸝
- cross-references to help students ⸝
- bullet-point summaries of each top⸝

The companion website hosts a wealt⸝ PowerPoint slides, flashcards, further re⸝ structured to accompany the textbook. I⸝ com/cw/alevelphilosophy.

Michael Lacewing is Senior Lecturer in⸝ University of London. He is the founder o⸝ and a consultant on philosophy at A L⸝ Association.

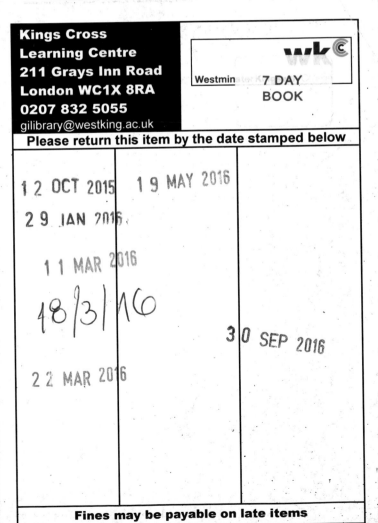

Praise for this edition:

'This excellent textbook covers an impressive range of material with admirable clarity and concision. The structure of Lacewing's exposition is such as to secure the central points, and then to provide readers with opportunities to "go further" – to venture more deeply and to explore topics in more detail. Highly pertinent use is made of a wealth of argumentation and illustration drawn from relevant anthologised textual sources. In addition, there are helpful syllabus checklists, chapter summaries, and well-chosen questions throughout. An invaluable guide.'
Dr Paul Dawson, *Head of Philosophy at King Alfred's School and Teacher of Philosophy at University College School, UK*

'*Philosophy for A2* has all the virtues that teachers and students have come to expect from Lacewing. It is crystal clear, accurate and authoritative. It is very difficult to find a Philosophy textbook which is truly accessible to sixth form students and equally acceptable to professional philosophers. But this book is surely both. The hard-pressed teacher will find here a resource that he or she can completely trust and rely upon. The student will find a text which is written in a clear, intelligible and engaging style. This is a model textbook and every school sixth form should possess at least one class set.'
Geoff Willis, *Senior Area Leader for Humanities, Literature and Languages, City of Stoke-on-Trent Sixth Form College, UK*

'Accessible for students at different levels and invaluable for teachers who want to ensure they cover all the relevant material for the new syllabus. Clear summaries of the main arguments and concise explanations of key extracts from the anthology make this textbook an essential resource for anyone taking the new A2 AQA Philosophy qualification.'
Agnes Orosz, *A Level Philosophy Teacher, UCL Academy, UK*

PHILOSOPHY FOR A2

Ethics and Philosophy of Mind

Michael Lacewing

Routledge
Taylor & Francis Group

LONDON AND NEW YORK

First published 2015
by Routledge
2 Park Square, Milton Park, Abingdon, Oxon OX14 4RN

Simultaneously published in the USA and Canada
by Routledge
711 Third Avenue, New York, NY 10017

Routledge is an imprint of the Taylor & Francis Group, an informa business

British Library Cataloguing in Publication Data
A catalogue record for this book is available from the British Library

Library of Congress Cataloging in Publication Data
Lacewing, Michael, 1971–
Philosophy for A2 : ethics and philosophy of mind / by Michael Lacewing.
pages cm
Includes bibliographical references and index.
1. Philosophy--Textbooks. I. Title.
BD21.L177 2015
107.6--dc23
2014043527

ISBN: 978-1-138-83787-4 (pbk)
ISBN: 978-1-315-73483-5 (ebk)

Typeset in Mixage
by Saxon Graphics Ltd, Derby

MIX
Paper from
responsible sources
FSC® C013604
www.fsc.org

Printed and bound by CPI Group (UK) Ltd, Croydon, CR0 4YY

CONTENTS

Westminster Kingsway College

Customer name: Tuan Jason HOANG
Customer ID: 20324713

Title: AQA philosophy for A2: ethics and
philosophy of mind
ID: SY189350
Due: 24 January 2018

Total items: 1
17/01/2018 13:35
Checked out: 1
Overdue: 0
Hold requests: 0
Ready for pickup: 0

Thank you for using the
PSP Asset Protection Self Service.

ACKNOWLEDGEMENTS

Thanks to Rebecca Shillabeer and Tony Bruce at Routledge for supporting this textbook, and to my colleagues at Heythrop College for supporting my work with A level philosophy. Thanks also to the AQA subject team for answering a number of queries on the interpretation of the syllabus. And a special thanks goes to Joanne Lovesey for her stellar work on compiling the glossary.

INTRODUCTION

The AQA A2 Level Philosophy continues the introduction, begun at AS, to some key concepts and methods in philosophy, studied as an academic discipline. It raises two big philosophical questions: 'How do we make moral decisions?' and 'Are my mind and body separate?' As with the AS, it introduces you to the debates over these philosophical questions by considering some of the very best attempts to answer these questions, the arguments of some of the very best philosophers in history as well as recent discussions.

For those readers who are familiar with my *Philosophy for AS* textbook, many of the points in this introduction are the same. But I include them here both as a reminder and for any readers who do not know the other textbook. There are also some points, particularly under FOLLOWING THE SYLLABUS (p. 2) and USING THE ANTHOLOGY (p. 3), that are different.

One aim of this textbook is, of course, to cover the ideas and arguments that are on the syllabus. But it aims at more than that. First, it aims to show you *how* to do philosophy – not just to tell you, but to show you, what philosophical thinking and philosophical writing is like. This is important because the A level aims to introduce the methods of philosophy, as well as the ideas. Second, it aims to get you *engaging* in the argument. The discussion is provocative and leaves many lines of thought hanging. So, for instance, you might come up with new objections or replies that haven't yet been discussed, or argue that a particular point is convincing or implausible. That's the idea. This textbook doesn't try to tell you what *should* be said, only (some of) what *could* be said. That leads to one important difference between this book and your essays. The book tries to be even-handed, and doesn't often draw firm conclusions.

In your evaluative essays, you'll be expected to defend a particular point of view.

How to use this book

How to do philosophy

Having completed the AS philosophy course, you'll have learned that philosophy involves reading and thinking in very particular ways. Chapter 1 is about how to reason, read, and write philosophically. It is repeated from *Philosophy for AS*, and included here so you don't need to keep turning to the other book. It is intended as a resource to which you can return again and again, as and when you need to. But you may want to remind yourself of how PHILOSOPHICAL ARGUMENT (p. 7) works and the best ways of ENGAGING WITH THE TEXT (p. 15) before going on to study Chapter 2.

Each paragraph of Chapters 2 and 3 is intended to be taken as a thought to be considered, re-read, and reflected on. *Philosophy needs to be read slowly, and more than once, to be understood.* You will probably find, in addition, that you are not able to completely understand a particular theory until you also understand rival theories that oppose it. And so, at the end of each major section (e.g. 'Ethical Theories'), you may feel that you need to return to earlier discussions, to think about them again in the light of what you learned later.

Following the syllabus

Ethics is covered in Chapter 2 and philosophy of mind in Chapter 3. Each chapter opens with a brief synopsis of what the chapter covers and what you should be able to do by the end of it. This is followed by the AQA syllabus, which I have structured by topic and subtopic. On the whole, I have continued to use the bullet points from the syllabus to structure the discussion, with each section further divided by the main ideas, arguments and objections. However, I have not followed the bullet points strictly or in the order they appear in the syllabus. I was able to explain the ideas, theories, objections and debates more clearly by rearranging them. The table of contents, with its many headings and subheadings, shows how each part relates to the others. There is also an INDEX BY SYLLABUS CONTENT on p. 355, which provides the page numbers on which each bullet point of the syllabus is discussed.

Additional features

Alongside the text, there are a number of features in the margin. Most commonly, there are questions that test your understanding and cross-references to other relevant discussions and ideas. To get the most out of the book, stop and answer the questions – in your own words – as you go along. The questions are the kinds that you'll find on the exam, so it is good practice for that. It is also worth following up cross-references, especially when you have read, but forgotten, the sections referred to. Understanding philosophy is often about being able to make connections. Also in the margin are occasional illustrations; definitions of technical terms; and references to philosophical texts where the argument being discussed can be found.

You'll frequently come across sections called 'Going Further'. These discuss more difficult ideas or take the theories and arguments further. So they will broaden and deepen your knowledge, and help you 'go further' in your understanding and evaluation of philosophical issues.

At the end of each main section covering a theory or debate, there is a list of 'Key Points', summarising clearly the main issues the section has covered. And at the end of each topic, there is a 'Summary' in the form of a list of questions, to show what issues have been addressed. Both the Key Points and the Summary should help with exam revision and testing your knowledge.

Using the anthology

The syllabus includes a list of texts. Many of the arguments identified in the syllabus content come from these texts. You aren't expected to read all the texts (though it would be good to try to read some of them), but you are expected to understand and be able to evaluate the central arguments they present. To help with this, you'll find these texts and the arguments they present discussed in 'Anthology' boxes. All the texts listed in the syllabus are discussed at some point, and they are included in the index by syllabus content, so you can look up the discussion of any text in order of author.

The syllabus for Ethics is very heavily based around texts, and the anthology includes a number of lengthy texts, including Mill's *Utilitarianism* and Aristotle's *Nicomachean Ethics*. So a substantial portion of the chapter is given to discussing them. For this reason, the chapter on Ethics is longer than the chapter on Philosophy of Mind. This is your opportunity to really 'get inside' a system of thought, a detailed exposition of a single theory. It is worth trying to read at least one of Mill or Aristotle, and not only the commentary provided here. It provides a different kind of experience about how philosophy is done.

By contrast, Philosophy of Mind is very focused on positions within an ongoing debate. With the exception of Ryle's *The Concept of Mind*, the texts for Philosophy of Mind are fairly short. However, some texts, for instance some of the papers by Chalmers, Jackson and Putnam, are very difficult and technical. In these cases, it is really just the core idea of the paper that is relevant to the A level. It is in the Philosophy of Mind that you will find the most challenging philosophical discussions on the A level. So although the chapter is shorter than the chapter on Ethics, it will probably take just as long to work through and understand.

Where the syllabus identifies a particular edition of a text, in print or online, I have used that edition for page numbers and quotations. Where the syllabus doesn't specify a particular edition, then I have indicated the edition or online source that I have used.

Glossary

The glossary provides brief definitions for an extensive list of terms. We have included terms that have a technical philosophical use, that identify an important philosophical concept, or that name a theory, argument or objection. While such terms are explained in the text, if you can't understand or remember the explanation, use the glossary to help you. It should also prove a useful resource for revision.

Companion website and further resources

You can find further resources supporting the study of AQA Philosophy on the Routledge companion website, www.routledge.com/cw/alevelphilosophy. The resources include

1. handouts based on this text, including material on philosophical skills, revision and exam technique
2. PowerPoint presentations
3. further-reading lists
4. helpful weblinks
5. flashcards, for revising and testing your knowledge of philosophical terms and the names of theories and objections
6. the AQA list of texts with links where provided, and
7. an additional chapter providing commentary on Descartes' *Meditations*, which the syllabus identifies as a key text for the A level as a whole.

HOW TO DO PHILOSOPHY

1

Philosophy is thinking in slow motion.

John Campbell

This chapter repeats Chapter 1 of my *Philosophy for AS: Epistemology and Philosophy of Religion*, amended as appropriate to be relevant to A2. It is included here for convenience, so you don't need to refer to the other book for information and reminders on how to do philosophy well.

This chapter covers three skills that you need to do philosophy well: reasoning (or argument), reading and writing. Assuming that you are studying for A2 Philosophy, so you have studied philosophy for a year, you will be familiar with how philosophy works. But you can read the chapter through now, as a reminder of the skills that are central, or come back to it when you need to.

Philosophical argument

At the heart of philosophy is philosophical argument. Arguments are different from assertions. Assertions are simply stated; arguments always involve giving reasons. An argument is a reasoned inference from one set of claims – the premises – to another claim, the conclusion. The premises provide reasons to believe that the conclusion is true. If the premises are true, the conclusion is more likely to be true. Arguments seek to 'preserve truth' – true premises will lead to a true conclusion. It is worth knowing a little bit more about arguments straightaway.

Deductive argument

Philosophers distinguish between two types of argument – deductive and inductive. Successful deductive arguments are *valid* – if the premises are true, then the conclusion *must* be true. In this case, we say that the conclusion is entailed by the premises. Here is a famous example:

> Premise 1: Socrates is a man.
> Premise 2: All men are mortal.
> Conclusion: Socrates is mortal.

A valid deductive argument with true premises is called *sound*. But a valid deductive argument doesn't have to have true premises. Here is an example:

> Premise 1: There are gnomes in my house.
> Premise 2: My house is in Oxford.
> Conclusion: Therefore, there are gnomes in Oxford.

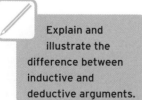

Give an example of a) an invalid argument; b) a valid argument with false premises; and c) a sound argument.

If the premises are true, then the conclusion must be true – so the argument is valid. But the premises aren't both true.

There are two ways that a deductive argument can 'go wrong'. First, it could be *invalid*: even if the premises are true, it is possible that the conclusion might be false. Second, it could be *unsound*: even though the conclusion is entailed by the premises, at least one of the premises is false.

Inductive argument

Explain and illustrate the difference between inductive and deductive arguments.

A successful inductive argument is an argument whose conclusion is supported by its premises. If the premises are true, the conclusion is *likely* to be true, but it is still possible that the conclusion is false. So inductive arguments are not described as 'valid' or 'sound'.

But they can also go wrong in just two ways. First, the premises might not make the conclusion more likely – they don't offer good reasons for believing the conclusion is true. Second, one of the premises may be false.

One type of induction is induction through enumeration, as in this famous example:

Premise 1: This swan is white.
Premise 2: This other swan is white.
Premise 3: That third swan is white.
…
Premise 500: That swan is white as well.
Conclusion: All swans are white.

The example shows that an inductive argument can be a good argument, but the conclusion can still be false!

Hypothetical reasoning

> A hypothesis is a proposal that needs to be confirmed or rejected by reasoning or experience.

There are other types of inductive argument, e.g. hypothetical reasoning. In hypothetical reasoning, we try to work out the best hypothesis that would explain or account for some experience or fact.

Medical diagnosis provides an example – what would explain exactly *this* set of symptoms? This isn't a matter of comparing this case with other cases which all have exactly the same symptoms. There may only be some overlap or the case might involve some complication, such as more than one disease being involved. We use hypothetical reasoning – if such-and-such were true (e.g. the patient has disease x), would that explain the evidence we have? The evidence supplies the premises of the argument, and the conclusion is that some hypothesis is true because it accounts for the evidence.

When we are using hypothetical reasoning, it is not usually enough to find some hypothesis that can explain the evidence. We want to find the *best* hypothesis. What makes a hypothesis a *good* hypothesis? Philosophers have argued for several criteria.

1. Simplicity: the best-known is probably Ockham's razor, which says 'Don't multiply entities beyond necessity'. Don't put forward a hypothesis that says many different things exist when a simpler explanation will do as well. A simpler explanation is a better explanation, as long as it is just as successful. For example, the

explanation that plants flower in the spring in response to an increase in light and temperature is a better explanation than saying that they flower in the spring because that's when the fairies wake them up. The second explanation is committed to the existence of fairies – and we shouldn't think that fairies exist unless there is something we cannot explain without thinking they exist.

2. Accuracy: a good hypothesis fits the evidence that we are trying to explain.
3. Plausibility: a good hypothesis fits with what else we already know.
4. Scope: a good hypothesis explains a wide range of evidence.
5. Coherence: a good hypothesis draws and explains connections between different parts of the evidence.

What makes a good hypothesis?

The best hypothesis will be the hypothesis that demonstrates all these virtues to a higher degree than alternative hypotheses. A lot of philosophy involves arguing about which theory provides the best hypothesis to account for our experience.

Understanding arguments

See UNDERSTANDING THE QUESTION, p. 314.

Understanding arguments is central to doing philosophy well. That is why throughout this book, you will be asked to outline and explain arguments. You'll be asked to do so in the exam, in 5- and 12-mark questions.

Understanding an argument involves identifying the conclusion, identifying the premises, and understanding how the premises are supposed to provide reasons for believing the conclusion. Use linguistic clues, like 'since', 'because', 'if … then …' and many others, to help you do this. It is also important to distinguish between what someone supposes for the purposes of argument, and what they actually want to assert.

Search the internet for 'argument mapping' to find lots of helpful information on how to construct argument maps and even free software for doing so.

Many arguments involve quite a complex structure, with some premises establishing an initial conclusion, which is then used as a premise to establish a second conclusion. In coming to understand an argument, it can be very helpful to create an *argument map*. This is a visual diagram of how the argument works. For example,

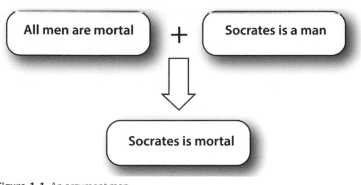

Figure 1.1 An argument map

Evaluating arguments

When you evaluate an argument, you are yourself *making* an argument. You are arguing that the argument evaluated is either a good or bad argument. In other words, the conclusion of your evaluation is that the argument evaluated is a good/bad argument, and you have to provide reasons to support this claim. There are three types of reason you can give, three different ways of evaluating arguments:

1. As already stated above, you can argue that one or more of the premises is false. If you are right, then the argument does not give you a reason to believe the conclusion, because it rests on a false premise.
2. As also already stated above, you can argue that the conclusion does not follow from the premises. If you are evaluating a deductive argument, you are claiming that the argument is not valid. If you are evaluating an inductive argument, you are claiming that the premises do not provide a (good or strong) reason to believe the conclusion. For example, with inferring the best hypothesis, you could argue that the conclusion is not the best explanation for the premises (e.g. that it isn't plausible or simple), or at least that the argument doesn't show that it is (e.g. there may be other explanations that haven't been considered).
3. You can also evaluate the formal features of an argument. Without worrying about whether it is true, you can ask whether it is clear,

whether the premises are relevant to the conclusion, whether the support offered by the premises has been demonstrated, and so on. You may want to offer an improvement on the argument, e.g. rephrasing it to be clearer, supplying missing premises, identifying assumptions, and so on.

Evaluating claims

In addition to evaluating arguments, you can evaluate claims on their own. In evaluating a claim, you provide an argument for thinking that it is true or false.

For any claim C (e.g. 'God exists'), there are four related ways of discussing it, as shown in this diagram:

C is true: God exists	C is false: God does not exist
1 Arguments for C being true	2 Arguments for C being false
3 Objections to arguments for C being false	4 Objections to arguments for C being true

When you are arguing for or against a claim, don't overstate your case. Your claim is only as strong as the reasons that you can provide for it.

See UNDERSTANDING THE QUESTION, p. 314.

In 25-mark questions, you are typically asked to evaluate a claim. You need to break this down into a series of arguments and their evaluation (discussed below in WRITING PHILOSOPHY, p. 16). After you've explained the claim, for each section of the answer, you should consider an argument for or against the claim, objections to that argument, and possible responses. You'll also need to indicate how *strong* you think the argument is, and weigh up the strengths of the arguments for the claim against the strengths of the arguments against. This isn't a matter of 'comparing strengths and weaknesses' on the page, but identifying what you think the *really important and critical* arguments or objections are. This is, of course, something that you need to argue for!

An aside: why reason?

Why, you may wonder, should we place so much importance on reasoning in this way? Is it worth it? Here are four quick reasons in favour of reasoning:

1. To discover the truth
2. To uncover poor reasoning, e.g. fallacies (see below) and sophistry
3. To recognise when, where, and how a dialogue ceases to be reasonable or instructive
4. To probe both sides of a controversial issue in a sensitive and intelligent way

Can I justify these claims? If I present an argument in favour of reasoning, then I'm using reasoning to justify reasoning, which is circular. Then again, if you object to reasoning for this reason, you are using reasoning to make your objection! An alternative justification of reason is to check the results of reasoning by a different method. Science does this all the time by hypothesis and observation. In many cases, we can confirm, by observation, that the conclusion of a piece of reasoning is correct. Some people are sceptical about reasoning or claim, for example, that all beliefs are equally 'reasonable'. For an excellent discussion dismantling this view, see Stephen Law's *Believing Bullshit*, Ch. 4.

To criticise an argument or claim is not necessarily to reject it. You can be concerned to reject bad reasons because you want to find stronger ones! To show respect to someone does not require that you agree with them. Taking someone else's thought seriously – so seriously that you test it rigorously in your mind – is to pay them a compliment.

It is important to remember that the *point* of philosophical argument is not personal victory.

Fallacies

A fallacy, as philosophers use the word, is not a mistake of fact or truth. A fallacy is an error in reasoning. More exactly, it is an argument in which the premises do not offer rational support to the conclusion. If the argument

See 'Fallacies', at
www.nizkor.org/
features/fallacies/;
'Fallacies: alphabetic
list (unique)', at
http://changingminds.
org/disciplines/
argument/fallacies/
fallacies_unique.htm;
and 'List of fallacies',
at http://en.wikipedia.
org/wiki/List_of_
fallacies

is deductive, then it is fallacious if it is not valid. If the argument is inductive, it is fallacious if the premises do not make the conclusion more likely to be true.

There are many types of fallacy; the *Nizkor Project* lists 42, *Changing Minds* 53, and *Wikipedia* over 100. It's good to become familiar with some of the main types. If you do, it is really important to understand *why* the fallacy is a fallacy.

Spotting fallacies has two purposes: 1) evaluating the strength of an argument and 2) improving it. When learning how to spot fallacies, try to develop the skill of reformulating the argument to avoid the fallacy. It is not always clear-cut whether a fallacy is being committed or not, and the answer depends on just how the premises are being deployed or further assumptions being made. The question is always ultimately about the strength of support the premises offer.

To learn how to avoid fallacies in your own work, it can be helpful to learn first how to spot them! Fallacies are always easier to spot in someone else's work, so start with people you don't know, then look at the work of other students, then try to spot them in your own work.

Reading philosophy

The syllabus includes a list of books and articles to read and think about. Reading philosophical texts is challenging, especially if you haven't read any philosophy before. You may not know much about the background of the text – when was it written and why? The form of the text is difficult – there can be long and complicated arguments, unfamiliar words, an unusual style of language from hundreds of years ago, and abstract ideas. It is unclear just how the text should be interpreted, and commentaries on the texts often disagree. The first thing to remember, then, is that it is *normal* to feel confused and challenged.

What can help? Here are some suggestions.

Approaching the text

For these first three points, you'll need to use a commentary on the text, or an introduction:

1. Contextualise: it can help to set the scene, but this shouldn't be restricted to a historical understanding. An awareness of central ideas is useful.
2. Identify what philosophical *problems* the text addresses.
3. Get an overview: look at the title, introductory and concluding paragraphs, and the chapter and section headings. Knowing the conclusion does not ruin the text (it isn't a detective story). Understanding the structure can help fit different arguments and claims together.

These next three points are about how to interact with the text:

4. For long texts, don't feel the need to start at the beginning. Start with what will best get you into the thinking of the author, e.g. connections to previous topics, points of interest, etc.
5. Don't get bogged down in details: reading the text more than once is helpful and often necessary. Read it quickly first, noting the main points, skimming what is most unclear; then read it again more closely.
6. Distinguish the text from secondary interpretation: for example, knowing what other people said Descartes said is not knowing what Descartes said.

Engaging with the text

1. Read slowly and actively: philosophy should not be read like fiction or even most non-fiction. Go slowly, take notes, and constantly question not only whether you've understood what the author is trying to say, but also whether what s/he says is true, and whether the arguments support the conclusions.
2. Look for signposts: sentences that indicate what the text is about, what has been, is being, or will be argued.
3. Ask what the passage of text offers: a new concept, a framework for understanding an issue, an argument for a conclusion?
4. Argument mapping: find the arguments. Identify premises, inferences and conclusions. Break arguments down into steps (there can be many interim conclusions).

5. Don't be afraid to challenge: try to find inconsistencies in the text, but also try to find ways to interpret the text to remove the inconsistencies.
6. Ask what interpretation best fits the purpose of the author. Does an interpretation presuppose ideas that were not available to the author?
7. Know the point of any example used: examples can seize the imagination and memory, but knowing its purpose and what it is supposed to show is central to understanding the text.
8. Look up key words in a dictionary of philosophy: don't be lazy, and don't use a normal dictionary (for philosophical words) as they won't capture or explain the relevant sense.

Beyond the text

1. Visualise: if you put the text, or the arguments within it, into some other visual form, that can help generate understanding.
2. Use secondary sources carefully: always question the authority of secondary sources, and always go back to the text.
3. Find different ways to think about and interact with the text. These will help you understand more than if you simply read it. For example, you might want to
    a. practise précis (either rewrite a passage more briefly in your own words or, if you have the text electronically, try deleting words while retaining the argument);
    b. rewrite a passage of the text in a different genre (e.g. a detective story);
    c. select quotations that make important points (good for revision);
    d. mark up the text for premises, conclusions, linguistic clues, etc.;
    e. do some argument mapping.

Writing philosophy

What you need to know

Different types of knowledge are needed to do well in philosophy. Each is tested by different types of question on the exam. The 3-mark questions ask you to define a term. The 5-mark questions ask you to outline and explain an important philosophical theory, a contrast or an argument. The 12-mark questions ask you to explain a longer or more complex argument, distinction, theory or the application of a theory. The 25-mark questions ask you to evaluate a claim.

See UNDERSTANDING THE QUESTION, p. 314.

1. *Understanding what the question is asking*: For each type of question, you need to understand what the question is asking you to *do*. So you need to know the difference between a definition, an outline, an explanation and what is needed for an evaluative essay.
2. *Knowledge of the issue*: You need to understand the relevant concept, argument or claim. Evaluating claims is most complex. You'll need to know what the options are, the key arguments defending and attacking the claim, the theories that philosophers have defended that pull different arguments and claims together into a coherent whole.
3. *Structure of arguments*: Knowing how an argument works (or doesn't) is more than knowing the conclusion and the premises used; it is understanding *how* the premises are supposed to connect together to support the conclusion. With your own arguments, you equally need to understand how they work, and you should present them with a clear structure.
4. *Relevance*: A good part of philosophical skill is a matter of selecting ideas, concepts, examples and arguments that you encountered in the material you studied that are relevant to the question. Knowing what is relevant is a special kind of knowledge, which involves thinking carefully about what you know about arguments and theories in relation to the question asked.
5. *Critical discussion*: When you evaluate a claim (25-mark questions), it is important to know that *presenting* ideas is distinct from *critically discussing* those ideas. You need to understand whether an argument succeeds or fails and why, and be able to present and compare arguments and counter-arguments to argue towards the most plausible position. You will usually need to draw on more than one source or author, and above all *think*.

Planning an essay

When you are answering a 3-, 5- or 12-mark question, what you need to do is straightforward. You don't need to make any choices about *what* concepts, theories or arguments to talk about, since that is specified by the question. You should still organise your thoughts before writing. But essays – both coursework essays and answers to 25-mark exam questions – need to be planned in more detail.

1.   Take time to understand the question in detail. This includes understanding what *kind* of question it is. Exam questions tend to be straightforward, but teachers ask all kinds of questions (explain and critically discuss, compare two positions, apply a theory to an example). Most weak essays are weak because they fail to answer the actual question.
2.   Keep the question in mind throughout writing, to ensure that your thought and planning stay relevant. Someone should be able to tell from the essay itself what question it is answering.
3.   If it is appropriate, think about challenging the question. Does it make assumptions that can be questioned?

Brainstorm to generate ideas of what you might discuss. (In an exam, recall the relevant revision plan.) One way is through 'successive elaboration' – take a single-sentence statement of a position, then make it more detailed, e.g. by providing some premises, and then think what would be necessary to establish the premises, etc. Another is 'conceptual note-taking', simply writing what comes to mind: even starting from 'I don't know anything about *x*' suggests and leads to others, such as 'I don't know what *x* means' and 'So and so defines *x* as…'. Half-formed thoughts are better developed when out on the page.

4.   If you are researching the essay, start by making the relevant ideas familiar, but make decisions on what to concentrate on, and narrow your research to achieve depth in a few central areas.
5.   An essay needs shape, it is always directed towards a conclusion, so you'll need to decide what to include and what to leave out.
6.   Don't aim to cover too much; three main arguments are usually enough. Even fewer can be fine if you go into real depth.

Plan an essay that argues for a particular position. You will often want to argue for or against a specific claim (as in a debate). But you don't have to. For example, you can argue that we can't know either way. Whatever your conclusion (your position), you'll need to defend it. Have it in mind throughout the plan and writing. The essay should read like one long argument for your conclusion (taking in various smaller arguments, objections and replies along the way).

7. The evaluative discussion is the most important part of the essay, so only introduce and explain material that you will use in discussion. You can think of this as two halves: the arguments in favour of your conclusion; and the objections to your arguments, or separate arguments against your conclusion, and replies to them. Make sure you consider the objections and counter-arguments – avoid being one-sided!

8. In light of all of the above points, write a plan which includes key points (definitions, arguments, objections, etc.) and the paragraph structure.

9. Each paragraph presents an idea. Paragraphs should not be divided on *length*, but as 'units of thought'. If you made a one-sentence summary of each paragraph, would the resulting account of the essay read logically?

Writing an essay

Once again, I'll just provide some advice on the most difficult writing task, the essay:

1. Plan the essay. It is very rare that good philosophical essays are written 'off the cuff', taking each thought as it occurs to you in turn. An essay is not (just) a test of memory, but of intelligence, which includes organisation and clarity.

2. However, new ideas will probably occur as you write. It is fine to deviate from the plan, but think through new ideas before incorporating them, to make sure they are good and to structure them.

3. The usual starting point for constructing an argument is explaining other people's ideas. The idea here is to be *accurate* and *sympathetic*.

An argument works best when the ideas are presented as strongly as possible – otherwise the opponent can simply rephrase the idea, and your counter-argument falls apart.

4.   In general, aim to be concise. Present the kernel of the idea clearly and relevantly. Stick to what you need to present in order to properly discuss the question. This can involve surrounding detail, since you need to show an awareness of the situation of the topic in the subject. But be selective and relevant.

5.   Never just *report* or *allude to* the arguments you have read – *make* the argument. To use a metaphor from war, you are not a reporter at the front line, but a combatant engaged for one side or the other.

6.   Use the three-part structure: make a point, back it up and show its relevance.

7.   In critical discussion, reflect on what a particular argument actually demonstrates, and whether there are counter-arguments that are better. You should be able to argue both for and against a particular view. Relate these arguments to each other, evaluating which is stronger and why. You need to work at shaping the material and 'generating a discussion'.

8.   Alternatively, you may want to relate a particular argument to a broader context, e.g. a philosopher's overall theory, other philosophers' ideas on the same issue, etc. – in general, work to understand the relation between the parts and the whole.

9.   Understand and be careful about the strength of your assertions. It is important to know whether your arguments indicate that all, some, most or typically … (e.g. lies are wrong, dualist arguments are flawed, etc.) and to distinguish between whether this is so or simply may be so.

10.   Never introduce new material in the conclusion. The conclusion should reflect the argument of the essay. Don't feel you have to personally agree with your conclusion! Essays are not confessions of belief.

11.   In an exam setting, you also need to keep note of the time, and leave time to review and correct what you've written.

A standard essay structure

1. Introduction: how you understand the question, what you'll argue for (and perhaps some indication of how you will discuss the question)
2. An explanation of the claim to be evaluated, perhaps including some of the relevant background theory, and either including or followed by …
3. The arguments in favour of the claim (give the arguments, and if you think they work, argue that the reasoning is valid and the premises are true)
4. Objections to these arguments and replies to the objections
5. Arguments against the claim
6. Objections to these arguments

Conclusion: a clear statement showing how the claim is supported/ defeated by the arguments discussed. This will require you to make some points, either as you go along or in the conclusion, about which arguments or objections are strongest and why.

> Alternatively, you may consider objections to each argument (in 3) in turn as you consider the argument.

General advice

When doing coursework essays:

1. Do not wait until you have finished your research to start writing the essay. If you find, as your research continues, that someone else has written what you've written, then reference it; if you find an objection, then explain it and explain why it is wrong, or, if the objection persuades you, rewrite what you've written as 'one might think …' and use the objection to show why it is wrong.
2. Rewrite the essay – almost no one does themselves justice in one draft.
3. Quotations do not substitute for understanding. Use them when you want to illustrate the precise wording of an idea or back up an interpretation.
4. Don't plagiarise.

In both coursework and exam essays:

5. Be precise, especially with words that have a philosophical meaning, like 'valid', 'assume', 'infer'.
6. Be clear. Being vague gives the reader the sense that you don't really know what you are talking about. Don't hide behind long words or technical terms – it rarely impresses people who understand them. Define technical terms and ordinary words that have a non-standard, philosophical meaning.
7. Don't use long and involved sentences. Use active, not passive, constructions; e.g. 'Plato argued …', not 'It was argued by Plato …'.
8. Include signposts. Generally speaking, the first sentence of a paragraph should give some indication to a reader as to where you are in the argument (e.g. 'A second criticism to the argument that …).
9. While it is acceptable to use the first person ('I'), this should not be to say 'I feel …' or 'I think …' or 'In my opinion …' as though such an assertion adds any weight to the plausibility of the conclusion. The whole essay is what you think, however it is phrased.

ETHICS

2

In this chapter, we look at two central debates in ethics. The first debate relates to deciding what the morally right thing to do is. We shall look at three theories. The first focuses on the consequences of the action, the second on the motive, and the third on being a good person. We then discuss how these theories approach a range of practical ethical issues.

The second debate concerns the question of whether ethical language states objective moral truths. Cognitivism claims that it does, while non-cognitivism claims that it expresses subjective attitudes. We shall look at a range of theories in each camp, and discuss the challenges that each position faces.

By the end of the chapter, you should be able to analyse, explain and evaluate a number of arguments for and objections to theories about how to decide what is morally right and whether ethical language can state objective truths or not.

> I shall make no distinction between the terms 'ethics' and 'morality'.

SYLLABUS CHECKLIST ✔

The AQA syllabus for this chapter is:

I. Ethical theories: how do we decide what it is morally right to do?

A. Utilitarianism:
✔ the maximisation of utility, including:
- the question of what is meant by 'pleasure', including Mill's higher and lower pleasures

- how this might be calculated, including Bentham's utility calculus
- forms of utilitarianism: act and rule utilitarianism; preference utilitarianism.

Issues, including:
- ✔ individual liberty/rights
- ✔ problems with calculation
- ✔ the possible value of certain motives (e.g. the desire to do good) and character of the person doing the action
- ✔ the possible moral status of particular relationships (family/friendship) we may have with others.

B. Kantian deontological ethics:
- ✔ what maxims can be universalised without contradiction, including:
  - the categorical and hypothetical imperatives
  - the Categorical Imperative – first and second formulations.

Issues, including:
- ✔ the intuition that consequences of actions determine their moral value (independent of considerations of universalisability)
- ✔ problems with the application of the principle
- ✔ the possible value of certain motives (e.g. the desire to do good) and commitments (e.g. those we have to family and friends)
- ✔ clashing/competing duties.

C. Aristotle's virtue ethics:
- ✔ the development of a good character, including:
  - 'the good': pleasure; the function argument and *eudaimonia*

- the role of education/habituation in developing a moral character
- voluntary and involuntary actions and moral responsibility
- the doctrine of the mean and Aristotle's account of vices and virtues.

Issues, including:
- ✔ can it give sufficiently clear guidance about how to act?
- ✔ clashing/competing virtues
- ✔ the possibility of circularity involved in defining virtuous acts and virtuous people in terms of each other.

D. Applications

Students must be able to critically apply the theories above to the following issues:
- ✔ crime and punishment
- ✔ war
- ✔ simulated killing (within computer games, plays, films, etc.)
- ✔ the treatment of animals
- ✔ deception and the telling of lies.

II. Ethical language: what is the status of ethical language?

A. Cognitivism:
- ✔ ethical language makes claims about reality which are true or false (fact-stating)
    - moral realism: ethical language makes claims about mind-independent reality that are true
        - ○ ethical naturalism (e.g. utilitarianism)
        - ○ ethical non-naturalism (e.g. intuitionism)
    - error theory: ethical language makes claims about mind-independent reality that are false (e.g. Mackie's argument from queerness).

B. Non-cognitivism:

✔ ethical language does not make claims about reality which are true or false (fact-stating)

- emotivism: ethical language expresses emotions (Hume and Ayer)
- prescriptivism: ethical language makes recommendations about action (Hare).

I. Ethical theories: how do we decide what it is morally right to do?

How should I live? This is a central question that we all face. Morality is intended to assist us in making such decisions and so guide our actions. 'Normative ethics' is the branch of philosophy that discusses theories of what we should do, while the application of these theories to particular issues, such as lying or war, is 'practical ethics'. We will discuss three normative ethical theories, utilitarianism, Kant's deontological theory and Aristotle's virtue ethics. We will then apply these theories to a number of practical issues.

A. Utilitarianism

There are different kinds of utilitarianism, which we will discuss in PREFERENCE UTILITARIANISM, p. 35, and RULE UTILITARIANISM, p. 50.

In its simplest form, utilitarianism is defined by three claims.

1. Act consequentialism: actions are morally right or wrong depending on their consequences and nothing else. An act is right if it maximises what is good.
2. Value theory: the only thing that is good is happiness.
3. Equality: no one's happiness counts more than anyone else's.

This is known as hedonist act utilitarianism. If we put (1) and (2) together, we see that the theory claims that an action is right if it *maximises* happiness, i.e. if it leads to the greatest happiness of all those it affects. Otherwise, the action is wrong. Our actions are judged not 'in themselves', e.g. by what *type* of action they are (a lie, helping someone, etc.), but in terms of what *consequences* they have. Our actions are morally right if they bring about the greatest happiness.

'Greatest happiness' is comparative (great, greater, greatest). If an action leads to the greatest happiness of those it affects, no other action taken at that time could have led to greater happiness. So an action is right only if, out of all the actions you could have done, this action leads to more happiness than any other. Just causing *some* happiness, or more happiness than unhappiness, isn't enough for an act to be morally right.

Act utilitarianism seems to provide a clear and simple way of making decisions: consider the consequences of the different actions you could perform and choose that action that brings about the greatest happiness. It makes complicated decisions easy and avoids appeals to controversial moral intuitions. The only thing that matters is happiness, and surely everyone wants to be happy. We can figure out empirically how much happiness actions cause, and so we can solve moral issues by empirical investigation.

> **What is act utilitarianism?**

ANTHOLOGY: BENTHAM, *AN INTRODUCTION TO THE PRINCIPLES OF MORALS AND LEGISLATION*, CHS 1, 4

Ch. 1 'The Principle of Utility'

Jeremy Bentham is considered the first act utilitarian. He defended the 'principle of utility', also known as the 'greatest happiness principle'. It is 'that principle which approves or disapproves of every action whatsoever, according to the tendency which it appears to have to augment or diminish the happiness of the party whose interest is in question'. Or again, 'that principle which states the greatest happiness of all those whose interest is in question, as being the right and proper ... end of human action'. (§2) So Bentham claims that in judging actions to be morally right or wrong, we should only take into account the total amount of happiness that the action may produce. Likewise, in our own actions, we should aim to produce the greatest happiness we can.

> **What is the principle of utility?**

Bentham's hedonism

Utilitarianism is so-called because it is concerned with 'utility'. In §3, Bentham makes the connection between utility and happiness:

> By utility is meant that property in any object, whereby it tends to produce benefit, advantage, pleasure, good, or happiness, (all this in the present case comes to the same thing) or (what comes again to the same thing) to prevent the happening of mischief, pain, evil, or unhappiness to the party whose interest is considered.

In §5, he clarifies what he means by 'interest':

> A thing is said to promote the interest, or to be *for* the interest, of an individual, when it tends to add to the sum total of his pleasures: or, what comes to the same thing, to diminish the sum total of his pains.

So, something has 'utility' if it contributes to your happiness, which is the same as what is in your interest. And happiness is pleasure and the absence of pain. The claim that pleasure, as happiness, is the only good is known as hedonism. In Ch. 5, Bentham goes on to list 14 'families' of pleasure, such as sensory pleasure, the pleasures of exercising one's skills, the pleasures of having power, the pleasures of memory, and the pleasures of benevolence. He also lists twelve families of pain, many deriving from similar sources as pleasure.

?

What does Bentham mean by 'happiness'?

Ch. 4 How happiness may be calculated

Bentham argued that we can measure pleasures and pains and add them up on a single scale by a process he called the 'felicific calculus' ('felicity' means happiness). If a pleasure is more intense, will last longer, is more certain to occur, will happen sooner rather than later, or will produce in turn many other pleasures and few pains, it counts for more. In thinking what to do, you also need to take into account how many people will be affected (the more you affect positively, and the fewer you affect negatively, the better). The total amount of happiness produced is the sum total of everyone's pleasures produced minus the sum total of everyone's pains.

> Briefly outline the central claims of Bentham's utilitarianism.

ANTHOLOGY: MILL, *UTILITARIANISM*, CHS 1, 2

John Stuart Mill begins his book on utilitarianism by remarking on how surprising it is that, with all the developments in knowledge over the last two millennia, there is still little agreement on the criterion for right and wrong. In science, we start from particular observations and work out the laws of nature from them. But our usual method of empirical induction doesn't work in ethics. Part of the difficulty is that we can't easily infer the principles of morality from particular cases, because we first need to know the principles in order to judge whether an action is right or wrong.

However, we shouldn't exaggerate the disagreement. Many philosophers agree that morality involves moral laws and they agree on what many of these laws are (e.g. concerning murder, theft, harming others, betrayal, etc.), even if they disagree about why these are moral laws. Mill then remarks that people's moral approval and disapproval is, as a matter of fact, strongly influenced by the effects of actions on their happiness. So the principle of utility has played a significant role in forming moral beliefs, even if this hasn't been recognised.

When Mill wrote *Utilitarianism*, there was a lot of misunderstanding of what utilitarians actually believed. Ch. 2 clarifies what utilitarianism is - what it really claims - by considering and replying to 11 objections which Mill argues arise from misunderstanding the theory. We will be able to consider only some of these in any detail, but it is worth setting them all out briefly here:

1. 'Utility' means what is useful, not what is pleasurable. Utilitarianism therefore ignores the value of pleasure.

    Reply: Obviously a misunderstanding. Mill reasserts Bentham's central claims. First, 'actions are right in proportion as they tend to promote happiness, wrong as they tend to produce the reverse of happiness'. Second, 'By happiness is intended pleasure, and the absence of pain; by unhappiness, pain, and the privation of pleasure.' Third, 'pleasure, and freedom from pain, are the only things desirable as ends'.

2. Utilitarianism only values pleasure. It does not recognise the 'higher' things in life or the dignity of human beings.
3. Happiness is unattainable.

    We will discuss these two objections in WHAT IS HAPPINESS?, next (p. 32).

4. We do not need happiness and many wise and noble people have lived without it.

    Reply: True, but what have noble people sacrificed their happiness for? Surely, it is the happiness of others. If not, then what a wasted sacrifice! Utilitarianism recognises the virtue of sacrificing your happiness for others – the aim remains to increase the total happiness in the world.

5. Utilitarians make right and wrong depend upon the agent's happiness.

    Reply: Another obvious misunderstanding. It is the happiness of everyone that is the criterion of right action.

For this reason, we should organise society and raise children in such a way that each person feels that their own happiness is bound up with the happiness of others, that they are made happy by making others happy.

to read

6. Utilitarianism is too idealistic, expecting people to be motivated by everyone's happiness in general.
7. Utilitarianism makes people cold and unsympathetic to others, considering only their actions and not their personal qualities.

We return to these two objections in THE VALUE OF MOTIVES AND CHARACTER (p. 45) and THE MORAL STATUS OF PARTICULAR RELATIONSHIPS (p. 48).

8. Utilitarianism is a godless theory.

    Reply: It isn't. Utilitarianism can easily be made compatible with Christian teachings about God. (Given his social context, Mill only mentions Christianity.)

9. Utilitarianism will lead to people sacrificing moral principles for 'expedient' immoral action.

    Reply: 'Expedient' usually means either what is in the person's own interest or in the short-term interest, as when someone lies to get out of a tricky situation. Where an action is 'expedient' in this sense and sacrifices the greater happiness of people generally, then utilitarianism condemns it. We will return to this issue in MILL, UTILITARIANISM, CH. 5 (p. 43).

For Mill's view on lying, see DECEPTION AND THE TELLING OF LIES, p. 134.

10. It is not possible to work out the consequences of an action for human happiness.
11. Utilitarians will be tempted to make exceptions to the rules.

We discuss these two objections in PROBLEMS WITH CALCULATION (p. 41) and RULE UTILITARIANISM (p. 50).

Having provided an overview of Ch. 2, we turn to one of its main themes - the nature of happiness.

What is happiness?

We consider Aristotle's theory of happiness in EUDAIMONIA, p. 72.

Mill agrees with Bentham that happiness is pleasure and the absence of pain. But the exact relation between pleasure and happiness needs further clarification. Happiness is not 'a continuity of highly pleasurable excitement', a life of rapture, 'but moments of such, in an existence made up of few and transitory pains, many and various pleasures, with a decided predominance of the active over the passive, and having as the foundation of the whole, not to expect more from life than it is capable of bestowing'. Thus variety, activity and realistic expectations play an important role in how our pleasures make up our happiness.

Is happiness, understood like this, attainable (objection 3)? Yes, says Mill, many people can experience it. The main obstacles are a poor education and poor social arrangements that lead to lack of opportunity and inequality. Of course, we can't expect good fortune all the time - we will all experience disease and the loss of people we love. But the main sources of human suffering are things that we can diminish over time.

? Why is it important to utilitarianism as a theory that we can achieve happiness?

Does utilitarianism degrade human beings in only valuing pleasure (objection 2)? In his essay on Bentham, Mill sympathises with the objection applied to Bentham's view of happiness. Bentham didn't really understand human nature, Mill argues; 'If he thought at all of any of the deeper feelings of human nature, it was but as idiosyncrasies of taste'. According to Bentham's felicific calculus, 'quantity of pleasure being equal, push-pin is as good as poetry' (push-pin was a very simple child's or gambler's game). Mill rejects the view that pleasures and pains are all equally valuable, and in *Utilitarianism*, he provides an alternative account of human nature that answers the objection.

Higher and lower pleasures

Mill argues that the claim that utilitarianism degrades human beings misunderstands what human beings take pleasure in. Some types of pleasure are 'higher' than others, more valuable, more important to human happiness, given the types of creatures we are and what we are capable of.

Which pleasures? How can we tell if a type of pleasure is *more valuable* (quality) than another, rather than just more *pleasurable* (quantity)? The answer has to be to ask people who know what they are talking about. If everyone (or almost everyone) who has experience of two types of pleasure prefers one type to the other, then the type that they prefer is more valuable. To ensure that they are considering the quality and not quantity of the pleasure, we should add another condition. A pleasure is higher only if people who have experience of both types of pleasure prefer one even if having that pleasure brings more pain with it, or again, even if they would choose it over a greater quantity of the other type of pleasure.

Mill argues that, as long as our physical needs are met, people will prefer the pleasures of *thought, feeling and imagination* to pleasures of the body and the senses, even though our 'higher' capacities also mean we can experience terrible pain, boredom and dissatisfaction. For example, ''Tis better to have loved and lost than never to have loved at all'. We can say the same about intelligence and artistic creativity – better to have the pleasures that they bring, even though they cause us pain and distress, than to be unintelligent or lack creativity.

Thus Mill compares a human being with a pig (the objection claims that valuing only pleasure is a 'doctrine worthy only of swine'). As human beings, we are able to experience pleasures of deep personal relationships, art and creative thought that pigs are not. We can experience new and deeper kinds of pain as a result. Yet we don't think that the possibility of pain would be a good reason for choosing to be a well-looked-after pig, rather

Aristotle's theory of pleasure is discussed in ARISTOTLE, NICOMACHEAN ETHICS, BKS 7.12–13, 10.1–5, p. 106.

Briefly outline Mill's test for higher pleasures.

Tennyson, 'In Memoriam A.H.H.'

than a human being. 'It is better to be a human being dissatisfied than a pig satisfied'. This preference, Mill thinks, derives from our sense of dignity, which is an essential part of our happiness.

In introducing this distinction between higher and lower pleasures, Mill rejects the felicific calculus, and adds the element of quality to the quantitative analysis of happiness that Bentham puts forward.

It is important to note that if Mill's prediction here is wrong – and people with the relevant experience do not prefer the pleasures of thought, feeling and imagination to other pleasures – then these are not higher pleasures. We can object that people do not reliably pursue the 'higher' pleasures of thought, feeling and imagination instead of the 'lower' pleasures related to the body and the senses.

Mill accepts the point, but argues that it is no objection. First, there is a difference between preference and action. We can choose what we know to be less good, whether from weakness of will or laziness or other factors. This doesn't undermine the claim that what we did not choose is more valuable.

Second, appreciating the higher pleasures can be more demanding. Our ability to experience the pleasure can be undermined by hard work, lack of time, infrequent opportunities to experience them, and so on. We may seek the lower pleasures simply because those are more readily available to us. This means that not just *anyone's* preference counts as deciding whether a pleasure is 'higher' or 'lower'. As with any question, we need to consult people who know what they are talking about. Having been to an art gallery once doesn't count as having experienced the pleasures of art, and listening to just one pop song doesn't count as having experienced the pleasures of pop music. Mill says that one pleasure is higher than another if almost everyone who is 'competently acquainted' with both prefers one over the other.

read

Preference utilitarianism

Bentham and Mill are hedonists. They argue that only happiness, understood in terms of pleasure, is valuable. But we can question whether this claim is correct. For example, Bentham says that 'pleasure', 'interest' and 'happiness' come to the same thing. Is this right, or can something be in my interest without my taking any pleasure in it? Or again, Bentham and Mill understand morality to require us to both produce happiness and decrease pain. But are these morally equal? Is it more important *not* to cause harm than it is to cause pleasure?

A third objection comes from Robert Nozick. He asks us to imagine being faced with the chance of plugging in to a virtual reality machine. This machine will produce the experience of a very happy life, with many and various pleasures and few pains. If we plug in, we will not know that we are in a virtual reality machine. We will believe that what we experience is reality. However, we must agree to plug in for life or not at all.

'The Experience Machine', *Anarchy, State and Utopia*

read

Nozick argues that most of us would *not* plug in. We value being in contact with reality, even if that makes us less happy. We can't understand this in terms of the 'pleasure' of being in touch with reality, because if we were in the machine, we would still experience this pleasure (we would believe we were in touch with reality). So we cannot argue, with Mill, that being in touch with reality is a 'higher' pleasure. It isn't a pleasure at all; it is a *relation* to something outside our minds. Nozick concludes that pleasure cannot be the only thing of value.

A different form of utilitarianism claims to be able to avoid these problems. Preference utilitarianism argues that what we should maximise is not pleasure, but the *satisfaction of people's preferences*.

1. The satisfaction of many of these preferences will bring us pleasure, but many will not. For instance, if people more strongly prefer not to suffer pain than to be brought pleasure, then that would explain the thought that it is more important not to cause harm.
2. If Nozick is right, we prefer to be in touch with reality, but not because it brings us pleasure. Having this preference satisfied is valuable.
3. We can also argue that people have preferences about what happens after their death, e.g. to their possessions, and it is important to satisfy these as well, even though this cannot bring them any pleasure.

4. We can also appeal to preferences to explain Mill's claims about higher and lower pleasures. He defends the distinction in terms of what people prefer. However, rather than talk about the value of types of pleasure, we could argue that whatever people prefer is of more value to them – whether or not most people would prefer pleasures related to thought, feeling and imagination.

In sum, preference utilitarians can argue that they offer a more unified account of what is valuable than hedonist utilitarianism. Pleasure is important, when it is, because it results from satisfying people's preferences.

Explain preference utilitarianism and one argument for it.

See DEDUCTIVE ARGUMENT, p. 8.

ANTHOLOGY: MILL, *UTILITARIANISM*, CH. 4

Going further: Mill's 'proof' of utilitarianism

Mill defends the claim that happiness is the only value in Ch. 4, his famous 'proof' of the principle of utility. The proof has two stages. In the first stage, Mill argues that happiness is good. In the second stage, he argues that it is the only thing that is good.

Stage 1: happiness is good

Mill argues that you can't strictly 'prove' that something is good or not. That is, it is not something that you can deduce from other premises. This is normal for 'first principles' in any area of knowledge, and a claim about what is ultimately good is a first principle in ethics. Nonetheless, we can give a reasoned argument about what is good.

First, some terminology. What is good is what we should aim at in our actions and lives. So what is good is an 'end' – the purpose – of our actions. Philosophers understand actions in terms of means and ends. Ends are why you do what you do; means are how you get it. So I might cross the street to post a letter. My end is posting the letter, my means is crossing the street. Now, of course, my posting a letter is also a means to an end, the end of communicating with someone. This, too, may be a means to an end. Perhaps I am asking them for a favour. So I cross the street in order to post the letter in order to ask someone a favour. What is the end of asking them for a favour? What am I ultimately aiming at? What we *should* aim at is what is desirable. So what Mill wants to show, first, is that happiness *is* desirable, and second, that *only* happiness is desirable. If he is right, then the answer to my previous question about why I am asking for a favour will be 'happiness'.

Since we can't deduce what is good, we have to appeal to evidence. Mill's argument that happiness is good has three parts.

1. 'The only proof capable of being given that an object is visible is that people actually see it … In like manner … the sole evidence … that something is desirable is that people do actually desire it ….'
2. 'No reason can be given why the general happiness is desirable, except that each person … desires his own happiness.'
3. 'This, however, being a fact, we have not only all the proof the case admits of, but all which it is possible to require, that happiness is a good: that each person's happiness is a good to that person, and the general happiness, therefore, a good to the aggregate of all persons ….'

read

Briefly explain Mill's argument that happiness is good.

See UTILITARIANISM AS
NATURALISM, p. 148

Explain Moore's
objection to Mill's
proof.

Explain the
objection that
Mill's proof commits
the fallacy of
composition.

Clarifying the argument

G. E. Moore objected that Mill commits the fallacy of equivocation in this argument. The word 'desirable' has two meanings. Its usual meaning is 'worthy of being desired'. Anything desirable in this sense is good. This is the sense it has in (2), since Mill is arguing that the general happiness is good. But another meaning could be 'capable of being desired'. To discover what is capable of being desired, look at what people desire. This is the sense it has in (1), it seems, since Mill links what is desirable to what people desire. But what people actually desire is not the same as what is *worthy* of being desired (good). People want all sorts of rubbish! Mill has assumed that what people desire just is what is good; he hasn't spotted that these are distinct meanings of 'desirable'.

Moore's objection misinterprets Mill's argument. Mill is asking 'What *evidence* is there for thinking that something is worthy of being desired?' He argues that people *in general* desire happiness. Unless we think that people *in general* all desire what is not worth desiring, this looks like good evidence. Is there anything that *everyone* wants that is not worth wanting? If we look at what people agree upon in what they desire, we will find evidence of what is worth desiring. Everyone wants happiness, so it is reasonable to infer that happiness is desirable (good).

Other philosophers have objected that Mill commits the fallacy of composition in (3). He seems to be saying that because each person desires their own happiness, everybody desires everybody's happiness (the general happiness). But this doesn't follow. For example, suppose that every girl loves a sailor (substitute 'own happiness'). From the fact that for each girl, there is some sailor that she loves, we cannot infer that there is one sailor (substitute 'general happiness') which every girl loves.

But this is also a misinterpretation of Mill's argument. At no point does Mill feel that he needs to defend the idea of impartiality in ethics. He simply assumes that ethics is concerned with what is good in general. He is not trying to infer that we ought to be concerned for others' happiness. Having argued that happiness is good, it follows from his assumption that ethics is impartial that we should be concerned with the general happiness.

Stage 2: only happiness is good

The claim that happiness is good is relatively uncontroversial. It is much more controversial to claim that it is the *only* good. Mill must argue that everything of value – truth, beauty, freedom, etc. – derives its value from happiness.

Now if people only ever desired happiness, he could use the previous argument to show that happiness is the only good. But clearly, people desire many different things. Of course, we may desire many things as a means to happiness, such as buying a nice house or having a good job. But it isn't obvious that everything we desire is a means to happiness, e.g. truth (being in touch with reality). So going by the evidence, many different things, and not only happiness, are good.

Mill's response is to clarify further what happiness is. Happiness has many 'ingredients', such as truth and freedom, and each ingredient is desirable in itself. We can explain this in terms of a distinction between 'external means' and 'constitutive means' to an end. We usually think of the relation between means and end as an instrumental relation; i.e. that performing the means achieves the further, independent end. Think about

Explain Mill's argument for the claim that happiness is good.

having a good holiday. Suppose you have to get up very early in order to catch the plane. You do this in order to have a good holiday, but it isn't part of having a good holiday. Getting up early is an external means to the end. But there is also another relation between means and ends, a constitutive relation. Later on, you are lying on the beach in the sun, listening to your favourite music. Are you doing this 'in order' to have a good holiday? Not in the same sense. This just *is* having a good holiday at the moment. Lying on the beach is a constitutive means to the end of having a good holiday. Having a good holiday is not something 'further' or additional that you achieve by lying on the beach. In these circumstances, here and now, it is what 'having a good holiday' amounts to.

> Explain the distinction between external and constitutive means.

The same applies to happiness, Mill argues. For example, when someone desires to know the truth 'for its own sake', their knowing the truth doesn't cause their happiness as some further and separate thing. Rather, in this situation, their happiness *consists in* their knowing the truth. Knowing the truth for its own sake is part of happiness for them. So, Mill claims, whatever we desire for its own sake is part of what happiness is, for us.

Why believe this? Mill argues that to desire something *just is* to find it pleasant. It is, he says, 'physically and metaphysically impossible' to desire something that you don't think is a pleasure. As pleasure is happiness, we only desire happiness, and happiness is the only good.

> 1) Outline and explain Mill's argument for the claim that happiness is the only good. 2) Does Mill succeed in showing that the only good is happiness?

Issues for (act) utilitarianism

Problems with calculation

On p. 27, we noted that act utilitarianism seems to offer a clear and straightforward way of discovering what is right and wrong. We need to consider how much pleasure and pain (or preference satisfaction) an action will cause. But the tenth objection Mill considers (see p. 31) is that it is not possible to work out the consequences of an action for human happiness. How can we know or work out the consequences of an action, to discover whether it maximises happiness or not? Surely this will be too difficult and too time-consuming for us to do. Bentham's felicific calculus (p. 28) is, in practice, mind-boggling, and we just can't get the relevant information (how intense each affected person's pleasure or pain will be, how long it will last, what other pleasures or pains it might cause in turn, etc.).

Preference utilitarianism might try to claim another advantage here. It is easier to know whether someone's preference has been satisfied than how much pleasure someone experiences. But this is very little improvement if we still need to compare the strength of different people's preferences and so on.

However, the objection misrepresents what utilitarians say. Bentham does not say that an action is right if it *actually* maximises happiness. He says it is right according to 'the tendency which it appears to have' to maximise happiness. We don't need to be able to work out the consequences precisely. An action is right if we can reasonably expect that it will maximise happiness. He also says that the felicific calculus need not be 'strictly pursued' before each decision or moral judgement. It just needs to be 'kept in view'.

This still means we must be able to work things out roughly. Mill thought this was still too demanding. Happiness is 'much too complex and indefinite' a standard to apply directly to actions. But we don't need to try, he claims, because over time, people have automatically, through trial and error, worked out which actions tend to produce happiness. This is what our inherited moral rules actually are: 'tell the truth', 'don't steal', and 'keep your promises' are embodiments of the wisdom of humanity that lying, theft and false promising tend to lead to unhappiness.

We will consider rule utilitarianism and its responses to these issues in RULE UTILITARIANISM, p. 50.

Explain the difference between saying that an act is morally right if it actually maximises happiness and saying an act is morally right if it appears to have a tendency to maximise happiness.

Mill calls these moral rules 'secondary principles'. It is only in cases of conflict between secondary principles (e.g. if by telling the truth you break your promise) that we need to apply the greatest happiness principle directly to an action. We shouldn't attempt to calculate happiness directly unless we have such a conflict. Only in cases of conflict will there be genuine exceptions to these rules.

Of course, our inherited morality still makes mistakes in what it thinks will or won't contribute to general happiness. So we can improve on the rules that we have. But saying this is quite different from saying that we have to consider each action from scratch, as though we had no prior moral knowledge.

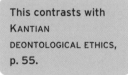

> Explain the problem of calculation and Mill's solution to it.

Individual liberty and rights

> This contrasts with KANTIAN DEONTOLOGICAL ETHICS, p. 55.

read

> Briefly outline the objection that act utilitarianism fails to rule out immoral types of action.

A second criticism of act utilitarianism is that no type of action is ruled out, in principle, as immoral. For example, if torturing a child produces the greatest happiness, then it is right to torture a child. Suppose a group of child abusers only find and torture abandoned children. Only the child suffers pain (no one else knows about their activities). But they derive a great deal of happiness. So more happiness is produced by torturing the child than not, so it is morally right. This is clearly the wrong answer.

Act utilitarians can reply that it is *very probable* that someone *will* find out, and then many people will be unhappy. Because we should do what is *likely* to produce the greatest happiness, we shouldn't torture children.

However, the theory still implies that *if* it was very unlikely anyone would find out, then it would be right to torture children. But other people finding out isn't what *makes* torturing children wrong.

This thought expresses two possible objections. First, we can point out that the example shows that happiness (or satisfying people's preferences) is not always morally good. For example, the happiness child abusers get from hurting children is morally bad. The fact that the abusers are made happy by what they do doesn't make their action better *at all*, but worse. So there must be some other standard than happiness for what is morally good.

Second, we can appeal to moral rights, understood in terms of restrictions placed on how people can treat each other. For instance, I have a right that other people don't kill me (the right to life). I also have a right to act as I choose as long as this respects other people's rights (the right to liberty). One of the purposes of rights is to protect individual freedom and interests, even when violating that freedom would produce some greater good. For example, my right to life means that no one should kill me to take my organs, even if doing so could save the lives of four other people who need, respectively, a heart, lungs, kidneys and a liver. Utilitarianism doesn't respect individual rights or liberty, because it doesn't recognise any restrictions on actions that create the greatest happiness.

Some utilitarians simply accept this. We have no rights. As long as we consider situations *realistically*, then whatever brings about the greatest happiness is the right thing to do. Counterexamples that appeal to very unlikely scenarios are unhelpful, because they have little to do with real life. In real life, act utilitarianism gives us the correct moral answer.

> Explain the objection that utilitarianism doesn't recognise individual rights.

ANTHOLOGY: MILL, *UTILITARIANISM*, CH. 5

Mill rejects this response, and provides a lengthy discussion of the problem, which he calls 'the only real difficulty in the utilitarian theory of morals', in Ch. 5. As he considers it, the problem is whether utilitarianism can give a plausible account of justice.

First, he analyses what justice is and argues that it is at its heart the concept of the moral rights of the individual. We think of each of the following kinds of action as a violation of justice:

1. violating someone's legal rights;
2. violating someone's moral rights (laws are sometimes wrong, so their legal rights are not always the rights they should have in law);
3. not giving someone what they deserve, in particular failing to return good for good and evil for evil;
4. breaking a contract or promise;
5. failing to be impartial when this is required, e.g. in relation to respecting rights, what people deserve or cases of public interest;
6. treating people unequally.

Explain Mill's
concept of
justice.

How does Mill try
to resolve the
conflict between
utilitarianism and
rights?

What is distinctive about justice is that it relates to actions that harm a specific, identifiable individual, who has the right that we don't harm them in this way. Duties of justice are 'perfect' duties. We must always fulfil them, and have no choice over when or how, because someone else has the right that we act morally. There are other cases of wrongdoing (e.g. not giving to charity) in which no *specific* person can demand this of us. Instead, we have some choice in how we fulfil the obligation to help others. These are 'imperfect' duties.

But *why* do we have the rights that we have? Mill says that '[w]hen we call anything a person's right, we mean that he has a valid claim on society to protect him in the possession of it, either by the force of law, or by that of education and opinion.' The reason why society should protect us in this way is the general happiness. The interests that are protected as rights are 'extraordinarily important'. They are interests concerned with security. We depend on security for protection from harm and to be able to enjoy what is good without fearing that it will be taken from us. The rules that prohibit harm and protect our freedom are more vital to our interests than any others. And so we protect these interests with rights, and these become the subject of justice. This contributes most to happiness in the long term. Hence, Mill says, 'I account the justice which is grounded on utility to be the chief part, and incomparably the most sacred and binding part, of all morality'.

Discussion

On Mill's view, we only have a right if our having that right contributes to the greatest happiness in the long run. We may wonder whether the rights that we usually take ourselves to have (e.g. related to individual liberty) really do this. Would society be more happy if people had less freedom in some cases? This is an important debate in political philosophy.

A clearer objection is that Mill's theory of rights doesn't offer a strong defence in particular cases. Suppose there is an occasion where violating my rights will create more happiness than not. A right protects the individual's interest against what may compete with it, e.g. the greater happiness on this occasion. Hence, my right to life prevents my being murdered to save the lives of many others. But if the ground of rights is the general happiness, this protection seems insecure. On the one hand, we have the demands of the greatest happiness. On the other hand, we have the individual's right, which turns out to be just the demands of the greatest happiness as well. If my rights are justified by general utility, then doesn't the happiness created by overriding my rights justify violating them? Utilitarianism can't offer any other reason to respect my right in this particular instance.

Mill can argue that this approach to conflicts between rights and happiness in individual cases doesn't understand utilitarianism in the right light. We need to consider happiness 'in the largest sense'. Rights protect our permanent interests, and thus serve the general happiness considered over the long term. We should establish that system of rights that would bring the most happiness, and then defend these rights. (Compare what Mill says regarding 'secondary principles' above, p. 42.)

But now we can object that Mill has given up on *act* utilitarianism. Mill seems to recommend that we don't look at the consequences of each act taken individually to see whether it creates the greatest happiness. He recommends that we create rights, which are a kind of rule, and enforce them even when they conflict with happiness in certain situations. Thus, he says, '[j]ustice is a name for certain classes of moral rules, which concern the essentials of human well-being more nearly, and are therefore of more absolute obligation, than any other rules for the guidance of life; and the notion which we have found to be the essence of the idea of justice, that of a right residing in an individual, implies and testifies to this more binding obligation'. When rights are involved, the right action is not the one that creates the greatest happiness, but the one that respects the right. It seems that, in the end, Mill must adopt RULE UTILITARIANISM (p. 50) to provide his account of rights and justice.

> Briefly explain the objection that utilitarianism cannot defend individual rights in cases of conflict with the general happiness.

> Can act utilitarianism respect and defend individual rights?

The value of motives and character

Utilitarianism is a theory about right action. It claims that an action is right if it leads to the greatest happiness. But, we may object, in such a theory, there is no recognition of the moral value of our *motives* for acting as we do. In particular, the desire to do good – to act as morality requires – is an important part of morality. In just considering actions, utilitarianism fails to consider the fact that we talk about good *people*; it doesn't recognise that our characters also have moral value.

As an objection to Bentham, this is fair. However, Mill has a developed response. He discusses these points briefly in Ch. 2 when replying to objections (6) and (7) (see p. 31). It is correct to say that utilitarianism considers people's motives for action as irrelevant to whether the action is morally *right* or not. However, that does not mean that it thinks motives have nothing at all to do with morality. They are relevant when considering someone's 'worth' as a person. Now, such a judgement rests on many factors, some of which have little to do with morality. But utilitarianism will say this: a motive or trait of character that tends to produce morally bad actions is itself a bad motive or trait.

Mill expands on this thought in his essay on Bentham. Morality as a whole is concerned not only with right and wrong action, but also with character. This is partly because our actions naturally arise from our character. But there is another reason. Having a good character is important to understanding what happiness is, and furthermore, it is itself one of the 'ingredients' of happiness. In MILL'S 'PROOF' OF UTILITARIANISM (p. 36), he argues that the desire to do good is one of those things that is desirable (good) for its own sake. For people who desire to do good because it is good, it is *part* of their happiness that they have this motive. Doing good is, in itself, pleasant to them.

For the utilitarian, this is the best possible psychology to have. What is good is maximising happiness, and here is someone who gets happiness from maximising happiness – what could be happier!

But then, we may object, utilitarianism is too idealistic, if it expects people to be motivated by 'the general happiness' all the time. Mill's response is that utilitarianism doesn't expect this. People can do the morally right thing irrespective of their motive. But utilitarianism does entail that children should be educated in such a way that promoting other people's happiness becomes part of their happiness.

This response depends on Mill's defence of happiness being the only good. If he is mistaken, if there are other goods which are valuable quite independent of their contribution to happiness, then we will understand the value of motives and character differently as well. For instance, if truth

> Explain Mill's claim that the desire to do good is valuable because it is part of happiness.

is valuable independent of happiness, then honesty is a valuable character trait, and not (only) because being honest forms part of our own happiness or brings happiness to other people, but just because it respects the value of truth.

Questions about the role of motives and character in morality are central to the other two moral theories we will discuss, KANTIAN DEONTOLOGICAL ETHICS (p. 55) and ARISTOTLE'S VIRTUE ETHICS (p. 70). In the first, we will discuss a completely different way of understanding the value of motives. In the second, we will discuss a theory of character that is closely related to Mill's in some respects, but with a different emphasis and a different conception of right action.

Is Mill's account of the value of good character traits correct?

ANTHOLOGY: MILL, *UTILITARIANISM*, CH. 3

Going further: Mill on conscience

An important part of moral motivation is a feeling of obligation, of duty. We feel bound not to murder or steal. We want to avoid violating our duty. But the same feeling doesn't mark thoughts about producing the greatest happiness. What would motivate us to act in accordance with the principle of utility?

People can be motivated to be moral by either 'external sanctions' or 'internal' ones. When someone does the right thing to avoid punishment or disapproval, or to gain some reward (from others or God), they are motivated by external sanctions. The internal sanction is a sense of duty, which Mill understands as the pain that we feel when we do not do what we believe we morally should do. This takes its 'purest' form when the thought is of doing one's duty whatever that is, just because it is one's duty, without regard to any other interests. This, Mill says, is the 'essence of conscience'. To avoid this pain, we do our duty.

As things stand, our conscience doesn't prod us to maximise happiness the way it prods us to avoid murder and theft. But that is because of how it has been cultivated. Conscience as it actually exists in each of us is 'encrusted' with all sorts of experiences – of sympathy, love, fear, religious teachings, and so on – acquired as we grow up. But human psychology is highly flexible and we could cultivate conscience to be associated just as strongly with the greatest happiness.

We already have a strong, natural emotion on which to base such an association, namely our social feelings, our desire to be in unity with others, our sympathy for others and need to live among them. Thus, we already grow up unable to disregard other people's interests, and this shapes not just what we think but how we feel and our character traits (as sympathetic, thoughtful, benevolent, etc.). If all the forces that shape conscience, including education and external sanctions, were directed to associating our conscience with the general happiness, then our feelings of duty would apply just as strongly to promoting the general happiness as they do to customary morality at the moment.

In this way, the motive of duty – the desire to do good and avoid evil for its own sake – would not only become part of happiness, it would also be directed towards the general happiness.

Explain Mill's theory of conscience.

The moral status of particular relationships

Many of the things that we do to make people happy are aimed at *specific* other people, our family and friends. We do them favours, buy them presents and generally spend our time and money on them. But act utilitarianism argues that in our decisions, we need to consider the *greatest* happiness that our actions could create. So shouldn't we spend much less time with the particular people we love and more time helping people who need help, e.g. through voluntary work, and likewise spend less money on the people we love and give much more money to charity? This would lead to greater happiness, because people who really need help will be made much more happy by the same amount of money or effort than people who don't really need anything.

There are different ways we can develop this thought into an objection. For instance, we can argue that utilitarianism is too idealistic, expecting people to give priority to needy strangers over those they know and love. Or again, we can argue that utilitarianism misses something morally important in counting each person equally. In the abstract, each person is equal, but *to me*, each person does not and should not count equally. It is morally right and good (or at least, not morally wrong) to show partiality towards those people one knows and loves.

Mill's response, in Ch. 2, is simply to say that on the whole, there are very few opportunities any of us have to benefit people 'in general'. And so only considering and contributing to the happiness of a few people is absolutely fine, and utilitarianism does not require more.

But there are two objections to this response. First, if it was true in Mill's day that people could not often benefit people 'in general', that no longer seems true today. There are many charities that work around the globe and welcome volunteer fund-raisers, and the news makes us continually aware of many different causes of suffering around the world. It is perfectly possible, therefore, to dedicate much of one's time and money to helping others 'in general', and there are many opportunities to do so. So it seems that utilitarianism does demand more.

Second, Mill's response doesn't address the objection that utilitarianism simply fails to understand the moral importance of particular relationships. If the general happiness is the ultimate end that we should seek in our action, then we should think of our friendships as a way to maximise the general happiness. Suppose a woman visits a friend in hospital. The friend thanks her. She replies, 'It was nothing, I was just doing my duty, maximising the general happiness in the world'. The friend can feel upset – the visit isn't personal, it is just a *means* to create happiness. If some other action would have created more happiness, the woman would have done that instead of visiting the friend.

Michael Stocker, 'The Schizophrenia of Modern Ethical Theories'

Or again, suppose a man is in a boating accident with both his wife and a stranger. Neither can swim, and he can only rescue one. We might think that he should simply rescue his wife. But if he thinks, 'Rescuing my wife will lead to greater happiness than rescuing the stranger', this seems to miss the particular importance that being married has, including its moral importance. The man has 'one thought too many', and we (and his wife!) can object to his way of thinking about what to do.

Friendship requires that the friend is valued as the individual person that they are, and that we act out of love for them. The motives that are involved in friendship seem to preclude a utilitarian understanding of morality. Yet doing something for a friend is morally good. Furthermore, attachments of love and friendship are central to our happiness, indeed to wanting to stay alive at all. But these attachments motivate actions that are not impartial between everyone's happiness. Utilitarianism fails to recognise the moral importance of partiality.

Some utilitarians have replied that morality is just much more demanding than we like to think. Can you defend spending money on your friends, rather than helping others through charity, when much of the world is in poverty or at war? However, Mill explicitly allows for partiality in his discussion of justice in Ch. 5. He would most likely argue that we are considering utilitarianism in the wrong way again. People have learned that having partial relationships is central to happiness, and so it does not maximise happiness to require people to give them up in favour of promoting the general happiness all the time.

To this response we may repeat the objection, made on p. 45, that Mill is giving up on *act* utilitarianism. Instead, he is appealing to general rules about living, and considering which of these rules would maximise happiness. And this is rule utilitarianism.

Rule utilitarianism

Rule utilitarianism claims that an action is right if, and only if, it complies with those rules which, if everybody followed them, would lead to the greatest happiness (compared to any other set of rules). Rather than considering actions individually in relation to whether they create the greatest happiness, we need to take the bigger picture. Morality should be understood as a set of rules. The aim of these rules is to maximise

---

Bernard Williams, 'Persons, Character and Morality'

1) Outline act utilitarianism and one objection to it. 2) Is an act morally right if it maximises happiness?

happiness. Actions are right when they follow a rule that maximises happiness overall – even when the action itself doesn't maximise happiness in this particular situation.

Rule utilitarians argue that this theory has a number of advantages over act utilitarianism, which we can see by considering how rule utilitarians respond to the objections raised above.

> Explain the difference between act and rule utilitarianism.

1. PROBLEMS WITH CALCULATION (p. 41): We don't have to work out the consequences of each act in turn to see if it is right. We need to work out which rules create the greatest happiness, but we only need to do this once, and we can do it together. This is what Mill says human beings have done over time, giving us our customary moral rules ('secondary principles'). Rule utilitarianism gives rules a *formal* place in its theory of whether an action is right.
2. INDIVIDUAL LIBERTY AND RIGHTS (p. 42): A rule forbidding torture of children will clearly cause more happiness if everyone followed it than a rule allowing torture of children. So it is wrong to torture children. More generally, as argued in the previous discussion, individuals have rights, which are rules, because if people have to follow these rules (respect people's rights), that leads to the greatest happiness. Mill's argument is correct, but it entails rule utilitarianism, not act utilitarianism.
3. THE MORAL STATUS OF PARTICULAR RELATIONSHIPS (p. 48): A rule that allows partiality to our family and friends will create more happiness than a rule that requires us to be impartial all the time. This secures the moral importance of such relationships – they are necessary to happiness. Of course, we shouldn't be completely partial. We still need to consider the general happiness, but we only need to act in such a way that, *if everyone acted like that*, would promote the greatest happiness. In the case of charity, I only need to give as much to charity as would be a 'fair share' of the amount needed to really help other people.
4. An act is not made right by maximising happiness but by being in accordance in a rule. If there is a conflict between following the rule and maximising happiness (e.g. telling a lie when 'no harm is done'), there will be no temptation for the utilitarian to say that we should break the rule. Even if the act does maximise happiness, this doesn't make it right. (This responds to objection (11) on p. 31.)

> Outline and explain how rule utilitarianism meets *two* objections to act utilitarianism.

Objections

Act utilitarians object that rule utilitarianism amounts to 'rule fetishism'. The point of the rules is to bring about the greatest happiness. If we only give as much to charity as we would need to if everyone gave to charity, then many people will not be helped, because not everyone will give what they should to charity. Surely, knowing this, I ought to give much more to charity; spending the money on myself would not be right. Or again, if I know that e.g. lying in a particular situation will produce more happiness than telling the truth, it seems pointless to tell the truth, causing unhappiness. The whole point of the rule was to bring about happiness, so there should be an exception to the rule in this case.

Rule utilitarians could respond by saying that we should amend the rule. However, life is complicated. *Whenever* a particular action causes more happiness by breaking the rule than by following it, we should do that action. If we try to add all the possible amendments to the rule 'don't lie' in order to make it always produce the greatest happiness, the rule will be impossibly long and we would lose any supposed benefits of rule utilitarianism. If we are going to be utilitarians, we should go back to act utilitarianism. What matters is the greatest happiness, and this is what makes an action right.

A better response from rule utilitarianism is to focus on the long term. If people try to follow act utilitarianism, this will lead to less happiness in the long term. For instance, people will no longer feel secure in their rights and there will be pressure on personal relationships to be given up in favour of impartiality. We may have to give up some happiness here and now to be more certain of the greatest happiness overall. Following rules provides this certainty.

As a form of utilitarianism, rule utilitarianism still faces a number of objections that we raised previously against act utilitarianism.

1. Is happiness the only thing that is valuable?
2. How should we understand the motive to 'do good'? Will a rule utilitarian want to follow the rule for its own sake or because it leads to the greatest happiness? Or can we defend something like Mill's solution, and argue that following moral rules *becomes part* of happiness?

> **?** Is it right to follow a rule that generally produces the greatest happiness, even when breaking that rule would cause more happiness in this situation?

3. Can rule utilitarianism recognise the importance of good character traits? Are character traits just motives to follow certain rules?
4. Can rule utilitarianism explain the moral value of particular relationships? For instance, if I form friendships because this maximises happiness, does that respect and value my friends for themselves, as the particular people they are?

There is also an additional objection that we can make that act utilitarianism doesn't face:

5. Can all of morality be summed up by rules? Isn't life too complicated for this? If so, we will need a different theory to explain what the right thing to do is when there are no rules that apply.

The rule utilitarian has a simple answer to this objection, though we can question whether it is adequate. One of the rules is 'When no other rules apply, do that action that maximises happiness'.

> Does rule utilitarianism provide the correct definition of a right action?

Key points: utilitarianism

- In its simplest form, act utilitarianism claims that an act is right if, and only if, it maximises happiness; i.e. if it creates more happiness than any other act in that situation.
- Bentham and Mill defend hedonism, claiming that happiness is pleasure and the absence of pain, and happiness is the only good.
- Bentham develops the 'felicific calculus' to work out how much happiness an act creates.
- Mill argues that some pleasures ('higher' pleasures) are more valuable than others. One pleasure is higher than another if almost everyone who has experience of both prefers one pleasure, even if there is less of it or it is accompanied by more pain.
- Mill argues that the pleasures of thought, feeling and imagination are higher than the pleasures of the body and the senses.
- We may object that pleasure and the absence of pain are not the only good. Nozick argues that we also value being in touch with reality.
- Preference utilitarianism argues we should maximise preference satisfaction. This theory claims to explain why pleasure is not the only

important thing and the distinction between higher and lower pleasures.

- Mill argues that happiness is desirable. The evidence for this is that everyone desires happiness.
- Moore objects that Mill confuses two senses of 'desirable', but we can reply that he misinterprets Mill's argument.
- Mill argues that happiness is the only good. It has many 'ingredients', which are constitutive means to happiness. An external means brings about a distinct end; a constitutive means constitutes that end in part (e.g. in a particular situation).
- How do we know which act will create the most happiness? Bentham replies that an act is right if we can reasonably expect that it will cause the greatest happiness, while Mill argued that our common-sense moral rules ('secondary principles') are a guide to what maximises happiness.
- We can object that some acts, such as torturing children for pleasure, are wrong even if they cause the greatest happiness. This shows that happiness is not always morally good. It also shows that utilitarianism doesn't respect individual rights or liberty.
- Some utilitarians accept that we don't have rights, but we can't test utilitarianism by unrealistic examples.
- Mill analyses justice as involving actions that relate to individual rights. These duties are 'perfect' in that we must always fulfil them. Imperfect duties, by contrast, leave us some room for choosing how to fulfil the duty, and they are not owed to specific individuals.
- Mill argues that we have rights because this produces the greatest happiness over the long term. Our rights protect what is most important to our happiness.
- We can object that if my rights are based on the general happiness, then in a situation in which the general happiness conflicts with my rights, there is no reason to respect my rights.
- If Mill argues that in such cases, we should still respect my rights, it seems he defends rule utilitarianism, not act utilitarianism.
- We can object that utilitarianism fails to recognise the importance of motives and character in morality. Mill responds that utilitarianism is about right action, not all of morality. Good motives and character are important in helping us do what is right, namely maximising happiness.

- But pursuing the general happiness doesn't feel like a moral obligation. Mill responds that it could do so if we formed people's conscience in this way.
- We can object that utilitarianism is too demanding in requiring us to be impartial about whose happiness we promote. It also misunderstands the moral importance of friendship and partiality in claiming that the reason why friendship is good is because it maximises the general happiness – it loses sight of the importance of the individual.
- Rule utilitarianism claims that an act is morally right if, and only if, it complies with rules which, if everybody follows them, lead to the greatest happiness.
- This theory avoids many objections to act utilitarianism, such as problems with calculation, individual rights and the demandingness of morality.
- However, act utilitarians object that it amounts to 'rule fetishism'. If breaking a rule would create more happiness on that occasion, we should break it. Rule utilitarians respond that people need to trust that others will abide by the rules, so we shouldn't break it. Following the rules will lead to the greatest happiness in the long run.
- Rule utilitarianism faces other objections to utilitarianism in general, namely whether happiness is the only good, the importance of good character and the moral value of particular relationships. We can also question whether morality can be summed up by rules.

B. Kantian deontological ethics

Deontology

Deontologists believe that morality is a matter of duty. We have moral duties to do things which it is right to do and moral duties not to do things which it is wrong to do. Whether something is right or wrong doesn't depend on its consequences. Rather, an action is right or wrong *in itself*.

Most deontological theories recognise two classes of duties. First, there are general duties we have towards anyone. These are mostly prohibitions; e.g. do not lie; do not murder. But some may be positive; e.g. help people in need. Second, there are duties we have because of our

> *Deon* (Greek) means 'one must'.

> Contrast
> UTILITARIANISM,
> p. 26.

particular personal or social relationships. If you have made a promise, you have a duty to keep it. If you are a parent, you have a duty to provide for your children. And so on.

We each have duties regarding our *own* actions. I have a duty to keep *my* promises, but I don't have a duty to make sure promises are kept. Deontology claims that we should each be most concerned with complying with our duties, not attempting to bring about the most good. In fact, all deontologists agree that there are times when we *should not* maximise the good, because doing so would be to violate a duty. Most deontologists also argue that we do not have a duty to maximise the good, only a duty to do *something* for people in need. As this illustrates, many deontologists think our duties are quite limited. While there are a number of things we *may not* do, we are otherwise free to act as we please.

? How does deontology differ from rule utilitarianism?

Going further: actions and intentions

Deontology says that certain types of action are right or wrong. How do we distinguish types of action? For example, a person may kill someone else. A conventional description of the action is 'a killing'. But not all 'killings' are the same type of action, morally speaking. If the person *intended* to kill someone, i.e. that is what they wanted to bring about, that is very different than if the killing was accidental or if the person was only intending to defend themselves against an attack.

Actions are the result of choices, and so should be understood in terms of choices. Choices are made for reasons, and with a purpose in mind. These considerations determine what the action performed actually is. So deontology argues that we do not know what type of action an action is unless we know the intention. We should judge whether an action is right or wrong by the agent's intention.

Explain why the relation between intention and action is important in deontology.

ANTHOLOGY: KANT, *FOUNDATIONS OF THE METAPHYSICS OF MORALS*, CH. 1

To understand Kant's moral philosophy, we need to explain a couple of terms and assumptions. First, Kant believed that, whenever we make a decision, we act on a *maxim*. Maxims are Kant's version of intentions. They are our personal principles that guide our decisions; e.g. 'to have as much fun as possible', 'to marry only someone I truly love'. All our decisions have some maxim or other behind them. Second, morality is a set of principles that are the same for everyone and that apply to everyone. Third, Kant talks of our ability to make choices and decisions as 'the will'. He assumes that our wills are rational; that is we can make choices on the basis of reasons. We do not act only on instinct. We can act on choice, and we can consider what to choose using reasoning.

In Ch. 1, Kant argues that the fundamental principle of morality is this: 'Act only on that maxim through which you can at the same time will that it should become a universal law'. Why does he come to this conclusion?

What, according to Kant, is a 'maxim'?

The good will

Kant begins his argument by reflecting on whether anything is morally good 'without qualification'. He argues that only the 'good will' is. Anything else can either be bad or contribute to what is bad. For instance, intelligence and self-control are good – but they can enable someone to do clever or difficult bad things, if that is what they choose. Power can be good, but it depends on what use we put it to. Nor is happiness good without qualification. If someone is made happy by hurting others, their happiness is morally bad. So we evaluate happiness by morality. Having a morally good will is a precondition to *deserving* happiness.

Kant then makes a second claim. What is good about the good will is not what it *achieves*. It doesn't derive its goodness

See INDIVIDUAL LIBERTY AND RIGHTS, p. 42.

Why does Kant say that only the good will is good without qualification?

from successfully producing some good result. Rather, it is good 'in itself'. If someone tries their hardest to do what is morally right but they don't succeed, then we should still praise their efforts as morally good.

Duty

What is our conception of the morally good will? We can understand it in terms of the concept of duty. Kant argues that to have a good will is to be motivated by duty. This is best understood by examples. Suppose a shopkeeper sells his goods at a fixed price, giving the correct change, and acting honestly in this way. Of course, this is the morally right thing to do. But this doesn't show that he has a good will, since acting like this is just in his self-interest. So we can act *in accordance* with duty, but without being *motivated* by duty. Kant controversially claims that this applies just as much to doing good things for other people when that is what we want to do and enjoy doing. Doing good things for others is right and should be praised and encouraged, but these actions don't necessarily have moral *worth*. But if someone was to do something good for others even when they didn't want to, but just because they believe that it is the morally right thing to do, *that* would show that they have a good will. So to have a good will is to do one's duty (what is morally right) *because* it is one's duty (because it is morally right). But what *is* morally right? What does a good will will? Here, things get tricky. A good will isn't good because it aims at certain ends, because there are no ends that are good without qualification. We can't, for instance, say that the good will aims at the general happiness, because happiness isn't always morally good. So the good will must, in some way, be good 'in itself', just on the basis of what it is like as a will. What makes a will good is something about the maxims it adopts. However, it can't be *what* the maxims say; i.e. what they aim at. A puzzle ...

Another puzzle arises if we consider this in terms of motives. What is it to want to do one's duty because it is one's duty, if we

Explain the distinction between acting in accordance with duty and being motivated by duty.

can't say what one's duty is? It can only be the thought of doing one's duty 'as such'. But what is that?

To solve these puzzles, we need to recall Kant's assumptions. Maxims are principles of choice. They are subjective – you have yours, I have mine. What makes them different is what they are about, what they aim at and why. But what they have in common is that they are all principles. Now, morality is a set of principles for everyone. So the concept of duty is the concept of a principle for everyone. So, somehow, the good will is a will that chooses what it does, motivated by the idea of a principle for everyone. This is 'not an expected result', Kant says.

How can this idea serve as a motive or criterion for the good will? Kant rephrases it: to have a good will, I should act only on maxims that I can also will everyone to act on. He later calls this principle the 'Categorical Imperative'. I can adopt this as a maxim, a principle of choice. I choose only to make choices on the basis of maxims that everyone could act on. But this maxim doesn't specify any particular end or goal (such as happiness). It only mentions the idea of a principle for everyone, a universal law.

We need to understand the Categorical Imperative in more detail. But first, an example: suppose I am tempted to make a promise with no intention of keeping it; e.g. I might borrow money (because I want the money) on the promise to pay it back, but I don't intend to pay it back. We can show that this is wrong. Suppose everyone acted on this maxim. Then everyone would know that everyone acts on this maxim. In that situation, making a false promise like this would be impossible. No one would trust my promise, and I can't make a promise unless someone believes it. So I can't will my maxim to be universal.

> Briefly outline Kant's concept of the good will.

> Explain Kant's argument from the concept of the good will to the Categorical Imperative.

ANTHOLOGY: KANT, *FOUNDATIONS OF THE METAPHYSICS OF MORALS*, CH. 2; RACHELS, *THE ELEMENTS OF MORAL PHILOSOPHY*, CH. 9.1

Hypothetical and categorical imperatives

criticism

An 'imperative' is just a command. 'Hypothetical imperatives' are statements about what you ought to do, on the assumption of some desire or goal. They specify a means to an end. So 'if you want to see the show, you ought to get to the theatre at least 15 minutes early' is a hypothetical imperative. In this example, the assumed desire or goal is explicit: the imperative is presented as a conditional, with the desire described in the antecedent ('you want to see the show'), and the command in the consequent ('get to the theatre at least 15 minutes early'). But hypothetical imperatives can leave the assumed desire or goal implicit; e.g. 'Eat at least five portions of fruit and vegetables a day' (if you want to stay healthy).

Why can't I just say 'I want to see the show but refuse to get there early' or 'I want to be healthy but refuse to eat fruit and vegetables'? Why *ought* I to do these things, given what I want? Because these are the means to my end. Kant argues that willing the end *entails* willing the means. It is an analytic truth that someone who wills the end wills the means. To will an end is to will an effect. But the concept of an effect contains the concept of a cause. Hence, to will an effect, you must will the cause. The cause is the means. (It is important here that you don't merely *want* the end, but actually will it.)

Criticism

Hypothetical imperatives can be avoided by simply giving up the assumed desire or goal. Suppose I don't want to see the show – then I don't need to get to the theatre early. Suppose I don't want to be healthy – then the imperative to get my 'five-a-day' doesn't apply to me. (Of course, it is odd not to want to be healthy, and we may wonder if I really do not want to be healthy – perhaps I do, but I can't be bothered … In this case, I want to be healthy, but I don't will it.) In other words, it is possible to 'opt out' of a hypothetical imperative.

This isn't true of morality, we usually think. Moral duties are not hypothetical. They are what we ought to do, full stop. They are your duty regardless of what you want. They are 'categorical'. Kant has also argued that moral duties aren't a means to some further end, because what makes an action good is that it is willed by the good will. All categorical imperatives – our moral duties – are derived from one, *the* Categorical Imperative: 'Act only on that maxim through which you can at the same time will that it should become a universal law'.

How are categorical imperatives possible? Why is there something that we ought to do, regardless of what we want? Kant argues that moral duties depend just on our being rational. We need to understand further just what this means.

response

Explain the distinction between a hypothetical and a categorical imperative.

The two tests

There are two different ways in which we could fail to be able to will our maxim to become a universal law.

1. 'Contradiction in conception': the situation in which everyone acted on that maxim is somehow self-contradictory. We saw an example of this in the case of making a false promise, above. Another example: suppose you want a gift to take to a party, but you can't afford it, so you steal it from the shop. Your maxim is something like: 'To steal something I want if I can't afford it'. This can only be the right thing to do if everyone could do it. However, if we could all just help ourselves to whatever we wanted, the idea of 'owning' things would disappear. Now, by definition, you can't steal something unless it belongs to someone else. Stealing presupposes that people own things. But people can only own things if they don't all go around helping themselves whenever they want. So it is logically impossible for everyone to steal things. And so stealing (at least stealing just because one wants something) is wrong.

Kant notes that the first test defines 'perfect' duties (duties of justice) while the second test defines 'imperfect' duties. See MILL, UTILITARIANISM, CH. 5, p. 43.

example

Why, according to Kant, is it wrong to steal?

Read again

2. 'Contradiction in will': this is more difficult to understand. The maxim is not self-contradictory, but we cannot rationally will it. Consider a refusal to help other people, ever. It *is* logically possible to universalise the maxim 'not to help others in need'. The world would not be a pleasant place, but this is beside the point. Kant does *not* claim that an action is wrong because we *wouldn't like* the consequences if everyone did it (many philosophers and students have misinterpreted Kant on this point). His test is whether we can rationally will that our maxim be a universal law. Kant argues that we *cannot will* that no one ever help anyone else. How so?

   a. A will, by definition, wills its ends (goals).

   b. As we said above, to truly will the ends, one must will the necessary means.

   c. Therefore, we cannot will a situation in which it would be impossible for us to achieve our ends.

   d. It is possible that the only available means to our ends, in some situations, involves the help of others.

   e. We cannot therefore will that this possibility is denied to us.

   f. Therefore, we cannot will a situation in which no one ever helps anyone else. To do so is to cease to will the necessary means to one's ends, which is effectively to cease to will any ends at all. This contradicts the very act of willing.

> **?** Explain Kant's tests of 'contradiction in conception' and 'contradiction in will'.

Morality and reason

Kant argued that it is not just morally wrong to disobey the Categorical Imperative, it is also irrational. As the tests show, disobeying the Categorical Imperative involves a self-contradiction. Through the Categorical Imperative, *reason* both determines what our duties are and gives us the means to discover them. Furthermore, we intuitively think that morality applies to *all and only* rational beings, not just human beings.

In Douglas Adams' *The Hitchhiker's Guide to the Galaxy*, Arthur Dent protests to the Vogons, aliens who are going to destroy the Earth, that what they are doing is immoral. But morality doesn't apply to beings that can't make rational choices, such as dogs and cats (pets misbehave; they don't act *morally wrongly*).

With this link, we can explain the nature of morality in terms of the nature of reason. Morality is universal, the same for everyone; so is reason, says Kant. Morality and rationality are categorical; the demands to be rational and moral don't stop applying to you even if you don't care about them. Neither morality nor rationality depend on what we want.

> **?**
> Are all and only rational creatures subject to moral duties?

The second formulation of the Categorical Imperative

ANTHOLOGY: KANT, *FOUNDATIONS OF THE METAPHYSICS OF MORALS*, CH. 2 (CONT.); RACHELS, *THE ELEMENTS OF MORAL PHILOSOPHY*, CH. 10.1

Kant gives a second formulation of the Categorical Imperative, known as the Formula of Humanity: 'Act in such a way that you always treat humanity, whether in your own person or in the person of any other, never simply as a means, but always at the same time as an end'. Why does he say this, and what does it mean?

Let us return to the idea of the good will. Only the good will is good without qualification. Another way of saying this is that it is the only thing of unconditional value. Everything else that is valuable depends, in some way, on the good will. For instance, intelligence is valuable for all sorts of purposes. In other words, it is valuable as a means to an end. Its value, then, depends on the value of its end. What gives its end value? We do, says Kant. Something is only an end if it is adopted by a will. It is our adopting something as an end that gives it value. Because I have desires and purposes, various things in the world are valuable *to me*.

So far, value is subjective. However, this does not apply to other people (or rational beings generally). Your value is not simply your value *to me* as a means in relation to some purpose or desire I have. It is not even your value to you (you might have very low self-esteem, and wrongly underestimate your value). We have 'intrinsic worth', which Kant identifies as 'dignity'. What gives us this dignity is our rational will. The will has unconditional value *as the thing which gives value to everything else*. So in the second formulation above, by 'humanity', Kant means our ability to rationally determine which ends to adopt and pursue.

Kant says that because people are ends in themselves, we must always treat them as such, and never 'simply' as a means. Note that he does not say we cannot use people as a means, but that we can't use them *only* as a means. We rely on other people in many ways as a means of achieving our own ends; e.g. people serving me in a shop are a means of getting what I want to buy. What is important, says Kant, is that I also respect them as an end.

To treat someone simply as a means, and not also as an end, is to treat the person in a way that undermines their power of making a rational choice themselves. It means, first, that we should appeal to other people's reason in discussing with them what to do, rather than manipulating them in ways they are unaware of. Coercing someone, lying to them or stealing from them all involve not allowing them to make an informed choice. If they are involved in our action in any way, they need to be able to agree (or refuse) to adopt our end as their own.

Second, treating someone as an end also means leaving them free to pursue the ends that they adopt. The value of what people choose to do lies in their ability to choose it, not just in what they have chosen. So we should refrain from harming or hindering them. This is to respect their rationality. Third, someone's being an end in themselves means that they are an end for others. We should adopt their ends as our own. What this means is that we should help them pursue their ends, just as we pursue our own ends. In other words, the second formulation requires that we help other people. This should be one of our ends in life.

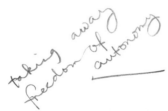
taking away freedom of autonomy

Explain Kant's reason for claiming that people are ends in themselves.

Explain what Kant means by the claim that we must treat people an end in themselves.

Issues for Kantian ethics

Problems with the application of the principle

In *Utilitarianism*, Ch. 1, Mill claims that when Kant attempts to deduce moral duties from the Categorical Imperative, he fails to show that there is any contradiction involved in being immoral. At best, he only shows that the consequences of everyone being immoral is something that we *wouldn't want*, but not something that we *cannot will*. However, Mill doesn't give us an argument supporting his objection, so we don't know why he thinks the two tests don't work in the examples Kant discusses.

But there are reasons to think the test is flawed. For instance, couldn't any action be justified, as long as we phrase the maxim cleverly? In stealing the gift, I could claim that my maxim is 'To steal gifts from large shops and when there are seven letters in my name (Michael)'. Universalising this maxim, only people with seven letters in their name would steal only gifts and only from large shops. The case would apply so rarely that there would be no general breakdown in the concept of private property. So it would be perfectly possible for this law to apply to everyone.

Kant's response is that his theory is concerned with my *actual* maxim, not some made-up one. It is not actually part of my choice that my name has seven letters, or perhaps even that it is a *gift* I steal. If I am honest with myself, I have to admit that it is a question of my taking what I want when I can't afford it. For Kant's test to work, we must be honest with ourselves about what our maxims are.

But here is another example. Say I am a hard-working shop assistant, who hates the work. One happy Saturday I win the lottery, and I vow 'never to sell anything to anyone again, but only ever to buy'. This is perhaps eccentric, but it doesn't seem morally wrong. But it cannot be universalised. If no one ever sold things, how could anyone buy them? It is logically impossible, which makes it wrong according to Kant's test. So perhaps it is not always wrong to do things which require other people do something different.

> Discuss, using one example, whether it is contradictory to will that everyone does what is immoral.

> Does the Categorical Imperative determine what we ought to do?

The intuition that consequences of actions determine their moral value

Criticism

Utilitarians object that Kantian deontology is confused about moral value. If it is my duty not to murder, for instance, this must be because there is something bad about murder. But then if murder is bad, surely we should try to ensure that there are as few murders as possible. If I *know* that unless I kill someone deliberately, many people will die, how can I justify *not* killing that person on the grounds that I cannot universalise the motive of murder? Surely it is only my duty not to kill because death is bad. So I should prevent more deaths. What makes a will good is that it wills good ends.

Kant's response, of course, is that there are no ends that are good without qualification. So this cannot be the right analysis of the good will.

But the disagreement goes deeper. Utilitarianism understands all practical reasoning – reasoning about what to do – as *means–end* reasoning: it is rational to do whatever brings about a good end. The utilitarian thinks it is just *obvious* that if something is good, more of it is better, and we ought to do what is better. Kant disagrees and offers an *alternative* theory of practical reasoning. Means–end reasoning is appropriate for hypothetical imperatives, but this is not all there is to practical reason. It is also irrational to act in a way that not everyone could act in. If rationality were only about means–end reasoning, then we couldn't say that any ends – such as other people – are obligatory. Morality becomes hypothetical. You only ought to do your duty *if* you want to be morally good. This treats morality like just another desire or purpose which we may or may not have.

Mill's response to this, of course, is that happiness is the only desirable end. But, once again, Kant has argued that happiness is not always good.

> See UTILITARIANISM, p. 26.

> **?** Is happiness always good?

> **?** Is it irrational to be immoral?

The value of certain motives and commitments

In THE VALUE OF MOTIVES AND CHARACTER (p. 45), we looked at the objection that utilitarianism does not recognise the moral value of motives. That particular objection cannot be levelled at Kant – he makes motives central to moral duty. In THE MORAL STATUS OF PARTICULAR RELATIONSHIPS (p. 48), we looked at two objections to utilitarianism that argued that a concern with 'doing the right thing' could turn out to be objectionable. The first was that utilitarianism makes morality too demanding by requiring us to be impartial between our friends/family and people we don't know. Kantian deontology doesn't require this. While we are required to help others, we are not required to be completely impartial or maximise happiness. (There is no contradiction in a maxim which aims to help others but not maximise happiness.) However, the second objection, concerning how we should understand the moral worth of motives involved in particular relationships of love and friendship, does apply to Kant's theory as it did to utilitarianism.

Kant makes the motive of duty (doing your duty because it is your duty) the *only* motive that has moral worth, and says that doing something good for someone else because you *want* to is morally right, but not morally good. But consider again the example of visiting a friend in hospital. If the visitor protests to her friend that she is just doing her duty, that her motive is simply to do what is morally right, then her friend can object. Kant seems to say that we have to want to benefit people because it is our duty to so, not because we like them. But surely, if I do something nice for you because I like you, that is a morally good action. Much of the time we do good things because we feel warmly towards the people we benefit. We can object that putting duty above feelings in our motives is somehow inhuman.

Kant can respond that he is not trying to *stop* us from being motivated by our feelings. His point is that, when we are choosing what to do, how we feel should not be as important as what it is morally right to do. Our feelings shouldn't *decide* the matter, our motive to do what is morally right should. But when you do something for a friend, should you think 'I'll do this because he is my friend; and it is morally right to do so'? Consider again the man rescuing his wife from drowning. If he thinks 'She's my wife and it is morally permissible that I rescue her', he has 'one thought too many'. His commitment to his wife means that he should stop at 'She's my wife'.

Perhaps Kant can reply that you don't actually need to have such a thought. His theory, after all, is how we can tell whether something is right or wrong, not how we should actually think all the time. So we can say that to be morally good, you only need to be willing to refuse to help your friend if that involved doing something morally wrong. And likewise for the man and his wife.

> Explain the objection that Kant does not recognise the value of being motivated by friendship.

> Is an action only morally good if it is motivated by duty?

Conflicts between duties

problem

response

> Briefly explain the objection to Kantian deontology from conflicts between duties.

ANTHOLOGY: RACHELS, *THE ELEMENTS OF MORAL PHILOSOPHY*, CH. 9.3

Kant argues that our moral duties are absolute. A duty is absolute if it permits no exceptions. Nothing can override a moral duty, because it is categorical. All other ends have their worth in relation to the good will. But the good will is motivated by duty.

This causes problems in cases in which it seems that two absolute duties conflict with each other. Should I break a promise or tell a lie? Should I betray a friend to save a life? If I am faced with a situation in which I must do one or the other, then Kant's theory implies that whatever I do must be wrong.

One response is to say that a *real* conflict of duties can never occur. If there appears to be a conflict, we have misunderstood what at least one duty requires of us. If duties are absolute, we must formulate our duties very, very carefully to avoid them conflicting. As we will see when discussing DECEPTION AND THE TELLING OF LIES (p. 134), Kant himself thought that some of our duties are very straightforward; e.g. our duty not to lie is simply that - *never* lie. But you can believe the rest of Kant's theory and not accept his view that duties are simple like this. For example, you could argue that 'don't lie' isn't a duty. Our duty could be something like 'don't lie unless you have to lie to save a life'. There will always be *some* maxim you can act on which you will be able to universalise. So it will always be possible to do your duty.

We can object that it is more realistic simply to say that (most) duties are not absolute. For instance, there is a duty not to lie, but it may be permissible to lie in order to save someone's life. Less important duties can 'give way' to more important ones. In cases of conflict, one will give way and no longer be a duty in that situation.

Rachels argues that Kant was right that we must be *consistent* in moral judgements. Our moral judgements must be based on reasons, and if some consideration is a reason in one situation, it is a reason for other people and in other similar situations. We can't think of ourselves as special, and allow ourselves to do what we would not want others to do. But Kant was wrong to think that consistency requires absolute rules, no exceptions. Instead, when we break a rule, we need a good reason to do so, a reason that we are willing to accept other people acting on as well.

However, this solution must reject the basis of Kant's theory of morality. His whole analysis of duty is that it is categorical. It is difficult to see how his understanding of why morality is rationally required could allow that duties can give way to each other.

This recommendation resembles PRESCRIPTIVISM, p. 180.

?

Should you act only on that maxim through which you can also will that it become a universal law?

Key points: Kantian deontological ethics

- Deontology claims that actions are right or wrong *in themselves*, not depending on their consequences. It identifies different types of action, and so judges whether they are right or wrong, on the basis of the agent's intention.
- Our duties are concerned with *our* actions, not attempting to bring about the most good. It can be against our duty to do what maximises the good.
- Kant argues that only the good will is good without qualification. The good will is motivated by duty. To have a good will is to do one's duty because it is one's duty.
- Kant argues that choices are made according to maxims, and that morality is a set of principles everyone can follow.
- He therefore concludes that it is morally right to 'Act only on that maxim through which you can at the same time will that it should become a universal law' (the Categorical Imperative). Acting on a maxim that does not pass this test is morally wrong.

- A hypothetical imperative tells you what you ought, rationally, to do, assuming a certain desire or goal. A categorical imperative tells you what you ought to do, irrespective of what you want.

- A maxim can fail the test of the Categorical Imperative in two ways: 1) it cannot be consistently universalised, because a situation in which everyone acted on it is impossible; 2) it cannot be willed in a universal form, because a situation in which it was universally followed undermines the operation of the will.

- As the test shows, Kant bases morality on reason. Reason and morality are categorical, apply to all rational beings, and are independent of our desires.

- Kant reformulated the Categorical Imperative as the Formula of Humanity: 'Act in such a way that you always treat humanity, whether in your own person or in the person of any other, never simply as a means, but always at the same time as an end'. This requires us to respect others' ability to make rational choices, and to help them achieve their ends.

- However, the Categorical Imperative delivers some counter-intuitive results.

- Utilitarians argue that an action is right if it brings about what is good. Kant replies that nothing is good without qualification except the good will.

- Utilitarians also argue that it is irrational not to maximise what is good. Kant replies that it is irrational to act on a maxim that not everyone could act on.

- We can object that Kant does not recognise the moral value of motives other than duty, such as friendship. One response is that Kant only requires us not to act on such motives if they conflict with our duty.

- We can object that Kantian deontology cannot allow duties to conflict, but in the real world, they do conflict.

C. Aristotle's virtue ethics

Utilitarianism and Kantian deontology focus on morally *right actions* – what is the right thing to do, and why? On these views, to be a good person is to be motivated to do morally right actions. By contrast, virtue ethics starts with what it is to be a *good person*. From this, it then derives an account of what a morally right action is, which it understands in terms of what a good person would do. An important claim of virtue ethics is that there is more to the moral life than actions.

ANTHOLOGY: ARISTOTLE, *NICOMACHEAN ETHICS*, BK 1

The good

Aristotle begins the *Nicomachean Ethics* with the question 'What is the good for human beings?' What is it that we are aiming at, that would provide a successful, fulfilling, good life? His discussion is very similar to MILL'S 'PROOF' OF UTILITARIANISM (p. 36). Or more accurately, since Aristotle got there first, and Mill was very familiar with Aristotle – Mill's proof resembles Aristotle's argument.

Our different activities aim at various 'goods'. For example, medicine aims at health; military strategy aims at victory. For any action or activity, there is a purpose (a 'why') for which we undertake it – its end. An analysis of the purposes for which we do things is an analysis of what we see to be 'good' about them. An answer to 'Why do that?' is an answer to 'What's the point?' – and 'the point' is what is worthwhile about doing that.

Now, complex activities, such as medicine, have many component activities, e.g. making pharmaceuticals, making surgical implements, diagnosis, etc. Where an activity has different components like this, the overall end (health) is better – 'more preferable' – than the end of each subordinate activity (successful drugs, useful implements, accurate diagnoses). This is because these activities are undertaken for the sake of the overall end.

We undertake actions and activities either for the sake of something further or 'for their own sake'. Suppose there is some end for whose sake we do everything else. Suppose that this end we desire for its own sake, not the sake of anything else. Then this end would be *the* good for us (§2).

Eudaimonia

People generally agree, says Aristotle, that this is '*eudaimonia*'. Before going any further with Aristotle's argument about the good, we should take time to understand what Aristotle means by eudaimonia.

Eudaimonia is the good for a human life. It is usually translated as 'happiness' but Aristotle says it is 'living well and faring well'. We have some idea of what it is when an animal or plant is living and faring well – we talk of them 'flourishing'. A plant or animal flourishes when its needs are met in abundance and it is a good specimen of its species. Gardeners try to enable their plants to flourish; zookeepers try to enable the zoo animals to flourish. So eudaimonia is 'the good' or the 'good life' for human beings as the particular sort of being we are. To achieve it is to live as best a human being can live.

There are a number of contrasts we can draw with our usual idea of 'happiness'.

1. We can talk of people being happy as a psychological state. But eudaimonia is not a state of mind, but relates to an activity – the activity of living. A good life is one that realises the full potential that a human life has.

2. Eudaimonia is not something subjective, but objective. To say someone is or was eudaimon is to make an objective judgement about their life as a good human life. It is not to say anything (directly) about their state of mind; nor is it a judgement the subject themselves has any special authority over. By contrast, if someone says they are happy or unhappy, it is difficult to correct them or know better.

3. Eudaimonia is not something easily changed. It does not come and go as happiness (in the usual sense) can. For it is an evaluation of a life (a life lived well) or a person (a good person) as a whole. These are very stable judgements.

satisfaction(?)

state we are aiming

Explain three differences between eudaimonia and happiness.

If eudaimonia relates to the *whole* of someone's life, then can you call someone eudaimon while they are still alive (§10)? Their life is not yet finished - something terrible may yet happen that would lead us to say that theirs was not a good life. On the other hand, it is absurd to say that they *are* eudaimon after they have died. We could say, once they are dead, that they *were* eudaimon, but then it is strange that we cannot say that they *are* eudaimon before they have died. We will see how Aristotle solves this puzzle once we have seen his proposal for what eudaimonia consists in.

Final ends

So, people agree that eudaimonia is the good. But they disagree on what eudaimonia is, e.g. pleasure, wealth, honour, or something else again (§§4, 5). It can't be just pleasure per se, Aristotle argues, since people can seek animal pleasures, but we're after the good for human beings. It can't be wealth - money is only useful as a means to an end, it isn't an end in itself. It can't be honour, since to have honour, others must honour you. What is it you want to be honoured (recognised, rewarded, praised) *for*? Whatever the answer, having *that* must be what is good.

Aristotle briefly raises the suggestion that the wise person wants to be honoured for their virtues. (We'll consider what a virtue is below.) But just *having* virtues, e.g. courage or intelligence, can't be enough for a good life, for two reasons. First, you can have virtue while asleep. Such inactivity isn't our end in life. Second, having virtue is compatible with suffering great misfortune in life. But this isn't a good life either. So we still don't know yet what eudaimonia is.

Given that people think pleasure, honour, or again, knowledge, are all good, is eudaimonia our *only* good (§7)? Call an end that we desire for its own sake a 'final' end. We can't give some further purpose for why we seek it. If there is just one end for the sake of which we do everything else, that is the good. If

Mill responds by distinguishing HIGHER AND LOWER PLEASURES, p. 33.

there is more than one end, there are various final ends, each of which is good. If pleasure, honour and knowledge are final ends, doesn't that show that eudaimonia is not our only good?

Not yet. Some final ends we might seek *both* for their own sake *and* for the sake of something else. Everything that we pursue for its own sake – such as pleasure, knowledge, honour, and so on – we also pursue for the sake of eudaimonia. How can we pursue something *both* for its own sake and for the sake of eudaimonia? We faced this puzzle when discussing MILL'S 'PROOF' OF UTILITARIANISM (p. 36). The solution was to distinguish between external means and constitutive means. Final ends are constitutive parts of eudaimonia. For example, we can pursue knowledge for its own sake and pursue it for the sake of living well if we understand acquiring knowledge as part of the good life. Everything we do is done for the sake of living and faring well.

By contrast, says Aristotle, we never want to live and fare well in order to achieve some *other* end. If there is a final end which we *never* seek for the sake of anything else, but only ever for its own sake, this will be a final end 'without qualification'. This is eudaimonia.

A further reason for thinking eudaimonia is our only good is that the good should be self-sufficient; i.e. it makes life desirable on its own. Eudaimonia is the most desirable thing, and we can't make it more desirable by adding something else to it. In fact, given what we've just said, to add some other goal, e.g. knowledge, to eudaimonia is just to make that other thing part of your eudaimonia. Eudaimonia is the only self-sufficient good.

The function argument

But we still don't know what eudaimonia is. So Aristotle embarks on an analysis in terms of the idea of *ergon*. This is often translated 'function', but as with translating eudaimonia as happiness, this is misleading. The ergon of a thing *can* be its function – the ergon of an eye is to see – but a more general

> Explain Aristotle's argument that eudaimonia is our only good.

account would be the 'characteristic form of activity' of something. 'Function' here is better understood in relation to 'functioning' rather than 'purpose'.

'Function' and 'virtue'

The 'characteristic activity' provides an insight into what type of thing something is (otherwise in what sense would the activity be 'characteristic'?). It thereby provides an evaluative standard for that thing: something is a good *x* when it performs its characteristic activity well. If the ergon of a knife is to cut, a good knife cuts well; a good eye sees well; a good plant flourishes (it grows well, produces flowers well, etc., according to its species).

In order to fulfil its ergon, a thing will need certain qualities. An *arête* is a quality that aids the fulfilment of a thing's ergon. It can be translated generally as an 'excellence', or more specifically, a 'virtue'. So sharpness is a virtue in a knife designed to cut. Good focus is a virtue in an eye.

Explain Aristotle's concepts of 'function' and 'virtue'.

The argument

Aristotle applies this entire account to human beings. Virtues for human beings will be those traits that enable them to fulfil their ergon. So, first, what is the 'characteristic activity' of human beings? At the most general level, we are alive. But this isn't distinctive of just us. So we shouldn't identify 'life' as our characteristic activity. We are a type of animal, rather than plant. We are conscious, have sense perception, etc. But again, we share this with many animals. But we want to know what the good for human beings, distinctively, is.

A human life is distinctively the life of a being that can be guided by *reason*. We are, distinctively, rational animals. Many commentators misunderstand Aristotle to be claiming that reason*ing* is our ergon. But Aristotle makes a deeper point – what is characteristic of us is that whatever we do, we do for reasons. All our activities – not just 'reasoning' – are, or can be, guided by reasons. Being guided by reasons is, of course, a matter of our psychology, and so Aristotle talks of the activity of the soul (*psyche*).

Now, we said above, that a good *x* (eye, knife, etc.) is one that performs its characteristic activity well, and that it will need certain qualities – virtues – to enable it to do this. Our ergon will be living in accordance with reason, and the virtues of a human being will be what enables this. Only the virtuous person can achieve eudaimonia. To fulfil our ergon and live well, we must be guided by the 'right' reasons – good reasons, not 'bad' reasons. So eudaimonia consists in the activity of the soul which exhibits the virtues by being in accordance with ('good' or 'right') reason (*orthos logos*). Finally, we must add – as noted earlier – that this must apply to a person's life as a whole. A day or even a year of living well doesn't amount to a good life.

Outline and explain Aristotle's function argument.

Testing the analysis

The next question might be 'But what is it to live in accordance with right reason?' The rest of the *Nicomachean Ethics* can be understood as an answer to this question. But before moving on to that issue, it is worth double-checking that this is a plausible account of eudaimonia. In §8, Aristotle argues that it is indeed consistent with other things we want to say about what is good for human beings.

1. There are three types of thing that are good for us – goods of the mind (e.g. intelligence, courage, etc.), goods of the body (e.g. strength, health, etc.) and 'external' goods (e.g. wealth, food, etc.). People generally agree that the goods of the mind are worth more than the others. We often think of the others as additional to, but not comprising, a good life. This agrees with the analysis; eudaimonia centrally concerns goods 'of the soul'.
2. We have said eudaimonia is living well. The analysis agrees, and spells out what it is to live well.

3. We can return to the suggestions in §5 (FINAL ENDS, p. 73) that the good life involves virtue, pleasure and prosperity, and now explain the truth in each.

    a. Virtue: as we said, to possess virtue is not enough; eudaimonia requires that one *acts* on it as well. The employment of good qualities and the achievement of good purposes are better than simply having the disposition to do so.

    b. Pleasure: people find pleasant whatever it is that they love. A virtuous person loves living virtuously – you shouldn't call someone 'just', for instance, if they dislike doing what is just. But that means that the life of the virtuous person will also be pleasant. Eudaimonia is therefore both good and pleasant.

    c. Prosperity: in order to *live* virtuously (e.g. to be generous), we will also need a certain amount of external goods. And so, enough good fortune is needed for a fully good life.

We can now solve the puzzle in §10 (EUDAIMONIA, p. 72): can we call someone eudaimon while they are still alive? Fortunes change, but living virtuously has a much greater permanence. A virtuous person deals with bad fortune in the best possible way, so only very rarely and through terrible circumstances, can someone virtuous fail to lead a good life. Now we understand that virtue is central to leading a good life, we can call someone eudaimon while they live, if they have sufficient external goods.

> Explain Aristotle's claim that eudaimonia involves virtue, pleasure and prosperity.

Going further: the rational 'soul'

We now have the outline of an answer to the question 'what is the good for human beings?' It is a life of activity in accordance with reason, and this requires the virtues. So what are the virtues?

not based on or governed by reasoning

See ARISTOTLE,
NICOMACHEAN ETHICS,
BKS 3.6-12, 7.1-10, p.
85.

Because our ergon is the activity of the soul in accordance with reason, a virtue is a trait of a person's 'soul'. In §13, Aristotle provides an analysis of the soul. We can divide it into an arational part, and a rational part (at least in analysis, even if there aren't literal 'parts'). The arational part can be further divided in two – the part that is related to 'growth and nutrition' (Aristotle thought that all life has soul) and the part related to desire and emotion. The desiring part we share with other animals, but in us, it can be responsive to reason. For instance, in someone who is tempted, but controls themselves, what they want yields to what they think is good. Someone with the virtue of temperance is not even tempted by what they think is not good. What they want 'speaks with the same voice' as their reason.

We can talk about the rational 'part' of the soul having two parts as well. There is the desiring part which can respond to reasons and there is the part with which we reason, which has reason 'in itself'.

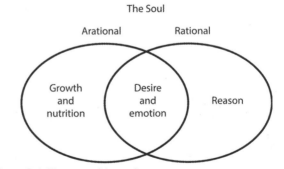

Figure 2.1 The parts of the soul

Virtues are traits that enable us to live in accordance with reason. They are, therefore, of two kinds – virtues of the intellect (traits of the reasoning part) and virtues of character (traits of the part characterised by desire and emotion).

ANTHOLOGY: ARISTOTLE, *NICOMACHEAN ETHICS*, BK 2

As we have seen, a virtue is a trait of mind or character that helps us achieve a good life, which Aristotle has analysed as a life in accordance with reason. There are two types of virtue – intellectual virtues and moral virtues. The central intellectual virtue for leading the good life, we will see, is PRACTICAL WISDOM (p. 99). In Bk 2, Aristotle concentrates on moral virtues, traits of character. Aristotle thought that the list of virtues isn't a miscellaneous collection, but grounded in a general, reasoned account of what virtues are. He presents that account in §§5-6.

Traits of character

Aristotle says that anything that is part of the soul (the mind) is either a passion, a faculty or a state (trait) of character. So since virtues are part of the soul, they must be one of these.

1. Passions: Aristotle's term 'passions' covers our bodily appetites (for food, drink, sex, etc.), our emotions, and any feelings accompanied by pleasure or pain. But these can't be virtues for three reasons.
    a. Just having a particular passion – feeling hungry or angry – doesn't make you a good or bad person.
    b. We don't choose our passions, but virtues are related to the choices we make. We cannot generally, just by an act of will, choose what we feel or want.
    c. Virtues concern how we are *disposed* to feel and act; they are not desires that actually motivate us.
2. Faculties: faculties are things like sight or the ability to feel fear. Virtues can't be these, since we have these naturally but we have to *acquire* virtue (see ACQUIRING VIRTUES AND BEING VIRTUOUS, p. 83).
3. So virtues must be states of character.

Aristotle defines states of character as 'the things in virtue of which we stand well or badly with reference to the passions'. Character involves a person's *dispositions* that relate to what, in different circumstances, they feel, how they think, how they react, the sorts of choices they make, and the actions they perform. So someone is short-tempered if they are disposed to feel angry quickly and often; quick-witted if they can think on their feet; intemperate if they get drunk often and excessively. What we find pleasant also reveals our character.

Character has a certain stability and longevity. Character traits last much longer and change less easily than many 'states of mind', such as moods and desires. But character can change, and so it is less stable and long-lived than personal identity. Yet it is central to being the person one is.

? What is a trait (or state) of character?

Virtues and the doctrine of the mean

What kind of state of character is a virtue? Some traits of character, such as being short-tempered or greedy, stop us from leading a good life - these are vices. Other traits of character, such as being kind or courageous, help us to lead a good life - and these are the virtues. Any virtue makes the thing which has it good and able to perform its characteristic activity well. So, in us, a virtue of character is a disposition to feel, desire and choose 'well', which is necessary if we are to live well and so achieve eudaimonia.

? What, according to Aristotle, is a moral virtue?

What does this involve? Aristotle compares living well with other activities, such as eating well or physical training. In these cases, the good nutritionist or good trainer needs to avoid prescribing too much food or exercise or too little. We achieve health and physical fitness by following an 'intermediate' course of action. However, what this is differs from person to person. A professional sportsman needs more food and exercise than most people. An 'objective' intermediate (or 'mean') is a mathematical quantity, halfway between the two extremes, as 6 is halfway between 2 and 10. But in human activity, the intermediate ('mean') is relative to each individual.

Now, in the 'art of living', so to speak, something similar applies. We can feel our passions either 'too much' or 'too little'. Virtue involves being disposed to feeling in an 'intermediate' way, neither too much nor too little. Some people feel angry too often, over too many things (perhaps they take a critical comment as an insult), or maybe whenever they get angry, they get very angry, even at minor things. Other people feel angry not often enough (perhaps they don't understand how people take advantage of them). To be virtuous is 'to feel [passions] at the right times, with reference to the right objects, towards the right people, with the right motive, and in the right way' (§6). This is Aristotle's 'doctrine of the mean'.

It is important to note that Aristotle's doctrine of the mean does **not** claim that when we get angry, we should only ever be 'moderately' angry. We should be as angry as the situation demands, which can be very angry or only slightly irritated. Given the very close connection between what we feel and how we choose to act, virtues are dispositions of choice as well, and there is a 'mean' for actions as well as for feelings.

What the right time, object, person and so on is, PRACTICAL WISDOM (p. 99) helps us to know. (We won't complete our account of virtue, therefore, until we have understood what practical wisdom is.) Practical wisdom is a virtue of reason. Our passions, we noted, are susceptible to reason. There can be right and wrong ways to feel passions, and the right way to feel passions is determined by reason. If we feel our passions 'irrationally' – at the wrong times, towards the wrong objects, etc. – then we don't live well. So, Aristotle concludes, a virtue is 'a state of character concerned with choice, lying in the mean, i.e. the mean relative to us, this being determined by a rational principle, and by that principle by which the person of practical wisdom would determine it' (§6).

> Explain Aristotle's doctrine of the mean.

Virtues and vices

The doctrine of the mean entails that we can (often, if not always) place a virtue 'between' two vices. Just as there is a right time, object, person, etc., at which to feel fear (or any emotion), some people can feel fear too often, about too many things, and towards too many people, or they get too afraid of things that aren't that dangerous. Other people can feel afraid not often enough, regarding too few objects and people. Someone who feels fear 'too much' is cowardly. Someone who feels fear 'too little' is rash. Someone who has the virtue relating to fear is courageous. The virtue is the 'intermediate' state between the two vices of 'too much' and 'too little'.

In §7, Aristotle presents the following examples. For many states of character, he notes, we don't have a common name.

We discuss courage in more detail in Aristotle, Nicomachean Ethics, Bks 3.6-12, 7.1-10, p. 85.

Table 2.1 Virtue as the 'mean'

Passion/ concern	Vice of deficiency	Virtue	Vice of excess
Fear	Cowardly	Courageous	Rash
Pleasure/pain	'Insensible'	Temperate	Self-indulgent
Giving/taking money	Mean	Liberal ('free')	Prodigal ('spendthrift')
Spending large sums of money	Niggardly	'Magnificent'	Tasteless
Important honour	Unduly humble	Properly proud	Vain
Small honours	'Unambitious'	'Properly ambitious'	'Overambitious'
Anger	'Unirascible'	Good-tempered	Short-tempered
Truthfulness (regarding oneself)	Falsely modest	Truthful	Boastful
Humour	Boorish	Witty	Buffoonish
Pleasant to others	Quarrelsome, surly	Friendly	Obsequious
Shame	Shy	Modest	Shameless
Attitude to others' fortune	Spiteful (rejoicing in others' bad fortune)	Righteously indignant (pained by others' undeserved good fortune)	Envious (pained by others' good fortune)

Work through the table, working out what state of character each word refers to. Use a dictionary if you need to.

Obviously, Aristotle notes, not all *types* of actions or states of character can pick out a mean. For example, being shameless is not a mean, but a vice, while murder is always wrong. Furthermore, we often oppose a virtue to one of the two vices, either because it forms a stronger contrast with that vice (e.g. courage-cowardice) or because we have a natural tendency towards that vice, so need to try harder to resist it (e.g. temperance-self-indulgence).

But we can wonder whether virtues and virtuous actions are always 'intermediate' in any meaningful sense. We will return to this issue in GUIDANCE ON HOW TO ACT (p. 112).

Can you think of a virtue that is not 'intermediate'?

Acquiring virtues and being virtuous

We now know what virtues are. But how do we acquire them? Virtues are necessary for eudaimonia, but because they are dispositions towards feeling passions, and passions are not under the direct control of the will, we can't simply choose to become virtuous.

In §§1-4, Aristotle argues that we acquire virtues of character through 'habit', in particular, the habits we form during our upbringing. (In fact, in ancient Greek, the word for a virtue of character, *ethiké*, is a variant on the word for habit, *ethos*.) To defend his claim, Aristotle argues, first, that virtues are not acquired just through teaching. If virtues could be taught directly, like a skill, it should be possible for there to be an adolescent 'moral genius' as there can be with other skills, like mathematics or gymnastics. But it's very unclear that the idea makes any sense.

Second, Aristotle argues that we are not virtuous just by nature. He points out that for what we can do naturally, we first have the 'potentiality' and then exhibit the activity. For example, you don't acquire sight by seeing; first you have sight, then you can see. But it is the other way around for virtues. We come to form dispositions to feel and behave in certain ways by what we *do*. We are not naturally virtuous, but we are naturally capable of becoming virtuous, just as we are not born musical but can become so: 'the virtues we get by first exercising them, as also happens in the case of the arts as well [e.g. learning to play a musical instrument]. For the things we have to learn before we can do them, we learn by doing them.' Hence, 'by doing the acts that we do in our transactions with other men we become just or unjust, and by doing the acts that we do in the presence of danger, and by being habituated to feel fear or confidence, we become brave or cowardly' (§1).

Aristotle concludes that whether or not we can lead a good life depends a great deal on the habits we form when we are young – in our childhood and early adulthood. Furthermore, because our character is revealed by what we take pleasure in, we need to learn to take pleasure in the things that we should take pleasure in, and be pained by what should pain us.

There is a puzzle in what Aristotle says. In order to become just, we have to do just acts. But how can we do just acts unless we are already just? The puzzle is solved by distinguishing between actions which are 'in accordance with' justice and just acts, properly so called (§4). The actions that we do when learning to become just are acts in accordance with justice. But a just act is an act that is not only in accordance with justice, but also done *as the just person does it*.

A fully virtuous action is one in which the agent knows what they are doing, chooses the act for its own sake (i.e. for the end at which that virtue aims, e.g. justice), and makes their choice from a firm and unchangeable character. A child, by contrast, may do what is just (such as not taking more than its fair share) because it is told to do so; or because it likes the person it is sharing with; or because it wants to please an adult, and so on. It neither truly understands what justice *is* nor does it choose the act *because* the act is just. As we develop in virtue, we understand more about what is good and develop a moral character, so we are more able to meet the conditions for fully virtuous action. We will also need to develop PRACTICAL WISDOM (p. 99).

See ARISTOTLE, NICOMACHEAN ETHICS, BKS 7.12-13, 10.1-5, p. 106.

See DUTY, p. 58, for Kant's similar distinction between acting in accordance with duty and being motivated by duty.

Explain Aristotle's theory of how we acquire virtues.

ANTHOLOGY: ARISTOTLE, *NICOMACHEAN ETHICS*, BKS 3.6-12, 7.1-10

Going further: Aristotle on courage and temperance

It is worth illustrating Aristotle's theory by looking at his analyses of some virtues in more detail. This should help us understand his doctrine of the mean and the link between virtue, emotion and action. Here we look at courage and temperance. We'll look at Aristotle on justice later (ARISTOTLE ON JUSTICE, p. 102).

Courage: Bk 3.6-9

In Bk 3.6, Aristotle says that courage is the virtue which is the mean regarding fear (and, to a lesser degree, confidence). A simple understanding of Aristotle's doctrine of the mean might lead one to think that courage is simply about having the right 'amount' of fear, neither too much nor too little. But it is immediately clear that this is not what Aristotle means by 'the mean'. For instance, we fear everything that can harm us, but it is right to have some of these fears and others are simply irrelevant to the question of whether someone is courageous. So, for example, we should fear disgrace – this is modesty and the absence of such a fear is shamelessness. Or again, someone might not fear the loss of money, but this isn't a matter of courage.

So part of what defines courage are the *kinds* of things that someone doesn't fear. A courageous person doesn't fear the most fearful, harmful things, of which death is the greatest. Aristotle goes on to argue that the courageous person doesn't fear death for a 'noble cause', especially death in battle. Some of his remarks betray his culture, and perhaps we would now identify courage in how someone deals with a painful illness just as much as courage on the battlefield.

The courageous person fears things that we all struggle to endure, but faces them *as* one should (§7). Most of us fear not only what we shouldn't or as we shouldn't, but also *when* we shouldn't or with the wrong *motive*. The courageous person feels fear, and acts in relation to fearful things, in accordance with the right rule, and the point of being courageous – the end of courageous action – is always some good and worthwhile goal.

Hence, we should distinguish being courageous (§8) from

1. facing danger because one is required by law or the threat of punishment (such people are motivated by shame or fear);
2. being calm in the face of danger because one is very experienced and knows what will happen (such people may not show courage when their knowledge gives out or something unexpected happens);
3. being driven by passion (anger, greed, lust) to do dangerous things (such people are not fully aware of the dangers involved, and are not acting on the right motive);
4. being calm and confident as a result of one's strength and past success (such people may not show courage when they fail or in sudden situations which they can't plan for – one's character is shown when action is needed quickly or spontaneously);
5. being unafraid because one is ignorant of the danger.

Can a thief be courageous in theft? Is Aristotle's account of courage too 'moralistic'?

Aristotle has said that the virtuous person takes pleasure in virtuous action. Does this apply to courage (§9)? Yes, but not obviously. Courageous action involves pain, but the end at which it aims must be pleasant. So it is only when acting courageously achieves its ends that it is pleasant.

Temperance: Bks 3.10–12, 7.1–10

As cowardice is the vice relating to fear, so self-indulgence is the vice relating to pleasure. But which pleasures? And what is the corresponding virtue?

We gain pleasure from many different objects and activities. We can assume, Aristotle says, a distinction between pleasures deriving from the body and those related to activities of the soul (§3.10). We don't call someone self-indulgent on account of their love of learning, or admiration, or friendship. So self-indulgence is a vice relating to bodily pleasures. But not even all of these. We don't call someone self-indulgent on account of their delight in seeing or hearing things, or even smelling things. Self-indulgence relates to the pleasures of taste and touch. In fact, Aristotle argues, it is really just touch. It isn't the tasting of things, such as a wine taster would engage in, that causes the problem. It is the consuming of such things. So self-indulgence relates to the pleasures of food, drink and sex.

Now, food, drink and sex are themselves necessary (§7.4), the pleasure they give is universal, and everyone desires them. But we can go wrong in desiring them (in general) *to excess*. But we can also go wrong in desiring *particular kinds* of food, drink or sex (§3.11). We can take pleasure in the wrong things, in the wrong way, on the wrong occasions, too much, and so on. Furthermore,

How does Aristotle's analysis of courage help us understand the doctrine of the mean?

Mill defends this distinction in terms of HIGHER AND LOWER PLEASURES, p. 33.

someone who is self-indulgent is pained, more than they should be, when they miss out on such pleasures; and they value such pleasures too highly, choosing them at the cost of other more valuable things.

We need to distinguish self-indulgence, which is a vice, from simply being weak-willed (the anthology text says 'incontinent', but that word carries quite a different meaning now!) (§7.1). Both the self-indulgent and the weak-willed person have desires for pleasure which are bad, and both of them act on these desires. The difference is that the weak-willed person knows that their desires and actions are bad, and they act against their choice. The self-indulgent person has lost sight of what is good. They think there is nothing wrong in pursuing pleasure as they do. Self-indulgence is worse than being weak-willed, and it is harder to correct.

So what is the opposite of being self-indulgent? We might naturally say that it is being 'self-controlled'. But this could mean either of two quite different states. There is the person who is self-controlled in the sense that they need to control themselves in the face of temptation ('continent' in the anthology text). This person is like the weak-willed person in that they have desires for pleasure which are bad and they recognise that these desires are bad (§7.2). However, unlike the weak-willed person, they are able to resist these desires, and do what is right.

But then there is also the person who is not even tempted by such pleasures. They do not have bad desires, but desire pleasure as and when one should, in accordance with the right rule. This person has the virtue of 'temperance'. (If someone doesn't enjoy such pleasures at all, they are 'insensible' – but this vice is very rare.)

So, in relation to bodily pleasures of food, drink and sex, someone can be either self-indulgent, weak-willed,

---

Explain the difference between being self-indulgent and being weak-willed.

Explain the difference between being self-controlled and being temperate.

self-controlled, temperate, or insensible. The temperate person will choose what is genuinely pleasant, and will only desire such pleasures if they don't get in the way of pursuing other ends, don't cost more than they can afford, and aren't 'unworthy' of human dignity (§3.11). Furthermore, because strong desires for these pleasures can easily lead us astray, and acting on such desires can increase their force over time, the temperate person's desires are moderate and few (§3.12).

Outline Aristotle's account of temperance.

Going further: virtue – past and present

There are many recognisable similarities between Aristotle's concept of an arête of character and our modern concept of virtue. Both are the grounds for calling someone good or bad, for praising or blaming them for what they feel and do. Both are clearly dispositions of feeling and closely related to the sorts of choices people make. If we start to list traits we would call virtues, we see a large overlap with Aristotle's list.

However, there are at least two very important differences. First, at least since the writings of St Paul, *strength of will* has been recognised as virtuous. When someone isn't disposed to act morally, but manages to do so by strength of will, we think highly of them. For instance, we might be more willing than Aristotle to call someone courageous who feels fear, but faces it down after a struggle with it. Or again, we are more likely to praise someone who resists the temptation of bodily pleasures as much as someone who doesn't feel their temptation. For Aristotle, having inappropriate desires actually shows a weakness of character; the properly virtuous person doesn't find acting well difficult. Of course, Aristotle accepts that it is better to act well through effort than not act well at all. But 'overcoming temptation' is not a sign of real goodness, but a sign of a weak or unvirtuous character.

Second, Aristotle's concept of eudaimonia is different from acting 'morally' as we would understand the term. And so the virtues he thinks are necessary for a good life don't match, and sometimes even conflict, with the moral virtues that we might accept. For example, he thinks we should have 'proper pride' (contrast the Christian idea of humility) and that we should aim to do public works of magnificence and expense. Aristotle has a sense of the best life involving 'cutting a figure' in society, achieving a certain recognition and 'honour'. Morality has since become more closely associated with self-sacrifice, and the traits we recognise as virtues more focused on securing welfare for others than recognition for ourselves. Whether this is a good or bad development in the history of ethics can be debated.

? Is Aristotle's conception of a good person more or less attractive than ours?

ANTHOLOGY: ARISTOTLE, *NICOMACHEAN ETHICS*, BK 3.1-5

Voluntary and involuntary actions

Virtue is concerned with choice, Aristotle has said. So as we are studying what virtue involves, we need to understand choice. But before we can do that, we need to understand the distinction between what is voluntary and what is involuntary, because we praise and blame what is voluntary, but not what is involuntary (§1). Aristotle discusses these issues in the first half of Bk 3.

There are two things that render our actions involuntary - force and ignorance. When we act voluntarily, by contrast, we know what we are doing, and we bring it about ourselves. Contrast three cases of standing on a train and stepping on someone's foot:

1. The train lurches, you lose your balance, and accidentally step on someone's foot. Stepping on their foot is involuntary, caused by force.

2. You shuffle your feet to get comfortable, and put your foot down on someone's foot without looking. Although moving your feet is voluntary, stepping on someone's foot is involuntary, caused by ignorance (that their foot was there).
3. You deliberately and knowingly bring your foot down on top of someone else's. This is voluntary.

Force

We can be forced to act not only by physical forces but also by psychological pressure (such as threat of pain). Where no one could withstand such pressure, we don't blame someone for what they do. This shows it is involuntary. However, we don't think of the prospect of something good or pleasant as 'forcing' us to act. When we act involuntarily, we do so with pain and regret.

Now, some actions that we do, we don't want to do. These might be called voluntary or involuntary. Aristotle gives the example of sailors throwing goods overboard in a storm. They want to save the boat, but they don't want to lose the goods. Such actions should be called voluntary. First, actions which we do to avoid a greater evil or in order to secure some good end are the right actions to *choose*. Second, we praise people for such actions, and we noted above that praise and blame attaches to what is voluntary.

So, the distinction between voluntary and involuntary actions relates to the *moment of action* in the particular circumstances one is in, not whether the action is generally desirable.

Ignorance

Some actions done as a result of ignorance are involuntary, some are simply 'not voluntary'. The difference lies in whether the action is one that causes us pain or regret. Suppose, again, you step on someone's foot while shuffling your feet. If you regret this, then stepping on their foot is involuntary. But if you don't care, then it is simply non-voluntary.

We should also distinguish acting *in* ignorance from acting as a result of ignorance. When drunk or really angry, you may do something without fully understanding just what you are doing. Here we say that your action is a result of your drunkenness or rage, rather than your ignorance. But your drunkenness or rage puts you in a state of ignorance. So you act in ignorance, but not from ignorance.

The kind of ignorance that makes an act involuntary relates to the particular circumstances of the action. You know what you are aiming at (you aren't ignorant of the end, e.g. 'to get comfortable'), and you can know relevant general truths (e.g. people have feet). But you don't know the particular circumstances of the action; e.g. what you are actually doing (stepping on someone's foot), what its consequences will be, what tools you are using to act with, or how (in what manner) you are acting. For instance, you might think you are gently helping, when you are actually annoyingly hindering.

> Explain Aristotle's distinction between voluntary and involuntary action.

Voluntary action

Voluntary action, then, is action that you bring about, in the knowledge of what you are doing.

Sometimes people say that actions done from desire or emotion aren't voluntary. But this is a mistake for four reasons.

1. If it were true, we would have to say that neither animals nor children ever act voluntarily.
2. There are many good actions that we can do from desire and emotion (such as being kind), and we ought to do them. It would be strange to say that what we ought to do is not voluntary.
3. Actions done from desire or emotion are pleasant, not painful. But we said involuntary actions are painful, while the prospect of what is pleasant does not force us.
4. Our desires and emotions are no less part of *us* than our reason. Acting on them is something *we* do.

Choice and deliberation

We need to distinguish what is voluntary from what we choose
(§2). Everything we choose to do is voluntary, but not everything
voluntary is chosen. For instance, spontaneous actions and the
actions of young children and animals are voluntary, but not
chosen in the sense intended here. So what is choice?

1. It isn't desire – someone who gives in to temptation acts
    with desire, but not from choice, while someone who resists
    temptation acts on choice, but against their desire.
2. It isn't 'wish', since you can wish for what is impossible and
    things you can do nothing about, but choice relates to what
    we can actually do. What we wish for is also the end we are
    aiming at. What we choose are the means to get there.
3. It isn't a kind of opinion – opinions are true or false, but
    choices are good or bad.
4. Instead, choice relates to voluntary action, where this is
    done on the basis of *deliberation*.

So what is deliberation (§3)? We don't deliberate about what we
can't change, such as the facts – we investigate these. We only
deliberate about things that we can change. In fact, we only
deliberate when we need to act differently on different
occasions. You don't deliberate about how to make a cup of tea
(once you've learned) – you just get on and do it! So deliberation
is a kind of reasoned thought about what we can change by our
efforts, and where we need to act differently on different
occasions.

Aristotle also claims that we don't deliberate about ends.
But is this right? For instance, I might study in order to get a
good grade (my end). But I might well deliberate about whether
to get good grades; for example whether it is worth the effort.
Or again, I may have two ends that conflict – being a good friend
and telling the truth – and I deliberate about which end to
pursue.

However, what Aristotle probably means is that we don't deliberate about ends *as ends*. When we deliberate, we always have some end in view, and whatever we are considering is as a means to that end. If I deliberate about whether to get good grades, I am considering this in light of some further end, such as going to university. If I deliberate about being a good friend or telling the truth, I do so in light of my final end – leading a good life.

We can now say what choice is. Choice is what we decide upon as a result of deliberation. So it is a deliberate desire regarding something that is in one's power.

Explain Aristotle's theory of choice and deliberation.

Going further: moral responsibility

Do people who are bad do bad things voluntarily and by choice? Before Aristotle, Socrates had argued that they do not. Everyone aims at what they believe is good. All bad action is acting from ignorance of what is truly good, so it is not voluntary. Aristotle accepts that bad people are ignorant of the good, but maintains that they still act voluntarily.

To know fully what the right act is involves understanding *why* it is right. Someone who is bad might know, as a child does, that action *x* shouldn't be done. But if they don't understand why, they don't really know what they ought to do. Put another way: given that we all aim at eudaimonia, what is good is the 'proper' object of wish – what is truly desirable (§4). This is, in fact, what the good person desires. Bad people desire what is not truly desirable, but they are ignorant of this fact. Most errors of this kind are caused by pleasure. What is bad can seem desirable if we think it is pleasant. And different states of character find different things pleasant; e.g. the just person finds justice pleasant, but the unjust man does not.

However, this does not entail that bad men act involuntarily. Aristotle offers four arguments for this claim.

1. We noted that choice relates to the means, the actions that we take. What it is in our power to do, it is in our power not to do. So we can choose to do either good or bad actions. So bad people do bad actions voluntarily.

2. We encourage people not to do bad actions, yet we don't encourage people not to do things that are out of their power. That would be pointless. So bad actions are done voluntarily.

To these arguments, we might respond that there is a *sense* in which bad people choose to do bad actions. But still they are not *morally responsible* for them, because they are pursuing what seems good to them. They do not know what is truly desirable, and it is this ignorance that influences their choices.

Aristotle's third argument responds to this objection.

3. Bad people became bad as a result of their choices. Therefore, they are responsible for becoming bad, and thus becoming ignorant of what is good.

Why believe this? In ACQUIRING VIRTUES AND BEING VIRTUOUS (p. 83), we noted that we acquire a particular state of character by acting in a corresponding way. For example, we become just by acting in accordance with justice. Thus, we are partly responsible for our character traits. We can choose how to act, knowing that how we act will make us good or bad people. A person, through choosing to act badly, becomes a bad person, and at that point, they have become ignorant of what is good.

Rather like becoming drunk and then not knowing what you are doing; or becoming ill through ignoring medical advice; or becoming ugly through lack of care and exercise; we are responsible for becoming bad through the choices we made. We can't, when drunk, choose to be sober; or when ill, choose to be healthy; or when ugly, choose to be beautiful; so when bad, we can't simply choose to become good. Yet despite this, our condition is voluntary and we are morally responsible for it. What appears good or pleasant depends on one's character traits. If the bad person is mistaken about what is good, this is as a result of their character traits. But as they are responsible for their character traits, they are responsible for their lack of knowledge of what is truly good. So the fact that they are doing something bad, thinking that it is good, does not count as the kind of ignorance involved in involuntary action (acting *from* ignorance), but as the kind of blameworthy ignorance (acting *in* ignorance) involved in drunkenness.

4. If we reject this argument, and claim that the bad man is not responsible for what he thinks is good, then we must apply the claim generally – *no one* is responsible for what seems good or bad to them.
   a. If the bad person is not responsible for their bad actions, and these are not done voluntarily, then the good person is not responsible for their good actions, and these are not done voluntarily.
   b. But we said earlier that what is good cannot force us to act, and that what is involuntary is painful and causes regret.
   c. So good actions are done voluntarily.
   d. Therefore, so are bad actions.

Of course, actions and character traits are not voluntary in the same way. Voluntary actions are under our control from start to finish. But with the development of character traits, it is only at the beginning – in choosing the actions that lead to certain character traits – that they are fully voluntary. After this, we gradually become a certain sort of person, and then we cannot simply choose to be a different sort of person.

> Outline and explain Aristotle's defence of the claim that bad people are morally responsible for their bad actions.

Key points: Aristotle's virtue ethics (I)

- All our activities aim at some good. If there is one good that all activities aim at in the end, this is the good for human beings.
- Aristotle argues that this good is eudaimonia, sometimes translated 'happiness', but better understood as 'living well and faring well'. Eudaimonia is not a psychological state, but an objective quality of someone's life as a whole.
- We seek final ends for their own sake. However, eudaimonia is the only final end that we seek *only* for its own sake. Other final ends, such as pleasure and honour, we also seek for the sake of eudaimonia.
- Something's *ergon* is its function or characteristic activity. Something is good when it performs its ergon well. An *arête* – a virtue – is a quality that enables a thing to fulfil its ergon.
- Our characteristic activity is to be guided by reason. Virtues are qualities that enable us to live according to reason. Our good, therefore, is the activity 'of the soul' which exhibits the virtues by being in accordance with right reason.
- Eudaimonia involves virtuous activity, pleasure (because we enjoy what we love doing) and prosperity (because we need some good fortune for virtuous activity).
- The soul has three parts – an arational part, a part characterised by desires and emotions that is responsive to reason, and the rational intellect.

- Moral virtues are traits of character, dispositions to feel, desire and choose in accordance with reason. A virtue lies 'in the mean', a disposition to feel passions neither too much nor too little, but 'at the right times, with reference to the right objects, towards the right people, with the right motive, and in the right way'. Practical wisdom judges what is in the mean relative to us.
- A vice is a disposition to feel or choose not in the mean, but either too much or too little.
- Character traits, and therefore virtues, are acquired through the habits we form when growing up. We acquire virtue by doing acts in accordance with virtue.
- A fully virtuous act is one in which the agent knows what they are doing, chooses the act for its own sake, and makes their choice from a firm and unchangeable character.
- Courage is the virtue concerned with fear. The courageous person faces truly dangerous things as one should and with the right motive.
- Self-indulgence is a vice concerned with bodily pleasures of food, drink and sex. The self-indulgent person desires these pleasures in excess or desires the wrong kinds of food, drink and sex, and is too pained when they miss out on such pleasures.
- The temperate person desires these pleasures as one should. The self-controlled person and the weak-willed person both desire these pleasures too much, but the self-controlled person makes the right choices while the weak-willed person gives in to temptation.
- Aristotle does not value strength of will as virtuous, but second-best to virtue. He also values achieving recognition as part of the good life.
- Voluntary action is action that you bring about, in the knowledge of what you are doing. Involuntary action is action that is forced or done from ignorance of what one is doing.
- Actions that are chosen are voluntary actions done on the basis of a decision resulting from deliberation.
- Deliberation is reasoned thought about what we can change. We do not deliberate about ends as ends, but always deliberate about the means to some assumed end.
- Bad people lack full knowledge of what is good. They desire what is not truly desirable, but what they find pleasant. However, they act in ignorance not from ignorance, because they are morally responsible for becoming bad people through choosing to do bad actions.

ANTHOLOGY: ARISTOTLE, *NICOMACHEAN ETHICS*, BK 6

Practical wisdom

We saw that Aristotle defines a virtue as 'a state of character concerned with choice, lying in the mean, i.e. the mean relative to us, this being determined by a rational principle, and by that principle by which the person of practical wisdom would determine it'. We have discussed choice and the mean. In order to complete our account of virtue, we need to understand what practical wisdom is.

Practical wisdom (*phronesis*) is an intellectual virtue, a virtue of practical reasoning. Aristotle draws a distinction between theoretical reason and practical reason (§1). Roughly, theoretical reason investigates what we can't change and aims at the truth. Practical reason investigates what we can change and aims at making good choices. Reasoning about what we can change is deliberation, so practical reason is expressed in deliberation. To make good choices, not only must our reasoning be correct, but we must also have the right desires (§2).

The person with practical wisdom deliberates well about how to live a good life (§5). So practical wisdom is 'a true and reasoned state or capacity to act with regard to the things that are good or bad for man'.

What practical wisdom involves

Practical wisdom differs from other sorts of knowledge both because of its complexity and its practical nature. Aristotle claims that it involves

1. a general conception of what is good or bad, related to the conditions for human flourishing;

VIRTUES AND THE DOCTRINE OF THE MEAN, p. 80.

CHOICE AND DELIBERATION, p. 93.

2. the ability to perceive, in light of that general conception, what is required in terms of feeling, choice and action in a particular situation;
3. the ability to deliberate well; and
4. the ability to act on that deliberation.

So it involves general knowledge, particular knowledge, an ability to reason towards a choice, and an ability to act on that choice.

There are different ways in which we can fail to deliberate well (§9).

a. We can deliberate with the wrong end. Our starting point is wrong, and so our choice is wrong. Our general knowledge of the good is faulty.
b. We can have the right end, and perhaps even achieve it. However, we don't understand the right means to the end, and so if we achieve our end, this is accidental or lucky. Either our knowledge of the particular circumstances or our reasoning is faulty.
c. We can fail to deliberate when we should or take too long.

So practical wisdom means deliberating with a good end, identifying the right means, and doing so in a timely way. In its fullest sense, practical wisdom involves deliberating from the most unqualified end, eudaimonia itself.

Point (2) above says that practical wisdom involves understanding what is required in a particular situation in light of a general understanding of what is good. The question that faces us on any occasion is how to achieve what is good – what the good life involves – in the here and now, in this situation. But there are no *rules* for applying knowledge of the good life to the current situation. What is right on a particular occasion is in accordance with 'right reason', but Aristotle has argued that this can vary from one occasion to another. Furthermore, this kind of insight is inseparable from making a good decision: we must

> **?** What, according to Aristotle, is practical wisdom?

not only understand the situation (which can involve considerable sensitivity), but also understand how to act well in it.

This makes it impossible to make generalisations about right and wrong, good and bad, that are true in all cases. Practical wisdom intuitively 'grasps' the particular facts involved in the case. This does not make ethics subjective, as there is a truth of the matter to be discovered. However, proving the truth of one view against another is not possible by argument alone. If you are blind, I may not be able to convince you of the colour of moonlight; if you lack insight into what is good, I may not be able to convince you of the goodness of being kind. If you can't understand the situation we are facing, I may not be able to convince you that the right thing to do on this occasion is to be generous.

And so, Aristotle argues, practical wisdom is not something that can be *taught*, for what can be taught is general, not particular (§8). Rules and principles will rarely apply in any clear way to real situations. Instead, moral knowledge is only acquired through experience.

The relation between practical wisdom and virtue

How does practical wisdom relate to virtue? We can imagine this objection: living a good life is a matter of being good, and this involves the virtues. So what use is practical wisdom?

A first, simple answer (§12) is this: the virtues (justice, courage, generosity, etc.) set our ends. Because we are virtuous, we aim at the good life, and we have a reliable conception of what this is (it involves justice, courage, generosity, etc.). But that isn't enough to live a good life, because it doesn't tell us what is good (courageous, etc.) *in this particular situation*. For that, we need practical wisdom to identify the (constitutive) means to our virtuous ends.

Further reflection tells us more. In ACQUIRING VIRTUES AND BEING VIRTUOUS (p. 83), we drew a distinction between acting in accordance with a virtue and doing a fully virtuous action. A

VIRTUES AND THE DOCTRINE OF THE MEAN, p. 80.

1) Explain why Aristotle claims that practical wisdom is not merely knowledge of moral rules. 2) Compare Aristotle and Kant on the nature of practical reason.

fully virtuous action is one in which the agent knows what they are doing and chooses the act for its own sake. Both this knowledge and this kind of choice depend on having practical wisdom. The knowledge involves understanding what is good in this situation, and choice depends upon deliberation, and good deliberation involves practical wisdom. So acting virtuously requires practical wisdom.

So Aristotle draws a distinction between 'natural' virtue and 'full' virtue (§13). He allows that we can have good dispositions from birth; e.g. someone might be naturally kind. But this doesn't amount to 'full virtue'. A naturally kind child doesn't fully comprehend the nature of their action, and could easily be misled into being kind for the wrong reasons or at the wrong time. Without practical wisdom, we can't have full virtue.

But practical wisdom also depends on virtue (§12). It is possible to deliberate from the wrong ends. A bad person can be very clever in achieving what they want. But cleverness is not practical wisdom, because practical wisdom also involves having general knowledge about what is good. This depends upon being virtuous, because what appears good to someone depends on their character traits. So on Aristotle's theory, we become both good and practically wise *together*.

> Explain why Aristotle claims that practical wisdom requires virtue and virtue requires practical wisdom.

ANTHOLOGY: ARISTOTLE, *NICOMACHEAN ETHICS*, BK 5

Going further: Aristotle on justice

What is justice?

In his other analyses of virtues, such as courage (p. 85) and temperance (p. 87), Aristotle understands what it is to act courageously or temperately by reflecting on the virtue. In a sense, the virtue defines the act. When it comes to justice, exceptionally, the analysis runs more in the opposite direction – the act defines the virtue. Justice, the virtue, is understood as the disposition to do what is just, to act justly and wish for justice. And we can provide a substantial account of what is just without referring back to the character trait of justice. Aristotle's account is largely deontological.

Aristotle argues that 'justice' has two meanings (§1).

1. In the 'wide' sense of justice, anything legal is just, and anything illegal is unjust. On his account of the law (but not perhaps ours today), the law instructs us to be virtuous (courageous, temperate, good-tempered, etc.) and prohibits us from being vicious. In this wide sense, then, justice is equivalent to virtue, at least in relation to how we treat other people. We shall put this meaning of justice to one side and focus on its narrow sense.

2. In its narrow sense, justice is fairness, and to be unjust is to act 'graspingly' (§2). Justice is concerned with those goods, such as money, safety or happiness, that are gained or in which we can obtain some advantage relative to other people. To be unjust is to seek to gain more than one's fair share of something good or avoid one's fair share of something bad. Justice is the principle that each person receives their 'due'. There are two kinds of justice as fairness.

    a. Justice in the distribution of what is good and bad (who gets what). Here, justice requires us to treat equals equally (§3). If people are unequal (e.g. what people are due depends on how well they do something), then we should treat their differences proportionally. So people should receive goods according to their merit (however merit is to be identified).

b. Justice in rectification. Here, some injustice needs to be set right or corrected (§4). The focus, then, is not on the people involved, who are treated as equals, but on the injustice. What is unequal needs to be made equal. For example, if two people have signed a contract, and one breaks the contract by taking more than their share of a profit, justice will require that the wrongdoer returns the illicit profit and makes some recompense. If one person has injured another, the victim has suffered. Justice in rectification compensates for this suffering and inflicts some form of suffering on the wrongdoer, removing their unjust 'gain' of avoiding suffering.

Justice, then, is intermediate between acting unjustly (having too much) and being unjustly treated (having too little). This virtue, unlike the others, *does* relate to an intermediate 'amount' of something (§5).

Development

We need to clarify what it is to act unjustly and what it is to be unjustly treated.

Aristotle distinguishes between unjust states of affairs, unjust acts, acting unjustly and being unjust.

1. In an *unjust state of affairs*, there is an unjust distribution – someone has more or less than they should – but this is not the result of anything that anyone has *done* (§7). For example, you may suffer some illness that means that you cannot work for a long time and end up poorer than others.

?

What is justice, according to Aristotle?

2. An *unjust act* is an act which results in injustice (someone has more or less than they should). It is merely unjust, and no more, if the person is acting involuntarily (e.g. they act from ignorance).

3. However, to do an unjust act voluntarily is to *act unjustly*. One acts unjustly, but is not an unjust person, if the unjust act is voluntary but not done by choice. In this case, the person acts with knowledge but has not deliberated. An example would be injuring someone through anger. Such a person is not a bad person, but they do act unjustly.

4. However, to do an unjust act by choice is to *be unjust*. In other words, the unjust person knows what they are doing (it is not from ignorance) and has deliberated about what to do (§5.8). This is the worst form of unjust act.

To be unjustly treated, the unjust action must be against your wishes (§9). You cannot be treated unjustly voluntarily – if you agree to the action, you are not unjustly treated. Nor can you treat yourself unjustly – if what you do is voluntary, then even if it harms you, you haven't acted against your wishes, so you haven't acted unjustly against yourself. So, for instance, if you give away a great deal of wealth or you accept more than your share of suffering, you do no injustice to yourself.

1) Explain Aristotle's account of the relation between justice and voluntary action. 2) Compare Aristotle and Mill on justice.

ANTHOLOGY: ARISTOTLE, *NICOMACHEAN ETHICS*, BKS 7.12-13, 10.1-5

Is pleasure good?

Like Mill, Aristotle claims that pleasure is good, and that eudaimonia involves pleasure. So he needs to answer objections that claim that pleasure is not good, and to clarify just how and when pleasure is good. He does this in Bks 7.12-13 and 10.2. We will not discuss all the objections he considers, as some are difficult and technical.

1. *Objection*: The temperate person avoids pleasure.
    Reply: Not true. What the temperate person avoids is an *excess* of certain *bodily* pleasures.
2. *Objection*: The practically wise person doesn't seek pleasure, but only avoids pain.
    Reply: Not true. The practically wise person does seek pleasure, but in accordance with reason. Furthermore, the fact that they avoid pain (in accordance with reason) shows that pleasure is good. As pain is bad and to be avoided, the contrary of pain, pleasure, is good and to be pursued.
3. *Objection*: Pleasure interferes with thought.
    Reply: Not true. The pleasures of thinking don't interfere with thinking, but assist it. It is pleasures that arise from other sources that interfere with thinking. It is generally true of pleasurable activities that each interferes with the others (see PLEASURE, VIRTUE AND FUNCTION, pp. 108-9).
4. *Objection*: Not *all* pleasures are good, for example bodily pleasures or taking pleasure in something bad or disgraceful. (Aristotle doesn't provide an example, but voyeurism - an invasion of someone's privacy, especially sexual privacy - provides a fairly clear example.)
    Reply: If we say bodily pleasures are not good, then how can we explain that their opposite, bodily pains, are bad? It is only *excess* of pleasure here that is bad. Disgraceful pleasures are not good, agreed. To explain this, we could say any of three things:

a. Disgraceful pleasures are not really pleasures, but only pleasant to bad people. All real pleasures are good, though.

b. The kind of pleasure involved in something disgraceful is a pleasure (e.g. looking at an attractive naked body), and so it is good in general. But such pleasure is not good when it is caused by or involves something disgraceful (such as an intrusion on privacy).

c. Pleasures are of different kinds, and only some pleasures are good. We will look further at this below.

Do we have any positive reasons for thinking that pleasure is good? Aristotle considers four arguments from another philosopher, Eudoxus, for the claim that pleasure is the *only* good (§10.2). He argues that Eudoxus is right that pleasure is a good, but not that it is the only good. (We will see further arguments from Aristotle in the next section.)

1. Every creature aims at pleasure. This is a good indication that it is, for each thing, the good. And what is good for all things is *the* good.

Aristotle agrees that this is the strongest reason for thinking that pleasure is good. However, he argues that pleasure is not the *only* thing that we aim at, it is not our only end (§10.3). There are other things which we seek out, such as seeing, knowing, being virtuous, that we would seek out even if they brought us no pleasure. The pleasure they bring is not *why* we seek them. They are FINAL ENDS (p. 73), not a means to pleasure.

With the next three arguments, Aristotle agrees that they show that pleasure is good, but not that it is the only good.

2. Everything avoids pain, so its contrary, pleasure, is good.
3. We choose pleasure for its own sake, not for some further purpose.
4. Adding pleasure on to any good makes it more desirable.

> Is there any good reason to think that pleasure is not good?

> This argument is almost identical to the first part of MILL'S 'PROOF' OF UTILITARIANISM, p. 36.

Explain why Aristotle claims that pleasure is not the only good.

In philosophy of mind, such feelings are known as QUALIA (p. 260.)

Explain Aristotle's analysis of what pleasure is.

So, we should conclude that pleasure is good, but not the only good.

Going further: pleasure, virtue and function

What *is* pleasure? We naturally think of it as a kind of subjective feeling, which we can only define by how it feels. But Aristotle argues that it is the unimpeded activity of our faculties (§7.12).

This is a very difficult claim to understand, but we can start by thinking about being 'in the zone', as we say now. Start with the activities of the senses, such as seeing (§10.4). Pleasure in the activity of a sense is caused most when that sense is at its best (e.g. when you can see well) and active in relation to its 'finest' object. Aristotle doesn't define this, but we can think of it as something on which we can really exercise that sense. So with vision, this is something that is (at least) interesting to look at, that we can explore and engage with through sight. Works of art and beautiful landscapes might provide examples. The same can be said of activities of thought – there is pleasure here in grappling with something that *exercises* our thought, but which *doesn't impede* it, e.g. through being too difficult to understand. We can extend this analysis to all our activities.

But pleasure is not something simply *caused* by, and separate from, such unimpeded activity. It 'completes' the activity. It is part of it, not a separate end, nor a state produced by the activity, as deliberating might produce a decision or looking might produce finding. The pleasure is *in* the activity itself and intensifies and supports it. Thus, when we enjoy an activity, we throw ourselves into it, and we can enjoy it less if other pleasures from outside the activity distract our attention.

If this is the correct analysis of what pleasure is, we can explain how pleasures can be good or bad, and how they relate to virtue and eudaimonia. Each kind of activity - eating, thinking, running, listening to music - has a corresponding kind of pleasure. So there are different kinds of pleasure. A pleasure is good when the activity that produces it is good and bad when the activity is bad.

In THE FUNCTION ARGUMENT (p. 74), we said that 'function' is best understood as 'characteristic activity'. Aristotle claims that different animals have different characteristic activities, and so they enjoy different pleasures. The pleasures that are most suited to human beings are, therefore, those that relate to our characteristic activity, namely living in accordance with reason. Now, it is the virtuous person who has the traits and the practical wisdom that enable them to perform this characteristic activity and this constitutes the good life for human beings. So what is 'truly' pleasant is what is pleasant to the virtuous person. It is these pleasures that form part of eudaimonia. People who are not virtuous may get pleasure from other activities, but such pleasure is not good or 'truly' pleasant.

> Compare and contrast Aristotle and Mill on pleasure.

ANTHOLOGY: ARISTOTLE, *NICOMACHEAN ETHICS*, BK 10.6-8

Eudaimonia and philosophy

In the second half of Bk 10, Aristotle returns to the question of what eudaimonia is. First, what has already been said (§6)?

1. Eudaimonia is not a state, but an activity (EUDAIMONIA, p. 72). You don't live the best life by being asleep or suffering such misfortune that you can do very little.

2. It is desirable for its own sake and it is self-sufficient (FINAL ENDS, p. 73).
3. It involves virtuous actions, as these are desirable for their own sake (ACQUIRING VIRTUES AND BEING VIRTUOUS, p. 83).

Aristotle has also just argued that eudaimonia involves pleasure. But we shouldn't make the mistake of thinking that the best life is one of pleasant *amusements*, even if this is what people with power and wealth spend time doing. People find different activities pleasant depending on their character. What is truly pleasant is what is pleasant to the good person, and this is a life of virtuous activity, not a life of mere amusement.

In PRACTICAL WISDOM (p. 99), we saw that Aristotle divides reason into practical reason and theoretical reason. We have discussed the place and role of practical reason in eudaimonia, since virtue, which is necessary for eudaimonia, is impossible without practical reason. But we have said nothing about theoretical reason.

Theoretical reason – the contemplation of truth – is what is 'highest' about human beings, Aristotle argues. Animals have a form of practical wisdom, in that they consider and act on what is best for themselves. But they do not contemplate general truths. This ability is our share in 'divinity'. Eudaimonia, therefore, must include excellent activity of theoretical reason, which is philosophy.

1. This activity is best, because theoretical reason is the best thing in us and with it, we contemplate what is best (the greatest, most wonderful and most divine things in the universe), not merely what is best *for us* (as in practical wisdom).
2. We are able to undertake this activity more continuously than any other activity, so it leads to the most continuously happy life.
3. It is the most pleasant activity – at least, its pleasures are most pure and enduring, unlike pleasures of the body.

4. It is the most self-sufficient activity. Nothing further arises from it (it is knowledge for its own sake), while in other virtuous activities, we normally gain something (honour, gratitude, friendship, power, etc.) beyond doing the action. We need fewer external goods for this than for any other virtuous activity. (To be generous, you need money. To be courageous, you need power. To be temperate, you need opportunities ....)

5. We are active in order to have leisure. 'Leisure' is undertaking those activities we wish to undertake. The virtues of politics aim at creating space for leisure, just as we only undertake war in order to achieve peace. They serve the activity of reason.

6. Finally, theoretical reason is what we most *are*, it is our characteristic activity.

7. Therefore, the best and most pleasant life for us, given our nature, will be a life of reason. The life of the philosopher (or more generally, a life dedicated to knowledge) will be the best life.

Aristotle concludes that we should strive to live such a life of theoretical reasoning as far as possible, to live in accordance with the best thing in us. But we are human, and require more than this. Hence the life of virtue more broadly is also part of eudaimonia, as he has argued all along. Having passions, having a body, living with others – these are all characteristically human too. Furthermore, the life of virtue doesn't require a great deal of external goods, and so while these are necessary, they are not central.

> Explain Aristotle's claim that the best life is the life of a philosopher.

Issues for Aristotle's virtue ethics

There are many issues that we may raise with Aristotle's virtue ethics, and the theory of human nature that underpins it. We can question his analysis of particular virtues, such as courage and temperance. We can question whether he is right about pleasure. We can question whether theoretical reason is the 'highest' thing in us. And much more. However, the syllabus directs us to three issues, and it is these that we will discuss here.

Guidance on how to act

A first issue is whether Aristotle's virtue ethics can provide us with any helpful guidance on how to act. Utilitarianism offers us the principle of maximising happiness and Kant offers us the test of the Categorical Imperative. Many philosophers have thought that Aristotle's doctrine of the mean should function in a similar way. But this leads to the objection that it isn't much help. First, 'too much' and 'too little' aren't quantities on a single scale. The list of 'right time, right object, right person, right motive, right way' shows that things are much more complicated than that. Second, this gives us no actual help with understanding, for example how often we should get angry, and how angry we should get. Just about anything could be 'in the mean' if the circumstances were right!

> Explain the objection that the doctrine of the mean provides no guidance on how to act.

In response, we can argue that Aristotle never intended the doctrine of the mean to be helpful in this way. We can't 'figure out' what it is right to do by applying a rule like the doctrine of the mean; we must have practical wisdom. Aristotle says explicitly that what is in the mean is 'determined by the person of practical wisdom'. And life is complicated; so practical wisdom isn't about applying easy rules either. It's about 'seeing' what to do, which requires virtues of character and lots of experience.

We can press the objection. Aristotle's theory of practical wisdom doesn't provide any guidance about what to do, either. If I have practical wisdom, it seems that I simply know what to do. But if I do not have practical wisdom, what then? Knowing that the right action is what a virtuous person would do doesn't help me, because I don't know what the virtuous person would do! Aristotle seems to admit as much when he says that practical wisdom requires virtue. Without a good character, I cannot understand what is truly good. But this means that knowledge of the good is not within everyone's reach. Either Aristotle's theory provides no guidance to anyone who isn't virtuous, or his theory is wrong because we are all sufficiently rational to understand what is right and wrong.

> Explain the objection that Aristotle's virtue ethics is no help to someone who is not already virtuous.

Aristotle argues that this is too simple. In discussing whether bad action can be voluntary (and therefore blameworthy) we saw that knowledge of the good can come in degrees, and we can improve or destroy our ability to know what is good by the kind of character we develop. If someone has a completely depraved character, perhaps they really don't know what is good or bad. But most people will have enough understanding of the good to make moral decisions. Furthermore, people can improve their knowledge of what is good by becoming more virtuous people.

The objection is thinking of guidance too much in terms of *rules*. Just because practical wisdom is not a set of rules, that doesn't mean it provides no guidance at all. Aristotle's theory suggests we think about situations in terms of the virtues. Rather than ask 'could everyone do this?' (as Kant suggests) or 'what will bring about the best consequences?' (as utilitarianism suggests), we can ask a series of questions: 'would this action be kind/courageous/loyal … ?' If we think of actions as expressions of virtue, this could be very helpful.

> Can virtue ethics be useful when thinking about what to do?

Conflicts between virtues

A second issue for Aristotle's virtue ethics regards cases of conflict between virtues. For example, can we show justice and mercy, or do we have to choose? Here, Aristotle's theory is in a similar position to Kant's deontology. He denies that conflicts between virtues ever take place. You need practical wisdom to understand what each virtue actually requires you to do in this particular situation. With such understanding, you will be able to discover a path of action which satisfies the demands of each virtue that is relevant to the situation. If you think that mercy requires injustice, or that justice demands being merciless, then you have misunderstood what justice or mercy actually mean in this situation. For example, perhaps we are motivated towards mercy in rectifying an injustice when someone appeals to difficult circumstances or ignorance of the effects of what they did. On Aristotle's analysis, such factors are directly relevant to judging the injustice of the act (whether it is unjust, or done unjustly, or done by an unjust person). So they are relevant to what justice in rectification requires of us.

See CONFLICTS BETWEEN DUTIES, p. 68.

One advantage that Aristotle's theory has over Kant's is that Aristotle explicitly rejects the claim that morality involves absolute or universal

? Can virtues ever conflict? What implications follow from your answer for Aristotelian virtue ethics?

rules. It is all a matter of context and judgement. This makes it easier to resolve potential conflicts.

Nevertheless, whether the theory is convincing in all cases can only be judged by looking at possible counterexamples. For example, could loyalty to a friend ever require you to be dishonest?

The possibility of circularity involved in defining virtuous acts and virtuous people in terms of each other

A third issue relates to Aristotle's accounts of virtuous action and the virtuous person. A simple reading, which causes the problem, is this:

An exception here is justice, which Aristotle defines in terms of the qualities of the act. See ARISTOTLE ON JUSTICE, p. 102.

1. an act is virtuous if it is an act that would be done by a virtuous person in this situation;
2. a virtuous person is a person who is disposed to do virtuous acts.

The difficulty with these definitions is that, taken together, they do nothing to clarify what a virtuous act is or what a virtuous person is. For instance, if we substitute the definition of a virtuous person in (1), we get 'an act is virtuous if it is an act that would be done by a person who is disposed to do virtuous acts in this situation'. The definition is circular, because we have used the term 'virtuous act' to define what a virtuous act is! We get the same problem if we substitute the definition of a virtuous act in (2): 'a virtuous person is a person who is disposed to do acts that would be done by a virtuous person'.

Explain the problem of circularity involved in defining virtuous acts and the virtuous person.

The problem is solved by paying closer attention to Aristotle's definitions. A (fully) virtuous act is indeed an act that a virtuous person does, when they know what they are doing and choose the act for its own sake (see ACQUIRING VIRTUES AND BEING VIRTUOUS, p. 83). However, a virtuous person is not simply someone who does virtuous actions. A virtuous person has the virtues, which are traits, including states of character and excellences of reason, that enable them to achieve eudaimonia (THE RATIONAL 'SOUL', p. 77). States of character relate to our choices and actions, but they are equally concerned with our passions and with what we find pleasure in (TRAITS OF CHARACTER, p. 79). And eudaimonia is defined not in terms of virtuous actions, but in terms of many activities 'of the soul', including feeling, thinking and choosing. So while (1) is correct, (2) is too simple.

We could press the objection a different way. We can't *tell* whether an act is virtuous without knowing whether a virtuous person would do it. And we can't tell whether someone is virtuous without seeing whether they do virtuous acts.

In reply, first, it is true that the criterion for an act being virtuous is that it is an act that a virtuous person would do. But we have a good *idea* of what a virtuous person is without being able to *name* particular individuals as virtuous or not. When considering 'what the virtuous person would do', we need not have any specific virtuous person in mind. So to judge whether an act is virtuous, we don't need to first judge that person *A* is virtuous and then figure out what *A* would do.

Second, it is true that we infer that someone is virtuous from what they do. But again, this is not the only evidence we have. Virtue is also expressed in emotional responses and pleasure, as well as the quality of someone's thinking. So there is no circularity in establishing whether an act or a person is virtuous.

> 1) Can Aristotle avoid the objection that virtuous actions and the virtuous person are defined circularly? 2) Is Aristotle's virtue ethics a plausible account of morality?

Key points: Aristotle's virtue ethics (II)

- Practical wisdom is a virtue of practical reason. It is 'a true and reasoned state or capacity to act with regard to the things that are good or bad for man'. It involves insight into what is good or bad in general, insight into what is good in a particular situation, and the abilities to deliberate well and act on that deliberation.
- There is no set of rules for applying general knowledge of what is good to particular situations. Practical wisdom simply grasps the particular relevant facts directly.
- So knowledge of what to do is so practical that it can't be taught, but requires experience.
- To do a fully virtuous action, we must aim at the right end. This is set by being virtuous. But we must also know what we are doing, understood as a means to that end. This is provided by practical wisdom.
- We cannot have virtue without practical wisdom, since virtue involves fully virtuous action. We cannot have practical wisdom without virtue,

since practical wisdom involves general knowledge of what is good, and this requires virtue.

- Exceptionally, justice is defined in terms of just acts, rather than the other way around. In its wide sense, justice is simply virtue in relation to others. In its narrow sense, justice is fairness in either distribution or rectification. It involves each person receiving their 'due'.

- The strongest reason to think that pleasure is good is that every creature aims at pleasure for its own sake. However, pleasure is not our only final end, so it is not the only good.

- Pleasure is the unimpeded activity of a faculty. It is not a *separate* psychological state caused by such activity, but part of the activity, a 'completion' and intensification of it.

- A pleasure is good if the activity which produces it is good. The pleasures most suited to human beings are those produced by living in accordance with reason. Therefore, what is truly pleasant is what is pleasant to the virtuous person.

- Theoretical reason is the best activity, the most pleasant and self-sufficient. Therefore, the best life is the life of the philosopher. However, eudaimonia is more generally the life of virtue as well.

- We can object that Aristotle's doctrine of the mean is of little use in helping us discover what is virtuous, since the mean is not the 'middle' nor the 'average' nor the 'moderate'. Aristotle can reply that the doctrine on its own isn't intended to be practically helpful in this way. Practical wisdom is needed to apply it.

- We can object that Aristotle's virtue ethics generally provide no guidance to anyone who isn't virtuous. Aristotle can argue that virtue comes in degrees, and many people have at least some knowledge of what is good, which they can use to become more virtuous. Furthermore, thinking about actions in terms of the virtues can be helpful in deciding what to do.

- We can object that virtues can conflict. Aristotle argues that they don't, and if you think they do, you have misunderstood what the virtues require. Practical wisdom is needed to recognise this.

- We can object that Aristotle defines a virtuous act as something a virtuous person does, and a virtuous person as someone who does virtuous acts. This is circular and uninformative. But Aristotle's definition of a virtuous person is independent and much richer. A virtuous person is someone who has the virtues, which are defined in terms of reason, eudaimonia, feeling and thinking, as well as choosing an action.

- To tell whether an act is virtuous, we do not first need to identify a virtuous person and then reflect on what they would do. We have an abstract conception of 'what the virtuous person would do' which we can use.

D. Applications

We said that ethical theories are intended to guide us in knowing and doing what is morally right. It is therefore very useful to consider theories in relation to practical issues, in order to understand the theories and their implications better. On each of the five issues we will discuss, there is much more to be said, but our primary purpose is to think about how the three theories we have examined – utilitarianism, Kantian deontology and Aristotle's virtue ethics – would deal with them.

Crime and punishment

Punishment is not revenge. Revenge is a reaction of a victim, or someone involved with a victim, and is inflicted by someone who has no formal authority to harm the wrongdoer. Punishment, at least in the context of punishment for breaking the law, is administered by someone impartial who represents a legal authority.

But like revenge, punishment involves depriving someone of some good, such as freedom, money or respect. This requires justification. How we can justify punishment – in fact, whether we can justify punishment – is closely connected to what we think punishment aims to achieve.

Utilitarianism

Bentham said that 'all punishment in itself is evil'. This is because punishment involves making the person who is punished less happy by depriving them of something good, such as freedom (a jail sentence) or money (a fine). Punishment can only be justified, according to a utilitarian, if this increase in unhappiness is outweighed by an increase in happiness. Our justification for punishing people needs to 'look forwards' to the effects of punishment.

Utilitarians have identified three beneficial effects of punishment.

1. Deterrence: 'internal' deterrence occurs when the punishment teaches the criminal a lesson, namely that crime is not worthwhile, and so prevents *them* from offending again. 'External' deterrence occurs when punishing criminals prevents *other people* from committing crimes.
2. Social protection: punishment stops the criminal from harming anyone else, e.g. by locking them in prison.
3. Reform/rehabilitation: punishment helps to change the criminal so that they won't commit crimes again in the future, not through deterrence, but by changing their desire to commit crimes and giving them more positive alternatives.

Outline and explain the possible beneficial effects of punishment.

However, simple utilitarian theories of punishment are open to some powerful objections. First, if the only rationale for punishment is the prevention of crime, then we would be justified in 'punishing' someone *before* they have committed a crime if we think there is a good chance they might. Or again, we could 'punish' someone who hadn't committed a crime in order to prevent some other bad thing happening. For instance, the police would be justified in claiming that they had caught a racist murderer (when they had just locked up someone innocent) in order to stop violent riots about the murder. But such cases seem grossly unjust. It is only right to punish people who are guilty of committing a crime. So punishment can't be justified by only looking at its effects. We have to 'look backward' to the crime itself – punishment needs to 'fit' the crime.

This is also the basis for the second objection. It might turn out that extremely severe punishments; e.g. hanging people for parking illegally, deter crime best of all. If the prevention of crime was all we were after, this would be justified. But again, punishment should fit the crime in being 'proportional' to it. Crimes that are not very significant should receive lighter punishments than crimes that are significant; and this has nothing to do with the effect of the punishment.

Explain the objection that utilitarianism justifies unjust punishments.

Why should only guilty people be punished, and punished proportionally to their crimes? Mill argues that utilitarianism can respect and explain these constraints. Punishment is a matter of justice, and justice relates to our rights. When someone's rights are violated, then the wrongdoer should be punished. But we have the right not to be punished for what we haven't done. We have this system of rights, and with it, a system of punishment, because it promotes the general happiness in the long run. The system of punishment itself should not infringe our rights – and so we should only punish the guilty.

MILL, UTILITARIANISM, CH. 5, p. 43

The rule utilitarian will agree. Only punishing the guilty, and in proportion to their crime, is a rule that will create more happiness than one that allowed us to 'punish' the innocent or to punish people disproportionately.

Is punishment justified by its effects?

Retribution and justice

Kant and Aristotle agree that punishment is a matter of *justice*. And they both hold that criminals *deserve* to be punished. They seek to justify punishment as an appropriate response to the fact of the crime.

Punishment is a form of justice in rectification, a response to an injustice. In ARISTOTLE ON JUSTICE (p. 102), we saw that Aristotle argues that justice (in the narrow sense) is the principle that each person receives what they are 'due'. Justice in rectification is a matter of setting right what is unjustly unequal. The wrongdoer has inflicted undeserved suffering and avoided it themselves – an unfair gain or advantage. Justice requires us to balance the scales, removing this unfair advantage, rather as a referee awards a penalty against a team that has committed a foul.

But this account faces several objections.

1. Is it really possible to think of all crimes as giving the criminal some form of 'advantage' and all punishment as removing this advantage? Suppose someone murders another person from hatred, and receives 25 years in prison. What is the advantage the murderer gained? To live life without a hated person around? Does the prison sentence somehow rebalance this advantage? Is this the best way of conceptualising why they should be punished?
2. By talking of 'gain' and 'loss', Aristotle's theory doesn't focus on the victim. It is almost as though it is the scales of justice that have been offended, rather than a particular human being.

3. What is *good* about this idea of justice? Aristotle needs to say more here relating justice to eudaimonia.

In response to (3), we can note that Aristotle repeatedly talks about the importance of having the right laws in society to enable citizens to develop virtue. In framing a law – and thus setting a punishment for a crime – we need to consider the virtue and eudaimonia of people in society as a whole. This justifies punishment on the grounds of its effects, as identified by utilitarians above. On this view, the *practice* of punishment is justified on the grounds of its effects on the virtue and eudaimonia of society. However, any *particular* punishment is justified deontologically on the grounds of justice.

> Explain an Aristotelian conception of punishment.

ANTHOLOGY: RACHELS, *THE ELEMENTS OF MORAL PHILOSOPHY*, CH. 10.3

Kant argues that utilitarian justifications of punishment violate the Categorical Imperative, particularly in its second formulation. They treat the person who is punished as a means to an end (less crime) and not as an end in themselves. Their punishment isn't being justified by what they have done, but by what punishing them might achieve. Rather than offering criminals rational, moral grounds for repentance, either they are seen as objects to be reformed; or their choices are thwarted by removing their freedom; or in attempting to deter them, we are offering them self-interested reasons not to commit crimes, rather than conveying the wrongness of the crime. But people, including criminals, have dignity and autonomy, and the right to decide for themselves how to live.

To be just, punishment needs to treat the criminal as an end in themselves. To treat someone as a rational being requires us to hold them responsible for their actions. We don't punish animals or young children in the same sense as we punish adults. Instead, our 'punishments' of animals and children are intended as a form of *training* them not to do whatever it is that they did. But in holding an adult responsible, we take their choices and conduct as the basis on which we respond to them. This is what punishment does.

In particular, rational beings are answerable to the Categorical Imperative. So when someone commits a crime, we can take them to be saying that their maxim is to be universalised. *This* (theft, murder, etc.) is how people are to be treated. In punishing them, we are treating them as they have *chosen* to be treated. On the most literal interpretation, the punishment should be to have the crime committed against themselves. For example, murder deserves the death penalty. However, the most literal interpretation is very counter-intuitive in many cases – theft deserves only a fine? Or perhaps also the infliction of a psychological state of insecurity? Rape deserves rape? No. The retribution works at a more abstract level – depriving someone else of their freedom (through theft, rape, etc.) deserves being deprived of one's own freedom.

However, utilitarians object that the infliction of further harm – adding the harm of punishment to the harm of the crime – needs some kind of good outcome to justify it. If punishment 'does no good' in terms of preventing crime, it is hard to see that we should continue it. But we can question this. Suppose depriving people of some good is not, in fact, an efficient way of preventing further crime. If so, is there really no point to punishment?

> Explain Kant's retributive theory of punishment.

> Can the punishment of criminals be justified?

War

War attacks people's lives, security, subsistence, peace and liberty. Clearly, these are very bad consequences, and no part of eudaimonia. War will therefore be condemned by utilitarianism and Aristotle's virtue ethics in most circumstances. For Kant, the motive for going to war is important. But can war be morally justified under certain conditions?

Questions regarding the justice of war are divided into three issues:

1. the justice of resorting to war ('jus ad bellum');
2. just conduct in war ('jus in bello');
3. justice at the end of war ('jus post bellum').

Resorting to war

According to deontologists such as Kant, the first, and perhaps most important, criterion for when a war is just is that the war is for a just cause. The only *maxim* on which fighting a war is defensible is because the war is for a just cause. Any other intention (e.g. to gain land or power), undermines the justice of the war.

Philosophers disagree over what constitutes a just cause. Kant cites the self-defence of the state against threats or aggressive actions by another state, but other philosophers have argued for the defence of others from aggressive attack, the protection of innocent people from aggressive regimes, and corrective punishment for aggressive past action. All involve 'resisting aggression', where aggression is the violation of basic rights by use of armed force.

A second criterion for a just war is that it must be declared by a legitimate state. To be legitimate, a state must be recognised as legitimate by its citizens and by other states; it must not violate the rights of other legitimate states; and it must respect the basic rights of its citizens. Kant also argues that any state that declares war without the consent of its citizens uses its citizens as a means to an end. He therefore argues that each declaration of war must be voted upon by representatives in a democracy.

Utilitarians, by contrast, focus on the *consequences* of going to war. Three such criteria for a just war have been suggested:

1. Given the great unhappiness that war involves, if there is another, less costly way of reaching the same end, it should be taken. Therefore, the declaration of war must be a last resort, following the exhaustion of all plausible alternative means of resolving the conflict.
2. Violence without likely gain cannot be justified. Therefore, a declaration of war can only be just if the state can foresee a probability of success in resolving the conflict through war.
3. The response of declaring war must be proportionate; i.e. the good that can be secured through war must outweigh the evil that will most likely occur. And in this calculation, the state must take into account not just the costs and benefits to itself, but those that will affect everyone involved in the war (e.g. including enemy casualties).

Aristotle's theory involves both types of consideration, deriving from his theory of justice and his theory of eudaimonia. War is not something to wish for, but is a response to some evil. And the only reason to wage war, he says, is to secure peace. The usual considerations, of the need to wage war for the right reasons, in the right way, at the right time, and so on, will apply.

> Compare deontological and utilitarian justifications of going to war.

Justice in war

Concerns with justice during war have focused primarily on how the enemy is engaged and treated. For example, there is a distinction between combatants and non-combatants. Only combatants may be targeted. While a utilitarian will justify this distinction on the grounds that we should minimise suffering, deontologists argue that it is wrong to *intend* the deaths of non-combatants. Some argue that it is wrong even to intend the deaths of combatants, as only the minimum use of force is legitimate.

This leads to a second principle, namely that the force used must be proportional to the end that the war seeks to achieve. Again, this can be justified by both utilitarian and deontological arguments.

Other widely accepted principles are easier to justify using deontological reasoning than utilitarian reasoning. For example, certain weapons, such as chemical weapons, or means of war, such as ethnic cleansing, are prohibited as 'evil in themselves'. Or again, armed forces are not justified in acting unjustly in war in response to the enemy acting unjustly. However, on Mill's theory of justice (p. 43), it may be possible to defend such principles on the grounds of rights and general happiness in the longer term.

Justice at the end of war

We can apply similar arguments to the end of war as well. For instance, given that a just war is fought to defend people's rights against violent aggression, at the end of the war, those rights should be secured. Or again, given that resorting to war and the use of force during war should both be proportional to the end, so we can also apply proportionality to any peace settlement. The settlement should not be a form of revenge,

? What does justice at the end of war require?

which will likely fuel resentment and further aggression, but involve reasonable terms and contribute to peace and happiness in the long term. However, this utilitarian consideration may conflict with a Kantian one, that aggressors should be punished. The two may be balanced by continuing the distinction between the political leaders and combatants who were the primary aggressors, and may be punished, and the rest of the citizenry, whose peaceful future should be protected.

Is war ever justified?

Pacifism argues that war is always unjust. There are both utilitarian and deontological arguments for pacifism.

On utilitarian grounds, we may argue that aggression by a state does not need to be resisted by war, as there are other means, less destructive but just as effective, such as a very widespread campaign of civil disobedience and international sanctions. However, we can object that while there are times when these responses work (e.g. Gandhi's campaign to free India from the British Raj, Martin Luther King's campaign for black civil rights), they only work when the aggressor is sensitive to claims of justice. But what if an aggressor responds to such campaigns with ethnic cleansing? War may be the only means to resist, and can therefore be justified.

A deontological argument for pacifism argues that war always involves violating our duties. But is this right? Kant didn't think so, and many deontologists argue that there is no duty not to kill another human being who is threatening one's life. If Adam attacks Barry, it would be unfair to allow Adam to gain at Barry's cost and Adam is responsible for the situation. So it would be wrong to prohibit Barry from resisting Adam, and Barry commits no wrong in resisting. However, the force Barry may use should be proportionate. If Adam is threatening Barry's life, Barry may kill Adam if no other option is available.

A third argument for pacifism is that while it is theoretically *possible* for a war to be just, if it meets the conditions described above, no *actual* war has or, given human nature, *can* meet the conditions for being just.

? Is war ever morally justified?

The treatment of animals

Utilitarianism

Bentham was aware that his identification of happiness – understood as pleasure and the absence of pain – as the only good had some radical implications. One is that animals are morally important. The question about who or what to consider when looking at the consequences of our actions is not 'Can they *reason*? nor, Can they *talk*? but, Can they *suffer*?' This line of thought has been more recently developed most famously by Peter Singer.

An Introduction to the Principles of Morals and Legislation, Ch. 17

Singer argues that the way we commonly treat animals – for food, clothing and medical experimentation – is not morally justifiable. We do not think that it is right to treat women worse than men just because they are women (this is sexism), nor to treat one race worse than another (this is racism). Likewise, it is wrong to treat animals differently just because they are not human. This is 'speciesism'.

Animal Liberation

We can object that with women and men, and different races, there is no difference in those important capacities – reason, the use of language, the depth of our emotional experience, our self-awareness, our ability to distinguish right and wrong – that make a being a person. But there is a difference between human beings and animals with all of these.

Singer responds that these differences are not relevant when it comes to the important capacity that human beings and animals share, namely sentience. For a utilitarian, an act (or rule) is wrong if it produces more *suffering* than an alternative. Who is suffering is irrelevant. When it comes to suffering, animals should be treated as equal to people.

Does this mean that we should prohibit eating meat, wearing leather and animal experiments? Not necessarily. First, there is the question of whether stopping these practices would reduce the amount of (animal) suffering in the world more than it would increase (human) suffering. Second, the utilitarian position only objects to suffering, not to *killing*. If you painlessly kill an animal and bring another animal into being, you haven't reduced the total amount of happiness in the world. We need only ensure that animals are happy when they are alive, and slaughtered painlessly. This would make eating meat much more expensive, because animals would have to be kept in much better conditions. Eating meat is only wrong when animals are not treated as well as they could be.

Outline the implications of utilitarianism for our treatment of animals.

Kant and deontology

Kant argues that there is a sharp distinction between human beings and animals. Because of our capacity for practical reason, human beings are ends in themselves. We have a rational will and can adopt ends. This is the only thing that is unconditionally good, and for everything else that is good, its goodness depends upon being adopted by a will. Animals do not have a rational will. They have desires, but to have a will is to be able to stand back from one's desires and reflect on whether or not they are good, whether or not to act on them. Animals are therefore not ends in themselves, and can therefore be treated as means to our ends.

However, Kant noted that while we do not owe duties *to* animals, that does not entail that we can treat them any way we want. Rather, we have the duty to others (and to ourselves) to be virtuous. That we protect and develop our ability to have a good will and do our duty is part of THE SECOND FORMULATION OF THE CATEGORICAL IMPERATIVE (p. 63). If we lack kindness towards animals, we may become unkind towards other people – and this would be morally wrong. Therefore, we need to treat animals in such a way that we don't damage our own abilities to be virtuous.

We can object that Kant's theory misses what is wrong about treating animals badly. Instead of saying that the harm to the *animal* is wrong, Kant says it is the harm to *ourselves*.

Second, we can note that babies also aren't rational or autonomous (yet) and neither are some people with severe mental disabilities. Can we treat them as means to an end, or do we have moral duties towards them? If we do, and yet these human beings do not have different psychological capacities from certain animals, then to deny those animals similar moral consideration would be speciesist, it seems.

A different deontological theory has been more recently defended by Tom Regan. He argues that we should assign rights to creatures who are a 'subject of a life'. By this Regan means having beliefs, desires, emotions, perception, memory, the ability to act (though not necessarily free choice) and a psychological identity over time. If a creature has these abilities, there is a way its life goes *for* it, and this matters *to* it. A right to life protects this. Although we can't know exactly which animals meet this criterion, we can be sure that almost all mammals (including humans) over the age of one do so.

> **Explain Kant's views on how we should treat animals.**

> *The Case for Animal Rights*

Because these animals have a right to life, Regan argues, we cannot kill them for any reason less important than saving life. Because we do not need to eat meat or wear leather to live, we should not use animals for these purposes. Regan also argues that an animal's right to life is equal to a human being's. We do not normally discriminate between 'more valuable' and 'less valuable' human lives, even though some people are capable of much greater things than others. So we should not discriminate between 'more valuable' human lives and 'less valuable' animal lives. This means we cannot justify medical experiments that involve killing animals by the human lives the experiment may help save.

Regan's view is very counter-intuitive. Our intuitive judgements that the lives of human beings are more valuable than those of animals, and that it is permissible to kill an animal when we *need* to, are very strong. But what are the arguments supporting these intuitions?

Is Kantian deontology right about how we may treat animals?

Aristotle and virtue ethics

Aristotle's theory suffers a similar flaw to Kant's. Animals have no share in eudaimonia, he argues, because they are incapable of either practical or theoretical reason. Our primary concern with eudaimonia has little place, therefore, for the consideration of animals.

However, more recent virtue theorists have argued that a different understanding of the relationship between human beings and animals provides arguments for greater concern. There may well be ways of treating animals that are not virtuous. However, the speciesism argument misses the point. It is not *just* the capacities of the being that determine how we should treat it, but also our *relationship* to it. There is a moral importance to bonding, the creation of special ties with particular others. We 'naturally' privilege those closest to us. Our bond to other human beings is special because we share humanity. However, we also form close bonds with other animal species, and there are aspects of our lives that we share in common, such as pleasure and pain, and all our lives are governed by a natural course of life for a species. Not to recognise the importance of animal suffering is to show a lack of compassion, while to treat an animal as a meat-growing machine or experimental object is to display a relationship with it that resembles selfishness and self-indulgence, because we reduce it from what it is in itself to something that exists only for our sake or our pleasure.

Does this mean that eating meat and animal experiments are wrong? There may be no one right answer, as a great deal depends on context. To eat meat for the right reason, in the right way, at the right time … may be permissible. We are left without a clear answer, but a sense of the difficulty of the question.

> **?**
> Does virtue ethics provide guidance on how we should treat animals?

Simulated killing

> This section is informed by the discussion in Garry Young, *Ethics in the Virtual World.*

Simulated killing is the dramatisation of killing within a fictional context, e.g. in video games, films and plays. It is not merely the description of a killing, as in a novel, but a fictional enactment of killing that the audience or gamer can see and hear. There is a difference – possibly a morally significant difference – between witnessing such a killing and playing the role of the killer. So we will first discuss simulated killing in the context of playing the killer in video games, and then discuss simulated killing in the context of watching films and plays.

We might wonder whether simulated killing should even be a moral concern. No one is actually killed; no act has been done that violates one's moral duty. For example, in a video game, all that actually happens is that pixels change. It's 'just' a game.

There are two responses to this line of thought. Obviously, if simulated killing is wrong, it is not wrong for exactly the same reasons that killing is usually wrong. But, first, we need not be concerned just with what is actually done (the simulation). Morality may take a concern with what is being represented (the killing). Is it morally acceptable to create or participate in any representation? While it has become widely socially acceptable to play violent video games, video games involving rape and paedophilia are banned in the UK. And yet we can say, just as truly, that such games are 'just' games, and no one is actually raped or molested. Our discomfort with saying this shows that simulations are not necessarily morally neutral just because they are simulations. Second, we can be concerned about the *effects* of simulated killing both on the people involved and on how they then treat other people in real life.

Playing the killer

UTILITARIANISM

This second line of thought is central to the utilitarian's concern. In playing a video game, no one is actually harmed in simulated killings, so as long as the gamer is enjoying themselves, there is a gain of happiness. However, could engaging in simulated killing increase the risk of harmful behaviour in the real world? Could it lead to an increased risk of

1. killing
2. aggressive behaviour more generally
3. other forms of antisocial behaviour, e.g. gamers being less responsive to others' distress, or
4. changes in gamers' attitudes towards violence in general?

(This last effect, unless such changed attitudes are themselves accompanied by decreased happiness, won't figure in a utilitarian calculus. However, it is something that virtue theorists will be concerned with – see below.)

Some people think, intuitively, that playing violent games *must* involve an increased risk of this kind. But the claim is an empirical one, and our expectations are sometimes contradicted by psychological research. Young argues that the evidence is not clear. Some studies on the *short-term* effects of simulated killing (effects for up to 75 minutes after playing) have indicated that there is an increased risk of aggressive thoughts, emotions and behaviour. However, others found that this increased risk only occurred in people with more violent personalities, while others found that it only occurred in boys, not girls. There have been very few studies looking at the *long-term* effects of simulated killing. Some reviews of the evidence have concluded that there is an increased risk of aggressive thoughts, emotions and behaviour and a decrease in empathy, but a number of the studies have been challenged as invalid or found an effect so weak as to be insignificant. There is some evidence that journals are also more likely to publish studies that find a link than studies that don't, so there is a bias in the published evidence. Therefore, the evidence that simulated killing leads to more aggressive behaviour, etc., is unclear, though perhaps we can say that there is an increased risk for *some* people.

Ethics in the Virtual World, pp. 57-9

As we saw in PROBLEMS WITH CALCULATION (p. 41), act utilitarians don't just consider the actual consequences of an action. They consider the 'tendency' or probability of the action having certain consequences. Rule utilitarians consider the consequences of the rule, in this case allowing simulated killings. The evidence so far is that we cannot say that simulated killing will probably increase actual immoral behaviour.

However, even if simulated killing increased aggressive behaviour, utilitarians will weigh the decrease in happiness that results from such behaviour in the real world against the pleasure derived from playing the game. Simulated killing will only be wrong if, on balance, it decreases rather than increases happiness.

Are we mistaken in trying to apply the utilitarian calculus to the act of simulated killing directly? Mill's alternative is to consider the 'secondary principles' of common morality (p. 42). But common morality doesn't provide an obvious guide here, given that video games of this sort have not been around very long. If we look to other games, such as children's play (cops and robbers, aliens, monsters), simulated killing is widely permitted and considered part of normal development (at least for boys).

Some people, therefore, might condemn playing violent video games as 'childish' behaviour that adults would be expected to outgrow. But the utilitarian force of such an objection is unclear. Does engaging in childish play decrease happiness? Perhaps an appeal to Mill's distinction between HIGHER AND LOWER PLEASURES (p. 33) adds some weight. Childish pleasures, such as those involved in simulated killing, will not count as higher pleasures for adults. Hence we may think worse of such a person who engages in such activity, but we will not condemn the activity itself.

> Explain the implications of utilitarianism for the morality of simulated killing.

KANTIAN DEONTOLOGY

Kantian concerns with simulated killing appeal to the same considerations as Kantian discussions of animals. Playing a game per se is no violation of one's moral duty. But if doing so damages one's rational will or leads to neglecting or violating one's duty to other people, then we can object. We could argue that just as treating animals with cruelty may lead to treating people with cruelty, so cultivating cruelty and an indifference to virtual suffering through simulated killing could undermine our willingness and ability to treat others as ends in themselves in real life. Kant notes that, at the time he was writing, butchers and doctors were not allowed to serve on English juries because they were hardened to suffering and death.

However, having reviewed the empirical evidence, it seems that there is not enough evidence to say that there is a link between simulated killing and neglecting one's duties to others.

Even if we don't fail in our duties to others, perhaps we somehow fail in our duty to ourselves. We could argue that repeatedly engaging in simulated killing erodes our sense of identity as rational, moral beings. But again, it is unclear whether this is true. *If* it does, then this would be a reason for thinking that it is wrong.

> Compare Kantian and utilitarian concerns with the morality of simulated killing.

VIRTUE ETHICS

A similar concern is central to Aristotelian virtue ethics. As discussed in ACQUIRING VIRTUES AND BEING VIRTUOUS (p. 83), we become just by doing just acts. The cumulative effect of playing games which involve simulated killing may lead to the development of character traits that are not virtuous, such as injustice and unkindness, or at least inhibit the development of character traits that are virtuous, such as justice and kindness. Simulated killing is wrong if it prevents the development of virtue, and so prevents the gamer from achieving eudaimonia.

Aristotle may be right that doing unjust acts develops the vice of injustice. But *simulated* killing is not an unjust act – no one is killed. So why think that *simulating* unjust acts will develop injustice? Once again, we can argue that the evidence doesn't support this claim.

Rather than focus on the development of character, we can ask whether a virtuous person would engage in playing video games that involve simulated killing. If so, then they will do so in the right way, with the right motive, and at the right times. What might that involve? For example, why would someone *want* to simulate killing someone else? Is taking pleasure in this activity virtuous?

Clearly, there is pleasure to be gained from violent video games – otherwise, they would not be so popular. But there may be more than one kind of pleasure one can take, and more than one motive for killing someone within the game. The virtuous person enjoys such pleasures appropriately, if there is an appropriate way to enjoy them. There may be morally better and worse ways of relating to simulated killing within the game. Is the point of the game just to kill people, or within the narrative, is killing a necessary means to some further goal? Does the gamer enjoy simulated killing as part of doing well in the game (so the motive is competitiveness) or just enjoy simulated killing for its own sake? And so on.

There may also be morally better and worse ways of understanding the relationship between the game and reality. It can be wrong for someone who confuses the two to play the game, but okay for someone who doesn't. Virtue ethics recognises that the right thing to do is not the same for everyone. The 'mean' is relative to each person. If there is any temptation to think of the game world as a model for the real world, playing such games is not virtuous. Someone could experience the rush of adrenalin as a helpful and safe expression of natural human aggression (good), or indulge in fantasies of actual killing during play (bad). And so on.

Relating this back to the empirical evidence: someone who draws a clear conceptual *and emotional* distinction between simulated killing and real life may be at no risk of being more aggressive after playing or developing bad character traits. Someone who cannot draw such a distinction may be at risk, and so should not play.

However, these remarks don't settle the question of whether the virtuous person would *want* to play such a game.

ACTING THE KILLER

Before turning to the morality of watching TV shows, films and plays that contain simulated killings, we can develop the points just made in relation to the actors in such a film or play. Acting takes place within a context which is governed by a whole set of conventions about what particular actions mean. Arguably, actors don't *imitate* real-life killings, and even in films, which may be more lifelike with special effects, etc., violence is typically unrealistic. Instead, actors pretend to kill (and to die) on the understanding that certain actions are to be understood as killings. Furthermore, actors – even method actors – are not supposed to feel *genuine* lethal rage towards their fellow actors during the scene, nor genuine bloodlust and excitement. (Method actors may feel the fictional counterparts of such emotions 'in character', but would not feel such emotions as themselves.) Suppose an actor confessed to feeling real murderous rage after the play or filming. This would be disturbing, to both them and us. Such feelings are not part of the conventions of acting, and indicate a blurring, in the actor's psychology, between the character and the actor.

What these remarks are meant to show is that acting takes place in a complex social context that sets acting apart from reality. The conventions protect the actors, enabling them to do their job without damaging themselves. Concerns about such a blurring are at issue in the discussion

? 1) How can Aristotle's doctrine of the mean be applied to simulated killing? 2) Is it morally acceptable to play the killer in video games?

of playing video games: does the gamer fail to distinguish themselves from their character? Is their morality compromised by the immorality of their avatar, either during or after the game?

An audience's perspective

Is there anything morally wrong with watching violent TV shows, films or plays? Such works are fictions, and it is common to talk about 'suspending disbelief' when immersed in a film or play. We 'make-believe' that what we are seeing is real. We don't believe it is – that would lead to very different emotions and actions (call the police!). But we pretend or imagine that it is real. Is it wrong to do this when what one is witnessing is a simulated killing?

It is worth noting that on each of our theories, killing is sometimes morally right, e.g. in war (Aristotle) or euthanasia (utilitarianism) or capital punishment (Kant). If a dramatic work explores this issue carefully, and convincingly presents a killing as the morally right thing to do, then it is hard to see what is wrong with imagining the simulated killing (at least on the assumption that such a killing *would* be morally right). So for the purposes of argument, let's assume that the killing that is simulated is morally wrong.

The approaches of our three theories to this question have been laid out above, so we can be brief. A utilitarian will be interested in the effects on the overall happiness of watching make-believe killings (or of a rule that allows simulated killings in TV shows, films and plays). There is no immediate decrease in happiness if the audience gets something positive out of the experience. So concerns will be limited to the longer term effects. As we might expect, the evidence is very similar to the evidence connecting playing violent video games to aggression in real life. There is some evidence the link is stronger in some groups of people than others, but overall, we don't have enough evidence to conclude that, in general, watching violence on screen or on the stage is likely to make one a less moral person. Even if there were a link, the risk of diminishing happiness needs to be weighed against the enjoyment gained by watching such works.

Let us take deontological and virtue ethical concerns together. Irrespective of consequences for how one acts, does watching simulated

Explain the different relations between simulated killing and morality within a fictional work.

killing damage one's character or good will intrinsically? Immoral simulated killings can take place within two fictional contexts. In one, the killing is represented *as* immoral, the killer as morally or emotionally wretched. The work can be understood as a morality tale – this is how not to be. But the killing can also be represented as moral – the morality *of the work* is different. This is the most problematic case. Is it wrong to imagine that something that is immoral is actually moral?

Kant would argue that it is certainly irrational. What is immoral *cannot* be moral. We can coherently imagine that contingent truths are different. But moral truths are established by a test of what is possible – so they are not contingent, but necessary. But even if this is so, is there anything morally wrong with imagining something impossible?

Again, understanding the relation between the work and moral reality is important. For example, do we think that the author intends the (immoral) values to be moral values only *within* the fiction? Or is the message that we should live according to the values portrayed? On the one hand, there may be something not virtuous about joining with the immoral imagination of the author. On the other hand, one may argue that it can help one understand morality more deeply. But this will only occur if one can keep one's distance from the 'morality' of the dramatisation. A virtuous person will be alive to the moral implications of the story being told, not simply in terms of its effects but in terms of its representation of what a good life is and the place of killing within it. Their make-believe will be coloured by this awareness.

What, if anything, is wrong with watching simulated immoral killing?

Deception and the telling of lies

Utilitarianism

A simple act-utilitarian approach to deception and lying would consider whether telling a lie creates greater happiness than telling the truth (or keeping silent). If it does, then it is morally right. If it doesn't, then it is morally wrong.

Mill's brief discussion of lying in *Utilitarianism*, Ch. 2, demonstrates that his version of utilitarianism does not evaluate actions just in terms of immediate or obvious consequences, but places them within a bigger picture. A person's being truthful is of great benefit to people's happiness generally, and our being able to trust what others say is not only the basis of social well-being but also a foundation of civilisation and virtue more generally. Weakening either our tendency to be truthful or other people's trust is, therefore, severely damaging to happiness. To tell a lie just for the sake of convenience is therefore morally wrong.

That said, Mill allows that lying is sometimes permissible; e.g. when it is the only way we can withhold information from someone who intends to do harm. We need to carefully consider which situations permit lying by weighing up the conflicting utilities involved. Suppose someone comes to your house to seek refuge from someone who wants to murder them. Soon after they have hidden, the would-be murderer arrives and asks you where they are. In this example, it seems fairly clear that lying will cause more happiness (or less unhappiness) than telling the truth.

> Explain Mill's position on the morality of lying.

Rule utilitarianism may argue that the rule 'don't lie' will, if everyone followed it, create more happiness than a rule that permitted lying. However, we can object, with Mill, that *never* lying will lead to harm in certain situations. We need a rule that allows for exceptions. It may be very difficult to put such a rule into words, since the situations in which telling the truth will lead to more harm than good are quite varied. We might lie to prevent someone from doing harm to others; or from doing harm to themselves; or because the truth would hurt (e.g. in cases of terminal illness or sexual infidelity); or because the truth would be damaging to some long-term good (e.g. in politics); or … It is hard to know what the right 'rule' for lying should be.

Kantian deontology

ANTHOLOGY: RACHELS, *THE ELEMENTS OF MORAL PHILOSOPHY*, CH. 9.2

In DUTY (p. 58), we saw that Kant rules out making a false promise as immoral because it involves a contradiction in conception. The same applies to lying in general. If you lie, you are following the maxim to tell a lie when you want to. If everyone told lies when they wanted to, people would stop believing each other. But you can deceive someone with a lie only if they believe you. So the maxim cannot be universalised, and lying is wrong.

> Briefly explain why Kant claims that lying is wrong.

Kant argued that lying is *always* wrong. The example of the would-be murderer who knocks on your door comes from his essay 'On a Supposed Right to Lie from Altruistic Motives'. *Even in this situation*, Kant says, you should not lie.

We can object, however, that one's maxim may be more specific than lying whenever one wants. For instance, you may adopt the maxim 'to lie when it is necessary to save a life'. Arguably, this can be universalised. Because in most situations, no lives are at stake, if everyone acted on this maxim, people would still believe each other most of the time.

Kant might reply that it would nevertheless fail in the case above. The would-be murderer knows that everyone lies when it is necessary to save a life. So they won't believe us when we answer their question about where their victim is hiding. So we can't deceive them.

Rachels responds that if they knew we would lie, they wouldn't bother asking. On the other hand, if they thought that we didn't know that they intend to kill someone, they might believe us. So is the maxim 'to lie when it is necessary to save a life' universalisable or not? It is unclear.

In his essay on lying, Kant adds a further argument against lying. We don't know what consequences will follow from our lying. Suppose we lie about the person hiding in our house, saying they ran down the street. Suppose that, unknown to us, they did exactly that. They left their hiding place and ran off. And so our lie sends the murderer straight to where the person is. We would be responsible, Kant claims, for this consequence. If we are tempted to lie because we think the consequences will be better than if we told the truth, it is possible that we are mistaken. We will have failed to do our duty, achieved nothing, and be responsible for the results. It is better to do our duty.

But, we can object, why aren't we similarly responsible if we tell the truth: if we say where the person is hiding, and the murderer finds them there?

The prohibition on lying also follows from THE SECOND FORMULATION OF THE CATEGORICAL IMPERATIVE (p. 63). To lie to someone is to treat them as a means to our own ends. They are not able to make an informed choice about what to do, but are manipulated in a way that they are unaware of. They can't share in our ends, because we have not been honest about what our ends are. We should not lie even when the other person's ends are immoral, and we are trying to prevent those ends being realised. We should not deceive the other person about our intention to thwart their ends. We must give them the chance to share *our* end of persuading them not to act on *their* immoral ends.

What seems to follow from Kant's deontology is that *if everyone were morally good*, then lying would always be wrong. But sometimes we need to protect ourselves (and others) from the wrong actions of others, and lying may be the only means of doing so. If the action someone intends to do would treat me as a means to an end, then we can, by lying, prevent this result. Kant himself recognises this in his *Lectures on Ethics*: 'if I cannot save myself by maintaining silence, then my lie is a weapon of defence'.

> Explain why lying involves treating the other person as a means, not an end in themselves.

> Is Kant right that lying is always wrong?

Aristotle's virtue ethics

When Aristotle discusses truthfulness, he opposes being truthful to boasting and mock-modesty (Bk 4.7). So his primary focus is on being truthful about oneself. But he also comments that 'falsehood is *in itself* mean and culpable, and truth noble and worthy of praise'. One way of understanding this is to say that deception and lying are acts, like adultery and murder (Bk 2.6), that have no mean. Lying is already an excess or deficiency in some way, and cannot be virtuous. An alternative interpretation is to say that truth is a final end, something that we should seek not for some further purpose, but for its own sake. This doesn't entail that lying is always wrong. Pleasure is a final end, but we should not always pursue it – there are appropriate and inappropriate ways of doing so. Perhaps the same can be said of truthfulness.

Aristotle is not particularly critical of boastfulness – to lie about what you have or can do, just because you enjoy lying, is contemptible but 'futile rather than bad'. To lie in order to gain or protect one's reputation is not particularly blameworthy, since having a good reputation, in Aristotle's eyes, is good. Someone who lies to gain money, on the other hand, 'is an uglier character'. These remarks indicate that there are better and worse motives for lying.

But they also suggest that lying is never virtuous. We might object, however, that as discussed above, there are occasions and motives that justify lying. Here we can appeal to our discussion of CONFLICTS BETWEEN VIRTUES (p. 113) and Aristotle's theory of practical wisdom. If there are few rules in ethics, it is unlikely that lying is *always* wrong. Instead, we will need practical wisdom to judge when it is justified and when it isn't. If we seek to deceive someone, to do so virtuously, we would need to do so at the right time, with the right motive, about the right truths, and in the right way.

This last point returns us to the point that there are ways of not sharing the truth other than lying. Perhaps the virtuous person will exhaust all the alternatives first before resorting to a lie.

> **?**
>
> How would a virtue ethicist attempt to justify a lie?

Key points: applications

- Utilitarians justify punishment by appealing to its effects. Deterrence, social protection and reform are all potential beneficial effects of punishment.
- We can object that utilitarianism will justify punishing someone before they have committed a crime. It will also justify disproportionate punishment. But punishment should fit the crime. Mill and rule utilitarianism can respond that a system of rights or a rule that rejects such punishment will lead to the greatest happiness.
- Punishment is justice in rectification, which Aristotle argues is a matter of rebalancing the scales of justice. The practice of punishment can be justified by its effects on the virtue and eudaimonia of citizens as a whole.
- We can object that not all crimes involve gaining an advantage, and that Aristotle misses the particular wrong done to the victim.
- Kant objects that utilitarian theories of punishment treat the criminal as a means to an end, not an end in themselves. We can justify punishment by pointing out that the criminal is being treated as they have themselves chosen to be treated by committing their crime.

- Utilitarians object that punishment cannot be justified if no further good arises from the punishment.
- Deontologists argue that to be just, a war must be in a just cause and undertaken for this reason alone, and declared by a legitimate state.
- Utilitarians argue that a just war can only be undertaken as a last resort, if likely to achieve its aims, and is proportionate in response to the harm threatened.
- Common principles of justice in war are that non-combatants must not be targeted, force must be proportional, no 'evil' weapons used, and that breaking these conditions is not justified by the enemy breaking them. Both deontologists and utilitarians can offer explanations of these principles.
- Justice after the war should secure people's rights, the peace settlement should be proportional, and non-combatants not punished.
- Pacifism argues that war is always unjust, either because there are equally effective but less destructive means of resisting aggression or because it always involves a violation of duties. Both claims can be challenged. If pacifism cannot be defended in theory, it can still be argued that no war can, in fact, meet the conditions of being just.
- Utilitarians argue that what matters is pain and pleasure, and so who is suffering is irrelevant. To think otherwise is speciesism.
- Utilitarianism claims that whether eating meat or animal experimentation is wrong depends on whether it produces more suffering than alternatives. Killing an animal painlessly, if you bring another animal into existence, won't reduce happiness, so is permissible.
- Kant argues that animals can be treated as means, as they don't have a rational will. However, we must not treat animals in ways that would lead us to become unvirtuous, and fail in our duties to other people.
- We can object that the harm done to the animal, not ourselves or other people, is what is wrong about harming an animal. We can also object that some human beings do not have rational wills, and we should treat animals with the same consideration we treat them.
- Regan argues that any creature that is a 'subject of a life' has a right to life. The right to life is equal in all cases.
- Virtue ethicists argue that how we should treat animals depends on our relationship to them, not just their capacities. We should be

compassionate and not treat them as existing just for our pleasure or benefit.

- Utilitarianism argues that playing the killer in video games, or watching simulated killings in dramatisations, is wrong if it leads to greater unhappiness than happiness, e.g. through effects on behaviour in the real world. Kantian deontology is likewise concerned by the effects of such activities on our doing our duty, and Aristotelian virtue ethics is concerned by the effects on our character traits.

- However, the evidence that there are such adverse effects from either playing such games or watching violent dramatisations is not clear. But some people may be susceptible to them.

- We can distinguish between different types of pleasure and different motives for playing video games involving simulated killing. A virtuous person would only gain pleasure from playing the killer if such pleasure is appropriate and they would only play such games at the right times, in the right way, with the right motive, and for the right reasons, and would correctly understand the relationship between the game and reality.

- A simulated killing may be presented as either moral or immoral within a dramatisation. We may raise concerns about imagining what is immoral as being moral, especially if the fiction indicates that we should adopt its values in the real world.

- Mill argues that lying is rarely justified because trust is so significant for our happiness. However, it can be justified in situations in which it will prevent significant harm.

- Rule utilitarianism is faced with the challenge of specifying exactly which rule concerning lying will maximise happiness.

- Kant argued that the maxim to lie when you want cannot be universalised, and so lying is always wrong. We may object that a more specific maxim may be universalisable, which would allow lying in certain circumstances, e.g. to save a life.

- Kant also argues that we should not lie because we believe it will lead to good consequences. It may not, and then we will have failed in our duty and be responsible for the bad consequences.

- To lie is to treat someone as a means to an end. However, we can argue that it is justifiable if we lie in order to prevent ourselves being treated as a means to an end.

- Remarks by Aristotle indicate that he thinks truth is a final end, and that lying always fails to be virtuous. But we may develop his theory to argue that there are few rules in ethics, and that practical wisdom may judge lying to be appropriate on certain occasions.

Practical ethics in exam answers

When you are asked just to explain how a theory deals with a particular practical issue, that is relatively straightforward. However, if you are asked to discuss and evaluate theories in relation to practical issues, it is easy to slip out of doing good philosophy into thinking in more 'everyday' ways. Doing well in exam questions on practical ethics involves thinking hard about the question in a philosophical way. Here are some tips to help:

See TWELVE-MARK QUESTIONS, p. 316.

1. While the facts (e.g. about simulated killing) are important, just talking about the facts is not philosophy. Nor is repeating what people generally say or feel about these cases. You are not doing social science, but discussing *justifications* for certain ways of making decisions.
2. Whether an action is right or wrong can depend on the facts, and as philosophers, we may not know all the facts. So philosophical arguments are often 'conditional'. It is not just acceptable, but good, to say 'if it turns out like this, then this follows (the action is right/ wrong)'. For example, you might say 'if capital punishment deters people from committing murder, then it is right' (if you are defending a utilitarian theory of punishment). Don't take much time to discuss whether capital punishment is or isn't an effective deterrent.
3. Avoid oversimplification wherever possible. Practical moral issues are very complex. In particular, if you are evaluating a theory, e.g. virtue ethics, by its success in practical cases, the complexity is crucial to being fair. Consider whether practical ethics 'ought' to be easy or not. Can we expect clear rules and algorithmic decision procedures in life? Is the presence of grey areas really a failure? Aristotle's theory suggests not.
4. Likewise, try to avoid objections that just point out our ignorance. For example, 'who knows what consequences follow from a lie?' is not helpful. This move is simply a refusal to do philosophy. A utilitarian

will quickly reply that we must simply do our best to work out the consequences. The same with 'who is to say what is right?' *You* as a philosopher are to say what is right, as you see it and to the best of your ability (this is not arrogance, but the contribution of a rational human being to a rational debate).

5.   Make a distinction between morality and legality. Whether a practice, such as simulated killing, should be legalised is a separate debate from whether it is morally acceptable.

6.   The premise of practical ethics is that we are searching for the (or a) right thing to do. Challenging this premise is unhelpful in this context. We will discuss some very interesting questions about whether morality is objective or not next. But such issues are usually best kept out of answers on practical ethics.

Summary: ethical theories

In this section on ethical theories, we have considered three theories:

1.   Utilitarianism: the theory that only happiness is good, and the right act (or rule) is that act (or rule) that maximises happiness

2.   Kantian deontology: the theory that one should act only on that maxim through which one can, at the same time, will that it be a universal law

3.   Aristotle virtue ethics: the theory that the good life for human beings is eudaimonia, which is the activity of the soul exhibiting the virtues and in accordance with reason.

In our discussion and evaluation of these theories, we have looked at the following issues:

1.   What is good? Is only one thing good?

2.   What is happiness? Is it pleasure? What is pleasure?

3.   Is an action right or wrong depending on its consequences, its motive, or its place in a virtuous life?

4.   What is the nature of practical reason? Is it means–end reasoning, a matter of what we can universalise, or insight into particular situations?

5. What is a virtue?
6. What is justice? What is the relationship between rights, justice and utility?
7. What is it to treat someone as an end in themselves?
8. How can we explain the moral value of particular relationships, such as friendships?
9. Can duties or virtues conflict?
10. What is it for an action to be voluntary?
11. What guidance can we expect or receive from normative moral theories?

We have also considered the application of these theories to five practical issues, crime and punishment, war, the treatment of animals, simulated killing, and deception and the telling of lies.

II. Ethical language: what is the status of ethical language?

Ethical language is talk about right and wrong, good and bad. 'What is the status of ethical language?' is a question about what statements like 'Murder is wrong' or 'Courage is good' mean. What is it that ethical language is doing? Are these statements of fact? Can ethical claims be true or false? Or are they something else, such as expressions of our approval or disapproval of certain actions or character traits? Our questions raise issues in metaethics.

We encountered a similar question regarding religious language at AS level. *Philosophy for AS*, RELIGIOUS LANGUAGE, p. 254

A. Introducing metaethics

What is metaethics?

Normative ETHICAL THEORIES (p. 26) provide an account of which actions, motives and character traits are right or good. They are intended to provide guidance on how to live. Metaethics, by contrast, does not do this. It asks about what morality is, philosophically speaking. It asks questions in philosophy of language, as we have just seen, but we can't answer those questions without also thinking about metaphysics, epistemology and philosophy of mind.

1. Metaphysics: suppose we think that ethical language states truths. Are these truths objective? Are they mind-dependent or mind-independent?
2. Epistemology: if there are ethical truths, how do we discover what these truths are? On the other hand, suppose we deny that ethical statements are true or false, arguing that they are expressions of subjective feeling. In that case, is there such a thing as moral reasoning? Can we provide reasons that justify our actions?
3. Philosophy of mind: what is it to hold a particular moral view, e.g. that murder is wrong? If 'murder is wrong' states a truth, then moral views are factual beliefs. On the other hand, if 'murder is wrong' expresses a feeling, then moral views are attitudes of approval or disapproval (or something similar). Is holding a moral view a matter of being motivated to act in certain ways, e.g. not to murder? If it is, what does this imply about the nature of morality?

What is metaethics?

Cognitivism and non-cognitivism

Theories of what morality is fall into two broad families – cognitivism and non-cognitivism. The distinction is now understood by philosophers to depend on whether one thinks that moral judgements express beliefs or not.

Cognitivism claims that ethical language expresses ethical beliefs about how the world is. To believe that murder is wrong is to believe that the sentence 'Murder is wrong' is true. So ethical language aims to describe the world, and so can be true or false.

Non-cognitivism claims that ethical language does not try to describe the world and cannot be true or false. It does not express beliefs, but some other, non-cognitive mental state. Different non-cognitivist theories disagree on exactly what this mental state is, but it is usually an attitude or feeling.

Outline three differences between cognitivism and non-cognitivism.

Mental states and 'direction of fit'

We can understand the difference between a cognitive mental state and a non-cognitive mental state in terms of the idea of 'direction of fit'. A man goes shopping, taking his shopping list with him. When shopping, he uses his list to guide what he puts in his basket. At the end of the shop, what is in his basket should 'fit' his list. If it doesn't, the mistake is with the basket, and the basket should be changed to fit the list. Now suppose that the man is being followed by a store detective. She makes a list of each thing that the man puts in his basket. At the end of the shop, her list should 'fit' his basket. If it doesn't, the mistake is with her list, and the list should be changed to fit the basket.

> Elizabeth Anscombe, *Intention*

The shopper's list is a list of what he wants. Desires have a 'world-to-mind' direction of fit. We seek to change the world to fit our desires and thereby satisfy them. They are not true or false, but represent how the world should be. By contrast, the detective's list is a list of what she believes is in the shopper's basket. Beliefs have a 'mind-to-world' direction of fit. We change our beliefs to fit the world, and thereby have true beliefs. They represent how the world is, not how we want it to be.

So which direction of fit do moral views have? Is the thought 'murder is wrong' a belief about how the world is, or is it like a desire to make the world a place in which there is no murder? Both answers are plausible and both answers face challenges.

> Explain the difference between cognitive and non-cognitive mental states in terms of their direction of fit.

Issues

Non-cognitivists argue that moral judgements are, like desires, motivating. Holding the view that murder is wrong involves being motivated not to murder. But, they continue, factual beliefs are not motivating. The sun is 93 million miles from the Earth – so what? Believing that fact inclines me to do nothing in particular at all. Because moral views are motivating, they are not beliefs, but non-cognitive attitudes.

Cognitivists can respond that some beliefs, including moral beliefs, are motivating. Or they can argue that moral beliefs aren't motivating. Instead, caring about what is morally good or right is motivating. It is possible, therefore (but perhaps psychologically very unusual), to believe that murder is wrong and not be motivated to refrain from murdering because one simply doesn't care about morality.

Cognitivism argues that what is right or wrong is something we can be mistaken about. It isn't just 'up to us' whether murder is wrong. People who think that murder is just fine are mistaken and vicious. Morality isn't simply a matter of taste. Non-cognitivism, therefore, faces the challenge of explaining why we make a distinction between morality and personal taste. Is non-cognitivism going to lead to scepticism or nihilism about morality, the view that there is no right and wrong (really)?

Non-cognitivism can argue that it is a simpler theory. It has a simpler metaphysics and a simpler epistemology. Cognitivism needs to explain how moral claims *can* be objectively true or false. Are there moral properties 'in the world'? What kind of property could they be, and how can we find out about them? Issues of rationalism and empiricism arise here.

We will discuss these issues and more, in detail, in the rest of this chapter.

See *Philosophy for AS*, KNOWLEDGE EMPIRICISM, p. 96.

Key points: introducing metaethics

Explain one challenge facing cognitivism and one facing non-cognitivism.

- Metaethics studies what morality is. It asks questions about the meaning of ethical language, the metaphysics of moral values, the epistemology of moral judgements, and the nature of moral views.
- Cognitivism claims that moral judgements express beliefs, are true or false, and aim to describe the world. Non-cognitivism claims that moral judgements express non-cognitive attitudes, are not true or false, and do not describe the world.
- Beliefs (and other cognitive states) have mind-to-world direction of fit; we change our beliefs to fit the world. Desires (and other non-cognitive states) have world-to-mind direction of fit; we change the world to satisfy our desires.
- Cognitivists face challenges from explaining moral motivation and the metaphysics and epistemology of objective moral truths. Non-cognitivists face the challenge of avoiding scepticism about morality.

B. Cognitivism

As we said, cognitivism is the view that ethical language expresses ethical beliefs about how the world is. The cognitivist argues that moral judgements aim to describe the world, and so can be true or false. Furthermore, we can be mistaken about whether a moral judgement is true or false. Our thinking it is true does not make it true.

Here are three quick arguments in favour of cognitivism:

1. We think we can make mistakes about morality. Children frequently do, and have to be taught what is right and wrong. If there were no facts about moral right and wrong, it wouldn't be possible to make mistakes.
2. Morality feels like a demand from 'outside' us. We feel answerable to a standard of behaviour which is independent of what we want or feel. Morality isn't determined by what we think about it.
3. Many people believe in moral progress. But how is moral progress possible, unless some views about morality are better than others? And how is *that* possible unless there are facts about morality?

But if there are truths about morality, what kind of truths are they? Moral truths seem to be quite different from empirical truths, which we can discover using our senses. One answer is provided by Kant's account of MORALITY AND REASON (p. 62). Moral judgements, such as 'Murder is wrong', are made true by a priori reason. The maxim involved in murder cannot be universalised.

However, we shall set Kant aside to discuss the two forms of cognitivism specified on the syllabus, MORAL REALISM (below) and ERROR THEORY (p. 156).

> Outline two reasons for thinking moral cognitivism is true.

> On a priori/a posteriori, see *Philosophy for AS,* TWO IMPORTANT DISTINCTIONS, p. 97.

Moral realism

Moral realism claims that good and bad are properties of situations and people, right and wrong are properties of actions. Just as people can be 5 feet tall or run fast, they can be morally good or bad. Just as actions can be done in 10 minutes or done from greed, they can be right or wrong.

What is moral realism?

There is a parallel between the metaphysics of ethical naturalism and MIND–BRAIN TYPE IDENTITY THEORY (p. 248) in the philosophy of mind and between ethical non-naturalism and PROPERTY DUALISM (p. 266).

These moral properties are a genuine part of the world. Whether moral judgements are true or false depends on how the world is, on what properties an action, person or situation actually has.

Moral realism in the last 150 years has focused on trying to clarify the precise nature of the relation between moral properties and natural properties; i.e. properties that we can identify through sense experience and science. This has led to two positions: ETHICAL NATURALISM (below) and ETHICAL NON-NATURALISM (p. 151). Ethical naturalism claims that moral properties are natural properties; ethical non-naturalism claims that they are a distinct kind of property.

Ethical naturalism

Ethical naturalism is a form of reductionism. It claims that the things in one domain – moral properties of goodness and rightness – are *identical* with some of the things in another domain – certain natural properties. The most plausible natural properties are certain psychological properties. The identity claim is a reduction because we have 'reduced' moral properties – which we might have thought were a different kind of thing – to psychological properties. I.e. there is *nothing more* to moral properties than being a certain kind of psychological property.

Utilitarianism as naturalism

UTILITARIANISM (p. 26) can be understood within the framework of ethical naturalism. It claims that the only good is happiness. We can interpret this to mean not simply that happiness is the only thing that is good, but that happiness is what goodness is. They are the same property. Happiness is a natural (psychological) property, and therefore, so is goodness. Because happiness is a natural property, so is maximising happiness. Whether an act maximises happiness is a (complex) natural property. According to utilitarianism, an act is right if it maximises happiness. Therefore, rightness is also a natural property.

Naturalism can argue that it solves some of the issues facing cognitivism. In particular, we now understand the metaphysics of moral properties. If goodness is just happiness, then there is no puzzle about what kind of thing goodness is. Furthermore, we can discover what creates happiness empirically. So we have an answer to the question about how we find out what is morally right and wrong: through experience.

What is ethical naturalism?

ANTHOLOGY: MOORE, *PRINCIPIA ETHICA*, §§36–41

This is how Moore understands Mill. Moore argues that Mill may not have realised that he was *defining* good as 'desired', but unless he does, MILL'S 'PROOF' OF UTILITARIANISM (p. 36) doesn't succeed. A brief reminder: Mill argues that happiness is desired. From this, he infers that happiness is good. This only works, says Moore, if Mill thinks that what is good is the same as what is desirable, and that what is desirable is the same as what is desired. So Mill must be thinking that goodness is the natural property of what is desired. Further evidence comes from Mill's claim, at the end of the proof, that 'to think of an object as desirable … and to think of it as pleasant are one and the same thing'.

Moore uses this interpretation to argue that Mill has committed a fallacy. We'll look at that objection below. However, in the previous discussion of Mill's proof, we argued that Moore has misinterpreted Mill. Mill takes what people desire (which is a natural property) as *evidence* for what is desirable (good). He does not say that goodness is the same property as being desired. And when he claims that what is good is what is desirable, nothing he says implies that he thinks that 'being desirable' (as opposed to being desired) is a natural psychological property. So we simply can't say whether Mill is a naturalist or not.

Explain utilitarianism as a form of ethical naturalism.

Going further: was Aristotle a naturalist?

Some philosophers have read Aristotle's function argument (THE FUNCTION ARGUMENT, p. 74) as presenting a reduction of the good to the natural, understood in terms of 'function'. The facts about human nature, in particular psychological facts about our desires, our needs and our ability to reason, are the basis for moral truths. There are facts about what our characteristic activity is, there are facts about what traits enable us to perform our characteristic activity well. And so it turns out to be a psychological fact whether a character trait, such as courage or being short-tempered, is good or bad.

However, exactly what eudaimonia consists in can't be identified with any natural fact. This is shown by the analysis of the relation between eudaimonia, virtue and practical wisdom. The person who has practical wisdom is not simply able to grasp some psychological fact about a situation that someone without practical wisdom cannot grasp. Instead, they understand the *reasons* for feeling, choosing or acting a certain way in a certain situation. This is why virtue is in accordance with 'right reason'. To make Aristotle a naturalist, we would have to provide an argument for thinking that whether some consideration is a reason or not is a matter of natural fact. We discuss moral reasons below.

> **?** Can eudaimonia be understood in terms of natural facts about human nature?

Objection

How can we establish that a moral property just *is* (identical to) some natural property? Given the different normative ethical theories that exist, claiming that goodness *is* happiness (or any other natural property) is obviously contentious. Such a claim isn't something that we can demonstrate by empirical reasoning – no scientific experiments will show that goodness is, after all, just happiness. We have to defend the identity claim philosophically. So from the psychological facts *alone*, we cannot deduce any moral knowledge. Only after we've established the identity claim by philosophical argument can we use empirical investigation to discover what is right or wrong.

Both non-cognitivists and ethical non-naturalists present arguments for thinking that no identity claim can be defended. Rather than summarise these arguments here, we shall move straight to the argument from non-naturalism.

Ethical non-naturalism

ANTHOLOGY: MOORE, *PRINCIPIA ETHICA*, §§6-14

The naturalistic fallacy

In *Principia Ethica*, G. E. Moore argued that moral properties are not natural properties. He did not argue that there is *no* relation between moral properties and natural properties. Moral properties may be *correlated* with certain natural properties. But they are not identical. Correlation is not identity. For example, having a heart is correlated with having kidneys – every animal that has a heart has kidneys and vice versa. But hearts and kidneys are not the same thing! Or again, having a size and having a shape are correlated – everything that has a size has a shape and vice versa. But size and shape are distinct properties. So even if goodness is correlated with happiness, say, that does not show that they are the same property.

Moore called the attempt to equate goodness to any natural property the *naturalistic fallacy*. Goodness, he claimed, is a simple and unanalysable property. It cannot be defined in terms of anything else (§6). Of course, we can say how people use the term (§8). But we can't give a definition that defines goodness in terms of its parts that together 'make up' goodness (§10).

Colours are similar. Yellow is a simple property, and no one can explain what yellow is to someone who doesn't know. You have to see it for yourself to understand what it is (§7). We can't define yellow – which is part of our visual experience of the world – in terms of wavelengths of light (§10). It might be

> **?** Why can't moral knowledge be established empirically?

> Objections from non-cognitivism are given in HUME, TREATISE OF HUMAN NATURE, BK 3, PT 1, p. 168.

> Explain the difference between correlation and identity.

correlated with these, such that seeing yellow is always caused by certain wavelengths of light. But it is a mistake to think that they are one and the same thing.

Unlike colours, goodness is not a natural property (§25). It cannot be investigated by empirical means. It is real, but it is not part of the natural world, the world of science.

The 'open question' argument

Moore supports his view that a definition of goodness is impossible by the 'open question' argument (§13). If goodness just is pleasure, say, then it wouldn't make sense to ask 'Is pleasure good?' This would be like asking 'Is pleasure pleasure?' This second question isn't a real question (the answer has to be 'yes'), but 'Is pleasure good?' is a real question – the answer can logically be 'yes' or 'no'. And so goodness cannot be pleasure, or any other property. 'Is *x* good?' is always a real question while 'Is *x x*?' is not. And so goodness cannot be defined as any other property.

Now, the question remains, what *has* the property of goodness? It makes perfect sense to say that pleasure is good in this sense (§9). But this is to accept that there are two things here, not one. There is the pleasure, and pleasure has this additional property, goodness. So goodness cannot be defined as pleasure or identified with it. Compare: when we say 'You weigh 60 kilos', we attribute you with the property of weighing 60 kilos. We don't think that you are the *same thing* as that weight – you are a person, not a weight! Likewise, we can meaningfully say that pleasure is good if we distinguish between pleasure and goodness (§12).

What, according to Moore, is the 'naturalistic fallacy'?

Explain Moore's open question argument.

What, according to Moore, does 'pleasure is good' mean?

Going further: is the 'naturalistic fallacy' a real fallacy?

Moore's open question argument doesn't work. Here is a similar argument. 'The property of being water cannot be any property in the world, such as the property of being H_2O. If it was then the question "Is water H_2O?" would not make sense - it would be like asking "Is H_2O H_2O?" So water is a simple, unanalysable property.' This is not right, as water *just is* H_2O.

The reason the argument doesn't work is because it confuses concepts and properties. Two different concepts - 'water' and 'H_2O' - can pick out the same property in the world. Before the discovery of hydrogen and oxygen, people knew about water. They had the concept of water, but not the concept of H_2O. So they didn't know that water is H_2O. 'Water is H_2O' is not *analytically* true. However, water and H_2O are one and the same *thing* - the two concepts refer to just one thing in the world. Water is identical to H_2O.

Likewise, the concept 'goodness' is a different concept from 'happiness'. 'Happiness is good' is not an analytic truth. We can accept that Moore has demonstrated this. But perhaps the two concepts refer to exactly the same property in the world, so that goodness is happiness. Moore's open question argument does not show that they are different properties.

Explain the claim that 'goodness' and 'happiness' are two concepts that refer to the same thing.

ANTHOLOGY: WARNOCK, *CONTEMPORARY MORAL PHILOSOPHY*, CH. 2 'INTUITIONISM'

Moore's intuitionism

If moral properties are not natural properties, then how do we discover them? How do we know what is good? In MILL'S 'PROOF' OF UTILITARIANISM (p. 36), he claims that we cannot prove what is good or not. To prove a claim is to deduce it from some other claim that we have already established. Moore agrees. But

See DEDUCTIVE ARGUMENT, p. 8.

unlike Mill, he does not think that we can argue inductively from evidence either. All we can do is consider the truth of the claim, such as 'pleasure is good', itself. Moore calls such claims 'intuitions'.

What does this mean? The claim that some truths can be known by rational 'intuition' is made by rationalism. But what is an intuition, and how can we tell if it is true? Are we supposed to have some special *faculty* of moral intuition? Moore leaves these questions open: 'when I call such propositions Intuitions, I mean *merely* to assert that they are incapable of proof; I imply nothing whatever as to the manner or origin of our cognition of them'. However, he has already said more than this. He has argued that these claims are not analytically true. And he has argued that we cannot know them through empirical investigation. So they must be some variety of synthetic a priori knowledge. He claims that we know claims about what is good to be true (or false) by considering the claim itself. Intuitions are 'self-evident' propositions.

A self-evident judgement rests on the 'evidence' of its own plausibility, which is grasped directly. This doesn't necessarily mean that everyone can immediately see that it is true. 'Self-evident' is not the same as 'obvious'. Our ability to make a self-evident judgement needs to develop first, and we need to consider the issue very carefully and clearly. Because moral intuitions are not known through the senses, the self-evidence of a moral intuition will be more like the self-evidence of a necessary truth, such as mathematics or claims about what is logically possible, than the self-evidence of a perceptual truth, such as the claim that there is a table in front of me. So, intuitionism does not need to claim that we have a faculty of intuition that 'detects' whether something is good or not, a bit like a supernatural sense. Intuitionism is simply a form of ethical non-naturalism that claims that some of our moral judgements are synthetic yet self-evident.

See *Philosophy for AS*, Intuition and deduction thesis, p. 104.

Principia Ethica, Preface

See *Philosophy for AS*, Necessary and contingent truth, p. 105.

?   What is intuitionism?

Varieties of intuitionism

Moore is an intuitionist about claims about what is *good*. He argues that we can define rightness in terms of goodness. Like Bentham and Mill, Moore claims that what is right is what produces the most amount of good. By contrast, Prichard is an intuitionist about what is *right*, what our duty is. Just as Moore argues that 'good' cannot be defined or analysed, so Prichard argues that we cannot define *obligation*. Now we often want to know whether something that we think may be our duty really is our duty. But, he argues, this is not something we can give reasons for. The only reason why something is my duty is because it is my duty, and that is the only reason I ought to do it. The fact that it causes happiness, for instance, is quite irrelevant. Our obligations are self-evident: we understand what they are by directly understanding, in each particular situation, what we ought to do.

Ross disagrees with both Moore and Prichard. Against Moore, he argues that we have intuitions about what is right. Against Prichard, he argues that it is not what is right in each particular situation that is self-evident. Rather, certain general principles about what is right are self-evident. Certain *kinds* of action - such as keeping our promises, gratitude, maximising the good, and not harming others - are our duty, and we can only know this by intuition. From these principles, we can then work out what we should do in each situation. Ross allows that these duties can conflict. In each case of conflict, one duty will 'give way' to the other. However, following Aristotle, there is no rule for knowing which duty should give way, nor is this a matter of intuition but a matter of judgement.

> Compare Moore, Prichard and Ross on which moral truths are known by intuition.

Objections

Warnock agrees with intuitionism that moral judgements are not like other kinds of assertion, such as descriptions of empirical facts (against naturalism) or expressions of taste (against non-cognitivism) or commands (against Kant). From this, intuitionists conclude that goodness must be some non-natural property that is quite different from other properties. But they don't tell us what this difference is.

First, they fail to tell us how morality is related to anything else. For example, isn't hurting someone what *makes* an action wrong? Isn't showing concern for another person something that *makes* the motive right? Intuitionists provide no explanation of how natural facts contribute to moral thinking.

Second, to say that we know moral judgements to be true or false 'by intuition' is only to say that we don't know them in any of the usual ways. The theory doesn't give us any real answer as to *how* we know truths by intuition. This leads to difficulties when people disagree over whether self-evident judgements are true. Because the judgements are supposed to be self-evident, any further reasons for believing them will not be as conclusive as considering the claim itself. So how can we establish that the claim is true in the face of disagreement?

Third, according to intuitionism, moral judgements differ from other kinds of factual judgement just in terms of their subject matter, what they are about. But in saying that a moral judgement attributes a property, say goodness, to some action, it seems that morality simply gives us information. But what has that got to do with how to live? Why are moral truths relevant to what to do, while other truths are not? Intuitionism doesn't give us an account of how or why morality motivates us.

Explain two arguments against intuitionism.

Error theory

ANTHOLOGY: MACKIE, *ETHICS: INVENTING RIGHT AND WRONG*, CH. 1, §9

Warnock's objections to intuitionism are developed by arguments presented by John Mackie. He agrees with naturalists and non-naturalists that we understand moral judgements to be cognitive. The way we use ethical language is to make objective claims about a moral reality. But, in fact, *there is no such moral reality*. *All* moral judgements are false. 'Murder is wrong' is false, and 'Murder is right' is false, because there are no objective moral properties. Ethical language rests on a mistake.

It is worth taking a moment to consider what Mackie means by 'objective'. At various points in Ch. 1, Mackie identifies the following features of an objective claim:

1. It can be something we know.
2. It can be true or false.
3. Its truth is independent of what we want or choose.
4. It is about something mind-independent.
5. It is about something that is part of the 'fabric of the world'.

These claims are not equivalent. Consider the claim 'that shirt is red'. We may well want to say that it is objective according to the first three criteria, but colours are certainly not mind-independent (colour depends conceptually on vision, which is a mental faculty), and it is hard to know whether we should say that colours are part of the 'fabric of the world' or not. This point will become important when we look at responses to Mackie's argument.

Mackie calls his argument an argument from 'queerness'. It is the oddity of moral properties that makes it implausible that they exist. The argument has two aspects, metaphysical and epistemological.

Epistemological queerness

If some actions, such as an act of courage, have the property of being objectively right; or again, if some states of affairs, such as being in pain or cowardice, have the property of being objectively bad – how could we know? Intuitionism, Mackie claims, says no more than that we have some special faculty – but, as Warnock also argued, this is a terrible answer that

> **What is error theory?**

> See *Philosophy for AS*, THE DISTINCTION BETWEEN PRIMARY AND SECONDARY QUALITIES, p. 44.

doesn't explain how we have this knowledge at all. If we think of our usual ways of knowing about the world – sense perception, introspection, hypothetical reasoning, even conceptual analysis – none of these can explain knowledge of morality.

The non-naturalist might well reply that it is not only knowledge of morality that faces this objection. We can't explain our knowledge of mathematics, necessary truths, the existence and nature of substance, space or causation in any of these ways either. Here, the objectivist is appealing to rationalist arguments about the scope of a priori knowledge. If we think we only gain knowledge in the ways empiricism allows, we will have to adopt an error theory for all these claims.

Mackie accepts the point: either empiricism can account for knowledge in these areas, or they all face the objection that they appeal to something 'non-natural'. To a significant extent, then, Mackie's argument depends on empiricism, rather than rationalism, being the correct account of our knowledge.

Mackie presses the argument from epistemological queerness by asking, as did Warnock, what the connection between natural properties and moral properties is. For instance, we commonly say things like 'that's wrong because it is cruel'. If we take cruel to mean 'causing pain for fun', then cruelty is a natural property. It is a psychological fact that something causes pain, and another psychological fact that someone's motive is taking pleasure in doing this. But what is the relation between these facts and the 'fact' that acting in this way is wrong? How can we establish whether it is wrong or not? It isn't an analytic truth, and we can't deduce it.

Therefore, it is better to say that there is no objective property of wrongness, and we don't know that things are wrong or right. Instead, moral judgements are simply our subjective reactions to certain actions and situations. (Mackie isn't saying that this is what moral judgements mean – that would be non-cognitivism. He is saying that they aim to be objective, but fail.)

If you haven't already, see *Philosophy for AS*, KNOWLEDGE EMPIRICISM, p. 96, to review the debate over knowledge between empiricism and rationalism.

Explain Mackie's argument from epistemological queerness.

Metaphysical queerness

If there were moral properties, Mackie claims, they would have to be very different from anything else in the universe. His argument for this claim rests on the connection between morality and motivation. Moral judgements motivate us – we avoid actions we believe are wrong and try to do actions that are right. But that means, if there were moral properties, simply *knowing* what is good or bad, right or wrong, would be enough to motivate us to act in certain ways. For this to be true, 'goodness', say, would have to have 'to-be-pursuedness' built into it.

If this is a confusing idea, that's Mackie's point. How could an objective property motivate us in this way? How could there be some direct, immediate relation between some fact of the world and our desires? Just to know something true about the way the world is doesn't entail being motivated to do anything about it. As we might say, the direction of fit is wrong.

> Explain Mackie's argument from metaphysical queerness.

Replies to Mackie

Mackie's argument from queerness appeals to two features of objectivity in particular – mind-independence and being part of 'the fabric of the world'. This last phrase is puzzling. It conjures up the world that science reveals to us – the fabric of the world is space, time, matter and perhaps causal relations between them. Obviously, morality can't be like this. Physics won't tell us right from wrong. But why should we think that all reality is like physical reality? Moral reasons and values, if they exist, aren't going to be like physical properties.

Are psychological states 'part of the fabric of the world'? They certainly exist – whether one is happy or in pain is a psychological fact. But, of course, it isn't a mind-independent fact. So not all objective facts are mind-independent in that sense; some facts are facts about our minds. Whether someone is in pain is a fact about their particular mind. But there are more general facts about the human mind, e.g. that we can feel pain. Perhaps moral facts are facts about our minds, and not all that 'queer' after all.

For example, Kant argues that both our intellect and our wills are rational. Rationality is 'built into' the mind. Kant himself doesn't talk about moral 'properties', but we could say this. Whether an action has the property of being wrong depends upon facts about the rational mind, namely whether the agent could universalise the maxim for their action without contradiction. Kant argues that it is objectively true or false whether a maxim can be universalised without contradiction. What makes it true or false is rationality, which is a property of the mind.

Or again, consider utilitarianism as naturalism. Mill argues that our experience *does* give us evidence of what is good. What is good is what is desirable, and the best evidence for what is desirable is what people generally desire. Once we recognise this, there is no particular epistemological difficulty in discovering moral properties. Furthermore, if we say that goodness *is* happiness, then there is no metaphysical queerness about goodness either. It is simply another natural property. Finally, given that we desire happiness, we can see how moral judgements are motivating. They are judgements about happiness, and this is something we are already motivated to pursue.

? Does Mackie show that objective moral properties don't exist?

See ARISTOTLE, NICOMACHEAN ETHICS, BK 1, p. 71.

Going further: Aristotelian non-naturalism

A non-naturalist response can take inspiration from Aristotle's virtue ethics. Aristotle argues that eudaimonia, our final end, involves living in accordance with reason. Virtue assists with this, and practical wisdom helps us discern the right reasons in any situation. By thinking more about reasons, perhaps we can answer Mackie's argument from queerness.

Non-naturalist epistemology

Following the Aristotelian model, we can understand moral judgements in terms of moral reasons. For example, to say that something is wrong is to say that the moral reasons against doing it are stronger than any moral reason in favour of doing it. Now the idea of a 'reason' only makes sense in relation to a rational creature – us. Reasons are always reasons for someone. That some natural fact (e.g. the suffering of an animal) is a reason (e.g. for us not to eat meat) is a 'relational' property – the fact is only such a reason in relation to us.

Understanding moral properties as reasons for action can be used to argue for objective moral truth. Whether some fact is a moral reason for or against some action is objectively true or false. Compare reasons for other types of belief. If radiometric decay indicates that the dinosaur bones are 65 million years old, this is a reason to believe that dinosaurs lived on Earth 65 million years ago. It is not *proof*, but it is a reason. Furthermore, it is an objective fact that it is a reason. The result of radiometric dating of dinosaur bones is a reason to think dinosaurs lived on Earth 65 million years ago, whether you think it is a reason or not.

Facts about reasons are not identical with natural facts. There is no scientific or empirical investigation into what reasons there are. Facts about reasons are normative facts. They are facts about justification and reasoning. These are non-natural facts.

Moral judgements, then, are statements about reasons. So they are statements about normative facts. Because they are statements about (normative) facts, moral judgements can be true or false.

Of course, it can be difficult to establish whether a natural fact constitutes a reason for action, and how strong this reason is. But the truth is often difficult to discover. Developing this knowledge is a matter of practical wisdom.

One model here is intuitionism. Suppose that to say something is good is to say that we have reason to desire it (it is desirable). Suppose that pleasure is good. Is it self-evident that pleasure is good, or can we give a further explanation? Suppose

We came across relational properties in discussing direct realism. See *Philosophy for AS*, pp. 32 and 49.

Explain how natural facts can be reasons.

Explain the claim that moral judgements are objectively true (or false) claims about moral reasons.

we can; e.g. pleasure is good because it forms part of a flourishing life for human beings. Is it, then, self-evident that being part of a flourishing life makes something good? If you give a further explanation, we can ask whether this explanation is self-evident, and so on.

Alternatively, non-naturalists may claim that no judgement is self-evident, because it is supported by other beliefs. When we then question those beliefs, we can give reasons for believing them, but must in turn assume others. Our reasoning, then, involves a matter of interpreting, applying and adjusting a *framework* of reasons. We test our claims and the reasons we give by their place in the framework.

In our reflections on reasons, we will be guided by trying to make sense of our moral attitudes generally. Reflection itself will be guided by what seems plausible or implausible to us. We justify moral judgements by appealing to the overall coherence, the balance between our judgements in individual cases and our general moral beliefs, the 'reflective equilibrium' we reach.

Compare intuitionism and the method of 'reflective equilibrium'.

Queerness again

But isn't the idea of 'truths about reasons' a very strange notion? Not really, the non-naturalist can argue. Reasons aren't strange, and we need them even to do science. Aristotle claims that certain facts about being human mean that a certain way of living is the best, most flourishing life. We therefore have reason to develop our characters in ways that allow us to live like this. This isn't strange.

We can object that if reasons are related to us, dependent on us, then surely they must be subjective, not objective. Facts are part of the world. The fact that the dinosaurs roamed the Earth millions of years ago would be true whether anyone had found out about it or not. But whether something is a reason or not depends on us.

This misunderstands the way in which reasons depend on us. There are lots of facts - for example, facts about being in love, or facts about music - that 'depend' on human beings and their activities (there would be no love if no one loved anything). But they are still facts, because they are independent of our judgements, and made true by the way the world, in this case the human world, is. You can make mistakes about whether someone is in love or whether a piece of music is baroque or classical.

But are *moral* reasons dependent on 'human beings' in general or on individuals? Take the case of animal suffering: surely this is only a reason for me not to eat meat *if I care* about animals. Or again, the fact that studying hard will increase my understanding of philosophy is only a reason to study hard *if I want* to understand philosophy. So what we (individually) have reason to do depends on what we (individually) want. So reasons aren't objective, they are subjective. Moral judgements are expressions of what we care about, not expressions of objective truth.

Are what reasons for action I have dependent on what I want?

Moral motivation

This last point returns us to Warnock's third objection to intuitionism (p. 156). Can non-naturalism explain the fact that moral judgements guide our behaviour? A truth, in and of itself, doesn't lead to action. For example, the fact that it is raining doesn't motivate me to pick up my umbrella unless I don't want to get wet. It seems that I need to *care* about the truth, and then the motivating force comes from the caring. But surely statements about right and wrong, good and bad are motivating *in their own right*. In that case, they are not like beliefs (about truths), but are like desires.

One response that naturalists and non-naturalists can make is to claim that moral judgements are *not* motivating. There certainly seem to be people - and perhaps all of us at certain times, e.g. when we are depressed – for whom statements about morality are not motivating. They just don't care about morality. Moral judgements, then, are only motivating to people who care about morality.

A second response is to agree that moral judgements are motivating, and this would be a puzzle if they were judgements about natural facts. But if we argue, as we did above, that moral judgements are about what we have reason to do, they will be motivating, because judgements about reasons are judgements about reasons *for us*. As long as we are rational, reasons will motivate us directly. Of course, that motivation can be interfered with because we are not completely rational, so we will not always do what we have most reason to do.

Explaining disagreement

What of Warnock's second objection, that intuitionism has nothing helpful to say in the case of disagreement over an intuition? We now have an epistemology that explains what happens. People are disagreeing over whether some fact is or is not a good reason for some action. When two people disagree morally, at least one of them is making a mistake, because they are not seeing certain natural facts as the reasons they are. If, Aristotle claims, we need both virtues and experience of life to gain sound moral insight, then it is not surprising that so many people make mistakes.

We can object, first, that it is not plausible that all cases of moral disagreement involve at least one person who lacks virtue and life experience! Second, if we press this line too much – if only a few people can gain moral knowledge – then the possibility of agreement on moral truth is very small indeed.

Explain two ways in which cognitivism can try to meet the challenge from moral motivation.

Outline and explain a non-naturalist account of moral disagreement.

Can moral disagreement be resolved rationally?

Key points: cognitivism

- Cognitivism claims that moral judgements express beliefs, can be true or false, and aim to describe the world.
- Cognitivism appeals to our experience of morality: we feel we can make mistakes, that moral demands are independent of us, that moral progress is possible.
- Moral realism claims that moral judgements are made true or false by objective moral properties. Ethical naturalism claims that moral properties are identical with some natural (psychological) properties. Ethical non-naturalism claims that moral properties are not natural properties.
- Utilitarianism can be understood as claiming that that the moral property 'goodness' is the natural property 'happiness'. Moore interpreted Mill's proof of utilitarianism in these terms, arguing that Mill thereby commits the naturalistic fallacy.
- Aristotle argued that eudaimonia is both the subject matter of morality and based on facts about human nature. Whether some character trait, e.g. courage, contributes to living well, and so is a virtue, is a matter of fact.
- However, it is unlikely that eudaimonia can be reduced to natural facts, since practical wisdom is sensitive to moral reasons, and these may not be natural facts.
- If moral properties are natural properties, this cannot be established by empirical investigation.
- Moore argued for the claim that goodness cannot be defined. To identify goodness with any type of natural property is a 'naturalistic fallacy'. This is shown by the open question argument.
- However, Moore shows only that moral concepts are distinct from natural concepts. He doesn't show that moral properties are not natural properties.
- Intuitionism claims that some moral judgements are self-evident; judgements that rest on being grasped directly. Intuitions are a type of synthetic a priori knowledge.
- Intuitionists do not agree on which judgements are self-evidently true. Moore argued that claims about goodness are intuitions,

Prichard argued the same for claims of particular obligation, and Ross for general principles of right.

- Warnock objects that intuitionism does not tell us how moral properties are related to natural properties, nor does it explain how we know moral truths by intuition, nor how we can be motivated by moral judgements.

- Mackie argues that moral judgements are cognitive, but false. They refer to objective moral properties, but no such properties exist. This is error theory.

- Mackie argues that if there were objective moral properties, it is a complete mystery how we could come to know them or how we could infer them from natural properties. And they would be metaphysically mysterious as well, since they would need to motivate us.

- We can object that some psychological properties are objective but not mind-independent in Mackie's sense. Kant can argue that an act is wrong if its maxim cannot be universalised, and this is a fact of rationality. Utilitarianism as naturalism can argue that moral properties are natural properties.

- On an Aristotelian non-naturalism model, a moral judgement that an action is wrong is true if the reasons against doing it are stronger than the reason in favour of it. This judgement is not a matter of proof or deduction.

- Natural facts can be understood as reasons supporting moral judgements. Reasons are relational, relating features of situations to moral agents.

- If reasons are objective, then there are objective (normative) facts about whether a natural fact is a reason or not.

- One model of how we can justify moral judgements on this view is intuitionism. Another argues that we interpret, apply and adjust a framework of reasons, trying to balance intuitions and reflection to reach 'reflective equilibrium'.

- We can object that whether some consideration is a reason for me depends on what I care about.

- We can also object that how moral judgements motivate us is left unexplained.

- One cognitivist response is to say that we must care about morality – and it is this, not moral judgements themselves, that motivates us.

- Another answer is to say that since moral judgements are about what we have reason to do, it is because we are rational that they motivate us to act.
- Cognitivists can argue that when people agree on the natural facts but disagree morally, they are disagreeing over whether the natural facts are reasons. At least one person is making an objective mistake.

C. Non-cognitivism

As described in COGNITIVISM AND NON-COGNITIVISM (p. 144), non-cognitivist theories of ethics claim that ethical language does not try to describe the world and cannot be true or false. Moral judgements do not express beliefs, but some other, non-cognitive mental state. Different non-cognitivist theories disagree on exactly what this mental state is.

Emotivism

Emotivism claims that moral judgements *express* the feeling or attitude of approval or disapproval. To say that 'Murder is wrong' is to express one's disapproval of murder. Ethical language is 'emotive'. So, in one sense, emotivism claims that morality is 'subjective'. However, there is an important distinction between emotivism and the theory that is called 'subjectivism'. Subjectivism claims that moral judgements *assert* or *report* approval or disapproval, and there is a difference between expressing disapproval and asserting it.

One form of subjectivism claims that to say 'X is wrong' is simply to say that it is generally disapproved of. But this can't be right, because it is not a contradiction to say 'Most people approve of X, but X is wrong nonetheless'. For example, racism has been very common historically. We may argue that 'racism is wrong' even while acknowledging that most people approved of it.

A second form of subjectivism, 'speaker subjectivism', claims that the meaning of 'X is wrong' is something like 'I disapprove of X' or again 'I think X is wrong'. This is a fact about oneself, so the statement can be true or false and is verifiable. Speaker subjectivism, therefore, is an unusual form of cognitivism: the facts that make moral judgements true are facts about the individual speaker's mind.

Speaker subjectivism entails that we cannot make mistakes about what is right or wrong. If I say 'Murder is right', I am simply stating 'I approve of murder'. If I am sincere, then I do approve of murder, and so murder is, indeed, right ('for me', we might say). But we naturally think that people *can* make mistakes about morality. Speaker subjectivism makes no sense of deliberation, trying to *figure out* what is right or wrong. Why should I bother to deliberate? *Whatever* I come to feel will be right!

By contrast, emotivism claims that moral judgements do not express *any* kind of truth or falsehood, because they are not cognitive. It can explain the objections to subjectivism above. To say that 'most people approve of racism' does not contradict 'racism is wrong', because 'racism is wrong' doesn't state something true or false. And one cannot be infallible in the sense of getting the answer right; there are no moral truths.

> **Explain speaker subjectivism and one objection to it.**

> **What is emotivism?**

ANTHOLOGY: HUME, *TREATISE OF HUMAN NATURE*, BK 3, PT 1

Many philosophers have interpreted Hume as defending emotivism, although that interpretation has recently been challenged. Our aim, however, is to extract the main line of argument from Hume that one could use in defence of emotivism. On this interpretation, Hume makes two main claims. The first is that cognitivism is false (§1). The second is that moral judgements are expressions of our feelings of approval and disapproval (§2).

The arguments against cognitivism

Hume gives two arguments against cognitivism. The first is this:

1. Moral judgements can motivate actions.
2. Reason cannot motivate action.
3. Therefore, moral judgements are not judgements of reason.

Cognitivism claims that moral judgements express beliefs, which can be true or false. And the faculty of judging what is true or false is reason. Hence, Hume's conclusion is a rejection of cognitivism.

Hume assumes (1) to be true. His argument for (2) depends on the claim that all judgements of reason are either relations of ideas or matters of fact. Before going any further, it is worth clarifying this claim.

Relations of ideas of can be discovered just by thinking, by recognising the truth of an analytic proposition or by deductive reasoning. To deny a relation of ideas is to contradict oneself. Matters of fact are claims about what exists, and they are established by perceptual experience and causal inference.

Hume argues earlier in the *Treatise* that we are always motivated by our emotions and desires. But, he claims, emotions and desires are not psychological states that can be true or false. As we can say now, they have a world-to-mind 'direction of fit'. By contrast, judgements of relations of ideas and matters of fact have a mind-to-world direction of fit. A psychological state that simply presents a truth can't motivate us to act, because there is no pressure to change the world to fit the mind. Simply understanding that some relation holds between two ideas doesn't entail that we should act one way rather than another. And knowing facts about the world might well tell us what exists, and how to achieve what we want. Knowing such things might *direct* our existing desires in one way or another. But how could it make us want anything in the first place? So judgements of reason cannot motivate action.

Hume's second argument against cognitivism is this:

4. There are only two types of judgements of reason, relations of ideas and matters of fact.
5. Moral judgements are not relations of ideas.
6. Moral judgements are not matters of fact.
7. Therefore, moral judgements are not judgements of reason.

The arguments for, and against, (4) were discussed at length at AS, so we won't repeat them here. If the claim is true, then empiricism about knowledge is true.

See *Philosophy for AS*, HUME, AN ENQUIRY CONCERNING HUMAN UNDERSTANDING, §4, PT 1, p. 99.

Treatise of Human Nature, Bk 2, Pt 3, §3

Explain Hume's argument against cognitivism from motivation.

See *Philosophy for AS*, KNOWLEDGE EMPIRICISM, p. 96.

What of (5)? Hume's main argument for this claim is that there is no relation of ideas that applies just to morality. Any relation that describes moral or immoral actions also applies to physical objects, but these aren't moral or immoral. Take murder, for example, which involves one thing killing another. A plant can kill another plant. There is nothing in the idea of 'killing' that gives us moral wrongness.

We can object that murder is not simply killing. It is wilful, premeditated killing. But, Hume responds, this just means that the action has a different *cause*. But the relation between cause and effect, which we describe as 'killing', remains the same. It is up to the person who wants to claim that moral judgements are relations of ideas to show what relations of ideas they are, and how they are unique to morality.

Similarly, if we claim that moral judgements are a matter of fact, we must identify *which* fact:

> Take any action allow'd to be vicious: Wilful murder, for instance. Examine it in all lights, and see if you can find that matter of fact ... which you call *vice*. In which-ever way you take it, you find only certain passions, motives, volitions, and thoughts. There is no other matter of fact in the case. The vice entirely escapes you, as long as you consider the object.

Hume concludes §1 by drawing a famous distinction between sentences that talk about what *is* the case (judgements of reason) and moral judgements, which talk about what *ought* to be the case. But how do we get from one to the other? How, for instance, do we get from the fact that some action will cause pain to the claim that we ought not to do it? What's the connection? '[T]his ought ... expresses some new relation [of which it] seems altogether inconceivable, how this new relation can be a deduction from others, which are entirely different from it'.

Outline and explain Hume's argument that moral judgements are not about matters of fact.

Moral judgements are expressions of feeling

Hume's answer is that we don't and can't *infer* an 'ought' from an 'is'. Instead, morality 'is more properly felt than judg'd of'. What arouses positive feelings of approval in us, we call virtuous; what arouses negative feelings of disapproval, we call vicious.

> [W]hen you pronounce any action or character to be vicious, you mean nothing, but that … you have a feeling … of blame from the contemplation of it. Vice and virtue, therefore, may be compar'd to sounds, colours, heat and cold, which … are not qualities in objects, but perceptions in the mind.

In this remark, Hume is drawing an analogy with secondary qualities. Primary qualities are properties that science says objects have (extension, shape, motion, number, solidity); and secondary qualities are properties that depend upon particular ways of perceiving objects (colour, sound, smell, taste, temperature). For example, colour, by definition, is something that is experienced in vision. According to science, the cause of what we experience as colour is vibrations of the electromagnetic field. This theory suggests that the world as we experience it through our senses and the world as science describes it are quite different.

See *Philosophy for AS*, THE DISTINCTION BETWEEN PRIMARY AND SECONDARY QUALITIES, p. 44.

Hume thought that this showed that secondary qualities exist only in the mind. Objects aren't coloured; instead, their parts have certain properties of size and motion and so on, causing them to emit or reflect wavelengths of light (which is a type of vibration, not itself a colour). It is not until we turn to human perceptual experience – something mental – that we need the concept of colour, that we come across 'colour experience'.

See *Philosophy for AS*, DO SECONDARY QUALITIES EXIST OUTSIDE THE MIND?, p. 46.

Hume is claiming that moral judgement is analogous. Good and bad, right and wrong, vice and virtue are not properties of actions and characters. Instead, moral judgements are expressions of our feelings (of approval and disapproval).

Explain Hume's claim that morality 'is more properly felt than judg'd of'.

Going further: replies to Hume's arguments

One way of escaping Hume's first argument is to claim that the first premise – that moral judgements can motivate actions – is false. To do good actions, we have to have the *desire* to be good as well. If moral judgements *don't* motivate us on their own, then this argument gives us no reason to believe that moral judgements aren't judgements of reason. However, this strategy leads us straight into his second argument. If moral judgements are judgements of reason, what type of judgements of reason are they?

Kant provides one account. We could argue that whether a maxim is universalisable or not is a relation of ideas, established by the test of contradiction. This was not a relation that Hume considered. A second account is provided by Aristotelian non-naturalism. Moral judgements are judgements of what reasons we have to act, so they are about *normative* matters of fact. Hume limits matters of fact to natural facts. He hasn't considered the possibility of non-natural facts.

Aristotelian non-naturalism also explains the connection between natural properties and moral judgements, bridging the gap between 'is' and 'ought'. Hume is right that we cannot *deduce* moral judgements from considering the natural facts; instead, we must *weigh up* the reasons that the natural facts give us. But once we recognise that whether a natural fact counts as a reason for believing a certain value judgement is itself a matter of objective fact, we can cross the gap.

Finally, we can turn Hume's analogy between moral judgements and secondary qualities against him. We can agree that moral reasons are like secondary qualities, but then argue that secondary qualities are not subjective. According to direct realist theories of perception, colours are properties of objects. When we perceive the colour of an object, we still perceive the object, but *as it appears to us*. 'Us' means 'human beings', not 'me' or 'you'. An object's colour is not subjective, because it is independent of how any *individual* person perceives it. To be

Explain one theory that claims that moral judgements are judgements of reason.

Explain one account of the relation between 'is' and 'ought'.

brown is to look brown to normal perceivers under normal conditions. Secondary qualities are no less real than primary qualities; it is just that they are a different *type* of property, one defined in terms of how we (human beings in general) perceive the world.

Likewise, moral judgements are defined in the context of human responses to the world. But what values there are doesn't depend on what any individual person finds valuable or not, just as the colour of something is independent of any individual person's perception of it. Whether some fact (e.g. animal suffering) is a reason to act in a certain way (e.g. stop eating meat) depends *in general* on human responses and our best account of eudaimonia; but it is independent of any individual's response, so it is not subjective.

> 1) Does the analogy between moral properties and secondary qualities show that moral values are objective or subjective? 2) Do Hume's arguments establish emotivism?

ANTHOLOGY: AYER, *LANGUAGE, TRUTH AND LOGIC*, CHS 1, 6; *THE CENTRAL QUESTIONS OF PHILOSOPHY*, PP. 22-7

Ayer's verification principle and its implications for religious language were discussed at AS. A brief reminder of the principle: it claims that a statement only has meaning if it is either analytic or empirically verifiable. A statement is analytic if it is true or false just in virtue of the meanings of the words. A statement is empirically verifiable if empirical evidence would go towards establishing that the statement is true or false.

> See *Philosophy for AS*, Verificationism, p. 254.

In Ch. 6, just as Ayer applies the principle to religious language, arguing that 'God exists' and other such statements are meaningless, he also applies the principle to ethical language. If I say 'murder is wrong', this is not analytic, nor can any empirical investigation show this. We can show that murder causes grief and pain, or that it is often done out of anger. But we cannot demonstrate, in the same way, that it is wrong. Moral judgements don't state truths or falsehoods, and are therefore literally meaningless.

> Explain why the verification principle entails that moral judgements are neither true nor false.

Instead, Ayer argued, they express feelings: 'If I say to someone, "You acted wrongly in stealing that money" ... I am simply evincing my moral disapproval of it. It is as if I had said, "You stole that money," in a peculiar tone of horror'. But not only does moral language express our feelings, as Hume argued, it also aims to arouse feelings in others, and so get them to act in certain ways.

In developing his theory, Ayer first distinguishes it from subjectivism (p. 151). He then compares it to Moore's intuitionism (p. 151). He agrees with Moore that '*X* is wrong' cannot mean '*X* would cause unhappiness' (or any other proposition substituting a natural property for 'wrong'). The open question argument shows that it is never a contradiction to say '*X* would cause unhappiness, but it is right to do it nonetheless'. So Ayer agrees that ethical naturalism is wrong.

But he also rejects non-naturalism. As an ethical non-naturalist, of course, Moore believed that moral judgements are about non-natural properties. While they are neither analytic nor empirically verifiable, they are nevertheless true or false. Ayer responds that Moore's intuitionism is unsatisfactory. We can't establish the truth or falsity of a moral claim by appealing to intuition unless we are able to provide some criterion for deciding between conflicting intuitions. Intuition itself is no way to verify a claim. Given the verification principle, only an empirical criterion will do. But there is no empirical test that will establish which intuition is correct and which is incorrect. And so, Ayer concludes, moral judgements are not genuinely meaningful, but simply express our feelings of approval or disapproval and arouse such feelings in others.

Explain Ayer's rejection of both ethical naturalism and non-naturalism.

Rejecting the verification principle

Ayer's theory depends on the verification principle. But the principle faces a famous objection. According to the verification principle, the principle itself is meaningless. The claim that 'a statement only has meaning if it is analytic or can be verified empirically' is not analytic and cannot be verified empirically. But if the principle of verification is meaningless, then what it claims cannot be true. So if the principle is true, it is meaningless, and so not true. Obviously, if it is false, it is false. Either way it is not true. Therefore, it does not give us any reason to believe that ethical language is meaningless.

Ayer claims that the principle is intended as *a definition*, not an empirical hypothesis about meaning. In other words, it is intended to reflect and clarify our understanding of 'meaningful' uses of words. Ayer accepts that the principle isn't obviously an accurate criterion of 'literal meaning', but that is why he provides arguments in specific cases, such as ethical language, which support it.

But in that case, the verification principle is only as convincing as the arguments that are intended to show that it is the right definition of 'meaningful'. If we do not find the arguments convincing, the principle provides no independent support.

> **Do Ayer's arguments show that emotivism is true?** [?]

ANTHOLOGY: WARNOCK, *CONTEMPORARY MORAL PHILOSOPHY*, CH. 3, PP. 21-4

However, emotivism does not depend on the principle of verification nor on Hume's theory of judgements of reason. As Warnock notes, emotivism as a *theory* really only developed with the work of Charles Stevenson. Warnock argues that Stevenson makes three central points.

First, Stevenson develops the distinction between beliefs and attitudes. As discussed in COGNITIVISM AND NON-COGNITIVISM (p. 144), a belief regards the truth of some claim - it is cognitive and has a mind-to-world direction of fit. An attitude regards what is to be done - it has a world-to-mind direction of fit and is non-cognitive.

Second, Stevenson develops the distinction between the descriptive and emotive meanings of words. He argues, quite independently of appeals to the verification principle or the scope of reason, that moral words have emotive meanings, which are neither descriptive nor analytic. The central ethical terms - 'right', 'wrong', 'good' and 'bad' - only have emotive meanings, of expressing approval or disapproval. But many moral terms ('steal', 'honesty', 'respect') have both descriptive and emotive meanings. To be told that someone is 'honest' is to learn something about them. For instance, they can't be honest while lying frequently! And whether someone lies frequently is a matter of fact. But the term 'honest' isn't just a description; it also has an emotive meaning of approval.

Stevenson's third claim analyses emotive meaning by connecting meaning to use. The purpose of moral judgements is not to state facts, but to influence how we behave through expressions of approval and disapproval. When we say that '*x* is good', we do not understand the judgement just by noticing that the speaker approves of *x* or even by noticing which features of *x* the speaker approves of. '*X* is good', and other moral judgements, are used both to express the speaker's attitudes and to influence the attitudes of other people. Moral terms are 'dynamic', and the main purpose of making moral judgements is to 'create an influence'.

One advantage of this theory is that it easily explains how and why it is that moral judgements motivate us. If moral language were just descriptive, stating how things are, why would that get us to act in certain ways? We need to care. And what we care about is captured in our attitudes to the world. Emotivism connects caring, approving, disapproving, with the very meaning of ethical words.

Explain Stevenson's theory of emotivism.

Objections to emotivism

ANTHOLOGY: WARNOCK, *CONTEMPORARY MORAL PHILOSOPHY*, CH. 3, PP. 24-9

Warnock argues that emotivism fails as an account of ethical language. First, being emotive and influencing people's attitudes is something that lots of non-ethical language does as well, e.g.

advertising. So we will need to say more to distinguish morality from advertising.

Second, ethical language doesn't always function to 'create an influence'. We may express our moral attitudes to others who already agree with them or that we know to be indifferent to our views – so influencing their attitudes is not the purpose. But this doesn't show that we aren't expressing a moral judgement.

Third, ethical language isn't particularly or necessarily emotive. The key moral terms 'good', 'right', 'wrong' and 'bad' may arouse emotions in others or express ours, but again, this depends on context. We do not think that it is always good to arouse emotions in others on moral issues, especially by using emotive language. Moral discussion can be, and sometimes should be, dispassionate.

> Explain two objections to emotivism.

The emotivist could reply to Warnock's objections by talking about 'primary' and 'secondary' uses. The *purpose* of ethical language, says emotivism, is to influence what people do. Without this, we would have no ethical language or judgements at all. However, that doesn't mean that it *always* has to be used for this purpose. This is normal – many types of language can be used in 'non-standard' ways in different situations. For example, it is possible to use fact-stating language to insult someone; e.g. 'You have a big nose'. That it is an emotive statement on this occasion doesn't make the *meaning* of the sentence 'emotive' – it states a factual claim. Likewise, language which is standardly emotive can be deployed without the intention to arouse emotion or influence action. Warnock hasn't shown that ethical language isn't 'essentially' emotive, only that it isn't always emotive.

> Is the purpose of ethical language to express our emotions and influence others?

There is, however, another objection that emotivism faces. What, *exactly*, is the emotion (or class of emotions) that moral judgements express? Can the emotivist draw a distinction between *moral* approval and disapproval and, say, *aesthetic* approval and disapproval? What makes approval moral or not moral?

Nothing emotivism says places limits on what we can approve or disapprove of. It identifies moral judgements with a particular *type* of

Explain the argument that morality cannot be understood *just* in terms of approval and disapproval.

Explain the objection that emotivism makes moral reasoning impossible.

judgement, one that expresses approval, etc., rather than a particular *content*. *Any* judgement that expresses approval or disapproval counts as moral. But this can't be right. Morality is about what is good or bad for human beings generally, given our nature and the types of problems life throws at us. It must relate in some way to what is good for people (or more broadly, animals, the environment, God).

Going further: moral argument

One of the most powerful objections to emotivism is that it oversimplifies ethical discussion. If I say 'abortion is wrong' and you say 'abortion is right', it seems that I am just expressing my disapproval of it and you are expressing your approval. I'm just saying 'Boo! to abortion' and you're saying 'Hurrah! for abortion'. I am also trying to influence your attitudes. But I am not doing so *rationally*, or by appealing to facts about what is good or bad. Trying to influence people without reasoning is just a form of manipulation. Emotivism reduces moral argument to propaganda.

Ayer responds that moral arguments are not arguments over moral judgements, but over facts: 'we do not attempt to show by our arguments that he has the "wrong" ethical feeling towards a situation whose nature he has correctly apprehended. What we attempt to show is that he is mistaken about the facts of the case.' When arguing over animal rights, say, we are constantly drawing facts to each other's attention. I point out how much animals suffer in factory farms. You point out how much more sophisticated human beings are than animals. I point out that it is unkind to kill animals for food. You respond that people are not motivated by unkindness, and indeed, farmers can be very kind to the animals when alive. And so on. But if we both agree on the facts, but still disagree morally, there is nothing left to discuss, says Ayer, no further argument can take place. Moral judgements always *presuppose* a system of values; but no arguments for these values can be given.

But if you and I disagree about a moral judgement, and moral judgements have no truth value, are we right to say that there is a 'disagreement' here at all? Isn't a disagreement when you think some claim is true and I think it is false?

Stevenson responds that a moral disagreement is a disagreement in *attitude*. It is a practical disagreement – no one can live both by the attitude that 'eating meat is wrong' and by the attitude that 'eating meat is right'. Attitudes can be discussed, because people do not have feelings or make choices in isolation. Any attitude has implications for other attitudes. If I disapprove of an action, I must also have similar feelings about similar actions, or my attitudes will not provide consistent guidance about how to live. Moral disagreement, then, can be about the relations between different attitudes. For example, deciding whether eating meat is right or wrong is complicated because there are many attitudes involved, sympathy towards the animal, attitudes towards death, feelings about the place of human beings in nature, and so on. It is difficult to work out how these attitudes can all be acted upon, and that is why people disagree.

We may still object that weighing up which attitudes to give up, which to keep, is a rational process. Emotivism does not give us an adequate account of deliberation. If you are unsure about whether something, lying say, is right or wrong, we can understand that you are trying to work out what your attitude towards lying *should* be. But why can't you settle the question of whether lying is right or wrong by simply noting whatever attitude you *already have* towards it? If emotivism is right, it seems that thinking hard about the question is irrational. We can put the point another way: emotivism doesn't explain how someone can *rationally* change their mind on a moral issue. First, they have one attitude, then they have another. But what *reason* do they have to change their mind?

Warnock develops the objection in a different way (p. 27): if moral judgements and arguments are about influencing people's attitudes, then a good moral argument will be one that is

> Explain Stevenson's claim that moral disagreements are disagreements in attitude.

> Can emotivism explain moral deliberation?

effective. That is all. There is no other, e.g. rational, criterion by which we might judge that it is a good or bad argument. Whatever I appeal to, to make you change your mind, no matter how irrelevant or far-fetched, if it makes you change your mind, it is a good argument. This is highly unsatisfactory.

We can take the point deeper still. We think of good arguments in terms of validity (for deductive arguments) and whether the premises give us a good reason to believe the conclusion. A valid argument is one in which if the premises are true, the conclusion has to be true. But according to non-cognitivism, moral judgements are not true (or false). So consider this argument:

1. It is wrong to murder.
2. If it is wrong to murder, then it is wrong to pay other people to murder for you.
3. Therefore, it is wrong to pay other people to murder for you.

We would normally say that this argument is valid. But according to emotivism, both (1) and (3) *don't state truths at all*, they express attitudes. And so the argument is not valid. So if emotivism is right, there can be no moral arguments.

> **?**
>
> Is emotivism a good theory of ethical language?

Prescriptivism

ANTHOLOGY: HARE, *THE LANGUAGE OF MORALS*, CHS 1, 5, 7, 10.2

R. M. Hare argued that moral words are not descriptive and *emotive* in meaning, as Stevenson argued. Instead, they are descriptive and *prescriptive*. 'The function of moral principles is to guide conduct.'

Prescriptive meaning (Ch. 1)

There are two types of prescriptive meaning, Hare claims. First, there are imperatives that tell someone to do something. Imperatives explicitly state what to do, e.g. 'Shut the door'. Hare argues that some moral judgements work in a similar way. For example, 'Eating meat is wrong' entails the imperative 'Do not eat meat'. How so? To accept the imperative, 'Shut the door' is to shut the door. To accept that eating meat is wrong is to not eat meat (Ch. 2, §1). So if you ask 'should I eat meat?', and I answer 'eating meat is wrong', then I have answered your question.

Second, there are value judgements. The most general value terms are 'good' and 'bad', which commend something. This commendation, although it is not explicit about what to do in the way imperatives are, provides guidance for our choices (Ch. 8, §1).

Hare criticises emotivism for mistaking the 'force' of moral statements. When I express a moral judgement, I am not trying to influence or persuade you, nor am I expressing my feelings (Ch. 1, §7). I am prescribing what you ought to do. Whether, *as a result*, you act as I prescribe is a different matter. Simply saying you should do *x* isn't an attempt to persuade you – that may require a lot of argument. The same distinction applies to stating a fact and trying to get someone to believe it.

> **?** What, according to Hare, are the two types of prescriptive meaning?

> **?** What is the difference between prescribing and persuading?

Good (Chs 5, 7)

We use the word 'good', says Hare, when we want to *commend* something to someone. We can talk about good chocolate, good teachers and good people. In each case, we are saying the chocolate, teacher or person is praiseworthy in some way. This use of language is quite distinct from *describing* something (Ch. 5, §4). Suppose I say 'That's a good strawberry, because it is sweet and juicy'. If we think 'good' as applied to strawberries just means 'sweet and juicy', then all I have said is 'That's a sweet and juicy strawberry because it is sweet and juicy'. But this isn't what I said. I commended the strawberry, I didn't merely describe it.

This, Hare argues, is what is correct about Moore's attack on the naturalistic fallacy (p. 151) and Hume's distinction between 'is' and 'ought' (p. 170). Because there is a distinction between describing and commending, nothing about being honest (i.e. telling the truth: descriptive meaning) can make me commend honesty (telling the truth is how to behave: prescriptive). More generally, nothing about the facts can *entail* a moral judgement.

However, 'good' is not purely a term of praise. Whenever we call something good, in each case there is a *set of standards* that we are implicitly relying on (Ch. 7, §1). Good chocolate is rich in the taste of cocoa. Good teachers can explain new ideas clearly and create enthusiasm in their students. A good person – well, a good person is someone who is the way we should try to be as people (Ch. 9, §1). When we use 'good' to mean 'morally good', we are appealing to a set of standards that apply to someone as a person. However, we have to *adopt* the standards. Because nothing about the facts entails a moral judgement, there are no facts that establish one set of moral standards as objectively correct.

The descriptive meaning of 'good' in any context comes from the set of standards that is being assumed. Its descriptive meaning picks up on the qualities that the something must have to be (a) good . . . (chocolate, teacher, person, whatever). Because 'good' is always used relative to a set of standards, it always has a descriptive meaning. If you know what the standard for a good teacher is, then you learn something factual about a teacher when I say 'she's a good teacher' (Ch. 7, §2).

This has an important implication: if we have two identical things, we cannot call one of them good and the other not good. Whenever we apply a standard in making a prescription, we are committed to making the same judgement of two things that match the standard in the same way (Ch. 5, §2). If I say this chocolate is good but that chocolate is not, I must think that there is some *relevant difference* between the two.

> Explain what Hare means by 'morally good'.

'Good' is used *primarily* to commend (Ch. 7, §4). For each type of thing that we describe as good, the standard is different, but in each case, we are commending it. However, we don't always use 'good' to commend (Ch. 7, §5). In fact, any word that both commends and describes can be used just to describe and not commend or disapprove. For example, we often use the word 'honest' to commend someone. But I can say 'If you weren't so honest, we could have got away with that!' This is an expression of annoyance, not praise. Likewise, I can agree that a 'good person' is one who is honest, kind, just, etc. But I can still think that good people are not to be commended, because, as Woody Allen said, 'Good people sleep better than bad people, but bad people enjoy the waking hours more'.

> Compare prescriptivism and emotivism on the meaning of 'good'.

Moral language (Ch. 10, §2)

The main features of 'good' are these:

1. It is used to commend, to provide guidance for choosing what to do.
2. It assumes a set of standards, features in virtue of which something counts as 'good' or not.
3. Two identical things must both be good or not. To think otherwise is logically contradictory.

In ethical language, 'good' refers, directly or indirectly, to being a good person. A good action, then, will be one that a good person does. Calling something or someone 'morally good' is intended to guide people's choices. The standards for who counts as a 'good person' are moral standards. However, moral standards are adopted, rather than being true or false.

The same features, Hare argues, apply to 'ought' and 'right'.

1. We say 'you ought to pay back the money' (in a particular situation) or again 'stealing is wrong' (in general) to guide people's choices and actions.

2. The standards that we are assuming in making these judgements relate to being a good person.

3. Two actions, in similar situations, must either both be right or not. If I think that it is wrong for you to steal from me, because it infringes my rights of ownership, then I must think that it is wrong for me to steal from you, because it infringes your rights of ownership – unless I can say that there is some relevant difference between the two cases. We must be willing to 'universalise' our moral judgements. Not to do so is logically contradictory.

Explain what Hare means by 'universalising' our moral judgements.

ANTHOLOGY: WARNOCK, *CONTEMPORARY MORAL PHILOSOPHY*, CH. 4

Warnock makes two objections to Hare's theory.

Ethical language

The first is that ethical language does not only prescribe, but has many other functions. Hare has in mind the situation in which someone asks what to do. But there are lots of other situations in which we use ethical language – we can exhort or implore someone, we can confess, we can complain, and so on.

However, Hare could reply that the central point of prescriptivism is that morality guides choices and actions. This isn't to say that, on every occasion, a moral judgement is being made to offer such guidance to the listener. The important point is that in holding a particular moral judgement, e.g. 'stealing is wrong', I am committed to acting on it.

We should accept this point, but Warnock points out that we needn't accept Hare's explanation of it. It is not only commending and prescribing that make a link between language and action. Language that expresses desires and attitudes *also* makes such links. Suppose I say 'I like apples', but I never eat apples, refuse anything made from apples, etc. There is something inconsistent here. Likewise, I can say 'I disapprove of stealing', but steal myself and never comment on others' thefts. Just by connecting ethical language to action, Hare hasn't shown that ethical language must be prescriptive. It could just as well express what we want or our attitudes.

Warnock argues that there isn't just one thing that ethical language does. It can be used many ways, and express many different psychological states.

Explain the objection that ethical language is not only prescriptive.

Moral reasoning

We saw that emotivism is open to the objection that it makes ethical discussion a matter of manipulation. Prescriptivism sees the 'guiding' aspect of ethics as a matter of prescription, rather than a matter of influencing someone through emotion. Hare argues that this makes ethical discussion more straightforward and rational.

First, we can ask about someone's reasons for prescribing what they do. Second, morality involves consistency – moral judgements must be universalised. For example, Singer claims there is *no relevant difference* between the suffering of people and the suffering of animals. If we are going to say that causing the suffering of people is wrong, we are committed to saying the suffering of animals is wrong – unless we can find a relevant difference. Moral disagreements can be about the consistency in applying certain standards, and reason can help resolve this.

See THE TREATMENT OF ANIMALS, p. 125.

Third, we can infer prescriptions from other prescriptions. A famous argument against abortion says 'Taking an innocent human life is wrong. Abortion is the taking of an innocent human life. Therefore abortion is wrong.' This has the same logical force, Hare claims, if we rephrase it as imperatives: 'Do not take innocent human life. Abortion is the taking of an innocent human life. Therefore, do not commit abortion.' To reject or refuse the conclusion, we must reject or refuse at least one premise. And so our prescriptions are logically related to one another. So we can use reason to discuss these relations.

Compare emotivism and prescriptivism on moral reasoning.

However, Warnock objects that, in fact, the *only* rationality Hare can find in moral arguments is consistency. In requiring us to universalise moral judgements, Hare's theory is similar to KANTIAN DEONTOLOGICAL ETHICS (p. 55). However, Kant argues that the standards for a good person (the good will) are themselves set by reason, and are therefore objective. Hare does not. Neither the empirical facts nor reason entails that we must have certain standards rather than others. If I argue that racism is morally right, and equality is morally wrong, *as long as I am prepared to universalise this claim*, there is no objective ground on which to disagree with me. Suppose you say 'But what if you were of a different race. Would you say you should be treated as inferior?' I can reply 'Yes.' Now what?

Hare argues that to prescribe that one's own interests be frustrated like this is irrational. And so his moral system will give us the Golden Rule of 'Do unto others as you would have them do unto you' - anything else would be inconsistent. But Warnock notes that while, of course, we don't *want* our interests frustrated, there is nothing irrational (unless Kant is right) in saying that they *ought* to be frustrated in certain situations. So I can defend stealing from you as long as I don't object *morally* to your stealing from me.

Suppose you say that we shouldn't steal because stealing would make life very difficult. This is *your reason* for prescribing that we shouldn't steal, implicitly appealing to the standard that the good person does not make life difficult. But Hare says that moral standards are not objectively correct. Suppose I do not adopt your standard - I have a different standard for 'good'. Then not only do I reject your moral judgement that stealing is wrong, I also don't accept your reason for this judgement as a moral reason. So, on Hare's view, there are no reasons to do a particular action *independent* of what standards we adopt. And so moral rationality is no more than consistency. But this does not rule out very objectionable values.

? 1) Do moral reasons depend on our values just as much as moral judgements? 2) Are moral judgements prescriptions?

Objections to non cognitivism

We conclude our discussion of non-cognitivism by looking at two further ISSUES (p. 145) that any non-cognitivist theory, including emotivism and prescriptivism, faces.

The authority of morality

If there is no objective moral truth, does it follow that 'anything goes'? If morality is a reflection of our emotions or attitudes, what authority does morality have over us? *Why* should we be moral? Where's the obligation? What is so important about particular emotions? I can do whatever I like, as long as I don't get caught. 'Morality' becomes no more obligatory than a matter of taste.

Non-cognitivists can argue that this is either an unfair simplification of their theories or a straightforward misunderstanding. Living as though there are no moral values is itself a choice or expression of feeling, and one that moral people will disapprove of morally. The theory that moral values are a reflection of our feelings does not imply that we should stop having moral feelings. We should disapprove of anyone who advocates that morality doesn't matter or is just a matter of taste.

But can we really justify interfering with how other people behave – when they behave 'immorally' – just because their actions don't accord with our feelings or choices? This seems very petty. But this isn't the reason we are interfering, claims the non-cognitivist. It is not because it offends us, but because they are being racist or cruel or cowardly or whatever.

The difficulty here is that my taking racist discrimination as a good reason to prevent an action is *itself* an expression of my feelings or the standards on which I make prescriptions. For the cognitivist, by contrast, that this is a good reason to interfere is a fact about reasons. The cognitivist claims to have the backing of reality.

> ?
>
> Does non-cognitivism undermine the authority of morality?

Moral progress

If there is no moral reality, we can argue, then our moral views cannot become better or worse. Obviously, they have changed – people used to believe that slavery was morally acceptable and now they do not. But how can we say that this is *progress* if there is no objective moral truth? There are two responses non-cognitivists can give.

First, they can claim that there can be very real improvements in people's moral views if they become more rational. This can happen in several different ways.

1. People may come to know certain facts that they didn't know before. In the case of slavery, people believed many things about slaves that were not true (one popular false belief was that they were stupid). Moral progress here means basing one's morality on the facts, not mistakes (Ayer).
2. People can become more consistent, more willing to universalise their principles (Hare). For example, Singer argues that if we were consistent in our feelings about preventing suffering, we would not eat meat. If he is right, then vegetarianism would be moral progress.
3. People can become more coherent in their moral judgements. Many of us have moral feelings that come into conflict with each other, e.g. over lying. Moral progress here would be a matter of working out the implications of our views, and changing what needed changing to make them coherent with each other (Stevenson).

Explain how non-cognitivism can account for moral progress.

Because people are ignorant, do not always think logically, and have not resolved the conflicts between their different feelings and conventions, there is plenty of room for moral progress. But moral progress just means becoming more rational in our moral thinking, not becoming more 'correct' in our moral judgements.

The second response non-cognitivists can give is this: if we disapprove of past moral codes and approve of our own moral code, then we will say that we have made moral progress. Society has moved from moral principles that were bad (i.e. principles we disapprove of) to moral principles that are good (i.e. principles we approve of). That is what moral progress is.

This response means that moral progress is relative to a particular moral point of view. If you disagree with me, you might claim that today's moral principles are much worse than those 200 years ago and so we have not made moral progress. But this is now just the familiar problem of how to make sense of moral disagreement, not a special problem about moral progress.

Key points: non-cognitivism

- Non-cognitivism claims that moral judgements express a non-cognitive mental state. Therefore, they do not aim to describe the world and cannot be true or false.
- Emotivism claims that moral judgements express approval or disapproval and aim to influence the feelings and actions of others.
- Emotivism is not subjectivism. Speaker subjectivism claims that 'X is wrong' means 'I disapprove of X', and so moral judgements can be true or false. On Ayer's emotivism, 'X is wrong' means something like 'Boo to X!'
- Hume gives two arguments for the claim that moral judgements are not judgements of reason. First, moral judgements motivate, but judgements of reason do not. Second, judgements of reason are either about relations of ideas or matters of fact, but moral judgements are about neither of these.
- He concludes that we cannot deduce a statement about 'ought' from statements about what 'is'. Instead, moral judgements are expressions of approval and disapproval.
- Hume also compares moral properties to secondary qualities, which he claims do not exist in the object, but in the mind.
- We can object that moral judgements do not motivate. We can also object that they are either about relations of ideas (Kant) or non-natural matters of fact (Aristotelian non-naturalism).
- We can agree that we can't *deduce* moral judgements from facts, but we can weigh up facts to provide reasons for moral judgements.
- We can also use direct realism's theory of secondary qualities to argue that moral properties are objective.
- Ayer argued that a statement only has meaning if it is either analytic or empirically verifiable. Moral statements are neither, so they are

1) Can non-cognitivism adequately explain moral progress?
2) Can moral judgements be objectively true?

- meaningless, neither true nor false. Instead, they express emotions, in particular, moral approval or disapproval.
- However, the principle of verification, according to itself, is not meaningful, because it is neither analytic nor empirically verifiable.
- Stevenson argued that moral judgements have emotive meaning. They express emotions, and are intended to influence the emotions and actions of other people.
- We can object that many types of language are emotive, so emotivism hasn't identified what is distinctive about ethical language. We can also object that ethical language doesn't always function to influence others or to express our emotions.
- Emotivists can reply that the primary function of ethical language is as they claim, and other uses are 'secondary'.
- We can object that emotivism cannot identify exactly which attitude(s) moral judgements express, and that morality must be understood in part in terms of what it is about.
- We may object that emotivism doesn't allow for moral reasoning. If moral judgements are attempts to influence others' feelings without appealing to reason, this is just manipulation.
- Ayer argued that all moral discussion is disagreeing over the facts, while Stevenson argued that there is also disagreement in attitude. As any attitude has complex implications for other attitudes, these disagreements can be complex.
- However, we can argue that emotivism cannot explain how someone would rationally change their mind. Furthermore, emotivism cannot explain how an argument containing a moral judgement could be valid if moral judgements cannot be true.
- Hare argues that ethical language is not emotive in meaning, but prescriptive. Prescriptive language either provides an explicit imperative or commends according to a set of standards.
- Description and prescription are logically distinct, which is why you cannot infer a moral judgement from natural facts.
- Moral standards must be adopted. They are not themselves objectively true or false.
- Standards apply universally, so to be consistent, speakers must be willing to universalise their moral judgements. If not, they must point to a relevant difference between cases.

- We can object that ethical language is not only prescriptive. While it is linked to action, the expression of many psychological states is linked to action.
- Hare argues that the requirement to universalise our prescriptions and the logical relations between prescriptions enables prescriptivism to recognise and explain moral reasoning.
- We can object that prescriptivism reduces rationality in morality to consistency. There are no rational limits on what someone can prescribe, nor on their reasons, as long as they are consistent.
- Non-cognitivism faces the objection that it reduces morality to an optional matter of taste. It can respond that we can still morally disapprove of people who treat morality in this way.
- We may object that if there is no moral truth, as non-cognitivism argues, we cannot talk of moral progress, because changes in moral views are neither right nor wrong.
- Non-cognitivists reply that moral beliefs can improve by becoming more rational, i.e. changing in the light of previously unknown facts or becoming more consistent or coherent. Furthermore, we can say that the change from previous views to current views is morally good (i.e. we express our approval of it).

Summary: ethical language

In this section on ethical language, we have considered two families of theories:

1. Cognitivism: the view that moral judgements express beliefs, aim to describe reality, and can be true or false.
2. Non-cognitivism: the view that moral judgements express a non-cognitive mental state, do not aim to describe reality, and are neither true nor false.

We looked at three cognitivist theories:

1. Ethical naturalism: the view that moral properties are natural properties. We considered utilitarianism as naturalism.

2. Ethical non-naturalism: the view that moral properties are non-natural properties. We considered intuitionism and Aristotelian non-naturalism.
3. Error theory: the view that moral judgements are all false, because there are no moral properties.

We looked at two non-cognitivist theories:

1. Emotivism: the view that moral judgements express approval or disapproval and aim to influence the feelings and actions of others.
2. Prescriptivism: the view that moral judgements are prescriptive, guiding our actions.

In our discussion and evaluation of these theories, we have looked at the following issues:

1. What is metaethics and how does it differ from normative ethical theories?
2. What is the difference between a cognitive and a non-cognitive mental state?
3. Is it a fallacy to think that moral properties are natural properties?
4. What is a moral 'intuition'? Which moral judgements are intuitions?
5. If there are objective moral properties, how could we know about them?
6. Do moral judgements motivate us?
7. What is a moral reason?
8. What is the best explanation of moral disagreement and reasoning?
9. If there are no moral truths, could morality be obligatory?
10. Is moral progress possible if morality is not objective?

PHILOSOPHY OF MIND

3

In this chapter, we examine three types of answer to the questions 'what is the mind?' and 'how does the mind relate to the body?' The first, substance dualism, argues that the mind is something that can exist independently of the body. The second set of answers claims that we can analyse and explain 'the mind' – which is not a 'thing' at all – in other terms, e.g. behaviour (behaviourism), 'functions' (functionalism) or neurophysiological processes (identity theory and eliminative materialism). The third answer agrees that the mind is not a thing, but argues that there is something about the mind that cannot be analysed in these other terms (property dualism).

In discussing these theories, we examine a wide variety of topics, such as the nature of consciousness, how we know that other people have minds and how the mind can cause physical events (e.g. bodily movements). By the end of the chapter, you should be able to argue for and against the theories discussed, and evaluate them in relation to different topics.

SYLLABUS CHECKLIST ✔

The AQA syllabus for this chapter is:

The mind-body problem: what is the relationship between the mental and the physical?

I. Dualism: the mind is distinct from the physical

A. Substance dualism

1. The indivisibility argument for substance dualism (Descartes)

Issues, including:
- ✔ the mental is divisible in some sense
- ✔ not everything thought of as physical is divisible.

2. The conceivability argument for substance dualism:
- ✔ the logical possibility of mental substance existing without the physical (Descartes)

Issues, including:
- ✔ mind without body is not conceivable
- ✔ what is conceivable may not be possible
- ✔ what is logically possible tells us nothing about reality.

B. Property dualism

1. Qualia
- ✔ qualia as introspectively accessible subjective/phenomenal features of mental states (the properties of 'what it is like' to undergo the mental state in question)
- ✔ for many, qualia would be defined as the intrinsic/non-representational properties of mental states.

2. The 'philosophical zombies' argument for property dualism:
✔ the logical possibility of a physical duplicate of this world but without consciousness/qualia (Chalmers).

Issues, including:
✔ a 'zombie' world is not conceivable
✔ what is conceivable is not possible
✔ what is logically possible tells us nothing about reality.

3. The 'knowledge'/Mary argument for property dualism based on qualia (Frank Jackson).

Issues, including:
✔ Mary gains no new propositional knowledge (but gains acquaintance knowledge or ability knowledge)
✔ all physical knowledge would include knowledge of qualia
✔ there is more than one way of knowing the same physical fact
✔ qualia (as defined) do not exist and so Mary gains no propositional knowledge.

C. Objections to dualism

1. The issues of causal interaction for versions of dualism:
✔ the problems facing interactionist dualism, including conceptual and empirical causation issues
✔ the problems facing epiphenomenalist dualism, including the causal redundancy of the mental, the argument from introspection and issues relating to free will and responsibility.

2. The problem of other minds for dualism:
✔ some forms of dualism make it impossible to know other minds
✔ threat of solipsism.

✔   Response: the argument from analogy (e.g. Mill).

II. Materialism: the mind is not ontologically distinct from the physical.

A. Logical/analytical behaviourism:
✔   all statements about mental states can be analytically reduced without loss of meaning to statements about behaviour (an 'analytic' reduction).

Issues, including:
✔   dualist arguments (above)
✔   issues defining mental states satisfactorily (circularity and the multiple realisability of mental states in behaviour)
✔   the conceivability of mental states without associated behaviour (Putnam's super-Spartans)
✔   the asymmetry between self-knowledge and knowledge of other people's mental states.

B. Mind-brain type identity theory:
✔   all mental states are identical to brain states ('ontological' reduction) although 'mental state' and 'brain state' are not synonymous (so not an 'analytic' reduction)

Issues, including:
✔   dualist arguments (above)
✔   issues with providing the type identities (the multiple realisability of mental states)
✔   the location problem: brain states have precise spatial locations which thoughts lack.

C. Functionalism:
✔   all mental states can be reduced to functional roles which can be multiply realised.

Issues, including:

✔ the possibility of a functional duplicate with different qualia (inverted qualia)

✔ the possibility of a functional duplicate with no qualia (Block's 'Chinese mind')

✔ the 'knowledge'/Mary argument can be applied to functional facts (no amount of facts about function suffices to explain qualia).

D. Eliminative materialism:

✔ some or all mental states do not exist (folk-psychology is false or at least radically misleading).

Issues, including:

✔ the intuitive certainty of the existence of my mind takes priority over other considerations

✔ folk-psychology has good predictive and explanatory power

✔ the articulation of eliminative materialism as a theory is self-refuting.

Overview: the metaphysics of philosophy of mind

Philosophy of mind is a branch of metaphysics, and different theories in philosophy of mind disagree on metaphysical questions about *what* exists and its nature. Questions about what exists are questions about ontology. In this section, I give a brief overview of the positions that we shall examine in this chapter. Not everything will be clear right away, as some of the terms will require further explanation. But it is worth having a sense of the options in philosophy of mind and how they relate to each other at the most general level.

According to a traditional metaphysics, a substance is an entity, a thing, that does not depend on another entity for its continued existence. It has 'ontological independence'. For example, this book is a (physical) substance.

> Metaphysics asks questions about the fundamental nature of reality. *Meta-* means above, beyond or after; physics enquires into the physical structure of reality – which may or may not be the fundamental nature of all reality. 'Ontology' comes from *ont-*, 'being', and *-ology*, 'study of'.

Substances are also understood by contrast with properties.

1.   Substances are what possess properties. The chair (substance) is solid (property). Properties can't exist without substances – they depend on substances to exist. Solidity depends on things being solid; the property 'being 1 metre long' depends on something being that long; and, Descartes claimed, thoughts can't exist without a thinker.

2.   Substances persist through changes in properties – something can change from being 1 metre long to being 1.1 metres long, e.g. by growing. Obviously, the property 'being 1 metre long' does not persist through this change. Or again, a thinker can think a series of thoughts – the thinker persists, the thoughts do not.

Explain and illustrate the difference between substances and properties.

A central question in philosophy of mind is 'is the mind a substance?' Can your mind exist independently, or is it dependent on something else in order to exist? In particular, is your mind dependent on your body, perhaps especially your brain, in order to exist at all? Many people believe, and many religions teach, that your mind can exist after death, i.e. the death of your body. This can mean many things, which we can't review here, but one common interpretation is that your mind is a separate substance from your body. If the mind is a substance, then the end of your body's existence is not the end of your mind's existence. The view that the mind and the body are separate substances is known as *substance dualism*. Substance dualism claims that there are two fundamental *kinds* of substance – mental and physical.

See the flow chart on the next page.

See *Philosophy for AS*, BERKELEY'S IDEALISM, p. 58.

We can contrast substance dualism with idealism, the view that minds are the *only* kind of substance, and so whatever exists is either a mind or depends on a mind. However, the most popular alternative to dualism is the view that the only kind of substance is physical. This view is *materialism* (on one meaning of that word). According to materialism, everything that exists, including whatever is mental, is either a material thing or it is dependent on some material thing to exist. (An updated version of materialism is physicalism, which replaces 'matter' with 'physical substance' because recent physics has analysed matter as interchangeable with energy in various forms.)

The most natural development of materialism is to say that instead of talking about '*the* mind', it is more accurate to talk about mental *properties*.

Mental properties include mental states, such as beliefs, and mental events, such as having a thought or feeling pain. If substance dualism is right, then mental properties are possessed by mental substances. However, according to materialism, mental properties are properties of a physical substance. You can think of the physical substance that has such properties as either the person or the brain.

Suppose materialism is true. Are mental properties (mental states and events) themselves types of physical property (physical states and events)? There are many different types of physical property, e.g. size, shape, motion, mass, various forms of energy, chemical properties such as molecular structure, biological properties such as genetic code, and many others. Are mental properties, such as thinking about snow or feeling sad, also physical properties? One might argue, for instance, that they are simply neurological properties, e.g. to think about snow *just is* for certain neurons to fire in one's brain. This view is known as the *mind–brain type identity theory.*

Alternatively, one might argue that mental properties are not physical properties and can't even be understood or explained in terms of physical properties. (Neurons firing is just a physiological process, like food being digested. How can consciousness *be* neurons firing any more than it could be digestion?) Although mental properties are possessed by physical substances, they are completely different from any of the other properties physical substances possess. This view is *property dualism* – there is only one kind of substance but two radically different kinds of property.

> There is a parallel between the metaphysics of property dualism and ETHICAL NON-NATURALISM (p. 151) in metaethics.

A third understanding of mental properties claims that they should be understood in terms of behaviour and dispositions to behave. Wanting to go for a drive, feeling cross, thinking about your mother – these are each a matter of being disposed to behave in certain, perhaps highly complex, ways. This view is *logical behaviourism.*

But perhaps thinking of mental properties just in terms of behaviour is too restrictive. We can talk more broadly in terms of the contribution of mental properties to how the person (or brain) functions, including the interactions of mental properties with each other, such as how one thought leads to another, how desires lead to emotions and vice versa, as well as how any and all of these lead to behaviour. This view is *functionalism.*

There are various ways of interpreting functionalism and logical behaviourism which involve different metaphysics. As they are usually interpreted, functionalism and logical behaviourism lie 'in between' the claim that mental properties are just types of physical property (type identity theory) and the claim that mental properties can't be explained or understood in terms of physical properties (property dualism). They are both forms of 'non-reductive physicalism'.

There are many more options in the philosophy of mind, but we will discuss just one. This view, *eliminative materialism*, claims that, not only are there no mental substances, there are no mental properties either (as we usually think of them). This is very counter-intuitive – no such things as having a thought or feeling a pain? But we shall leave the arguments for the view for when we discuss it properly.

As the examples so far indicate, many philosophers think that mental properties can be categorised in terms of 'thought' and 'consciousness'. They pick out the two most important aspects of what we mean by 'having a mind'. What distinguishes things that have minds (or mental properties) from things that don't is that things with minds have a 'point of view', a 'perspective', on the world. Things with a point of view experience the world, there is a 'subjectivity' to their existence, they are not just objects. And this involves ideas of being conscious and of being able to experience and think about things, to have beliefs and desires.

So the question 'how does the mind relate to the body?' has two components: how do thoughts relate to the body? and how does consciousness relate to the body? We will discuss both, but we will spend more time, particularly in objections and replies, discussing consciousness.

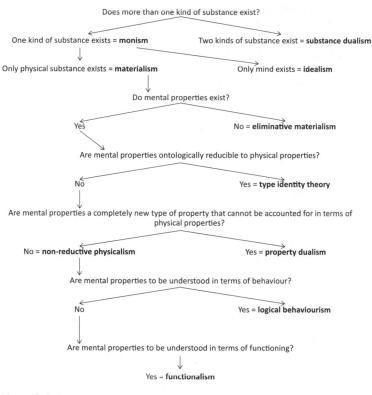

Figure 3.1 Flow chart of positions in philosophy of mind

I. Dualism: the mind is distinct from the physical

A. Substance dualism

As noted above, a central question in philosophy of mind is 'is the mind a substance?' Substance dualism argues that it is. It holds that there are two fundamentally different types of substances: physical (or material) substances ('bodies', physical objects) and mental substances (minds). It claims that minds do not depend on bodies in order to exist, i.e. minds can exist separated from any body. Minds and bodies are ontologically distinct and independent. People who believe that the mind is the soul, and the soul can continue to exist without a body after death, are usually substance dualists.

If mental substance exists, it will be very unlike matter. For instance, we shall see that Descartes argues that it does not exist in space and does not have any parts.

> Explain the claim that the mind is 'ontologically distinct and independent' from the body.

The syllabus specifies just *Meditation* VI. For a more detailed discussion of Descartes on mind and body, see the commentary on Descartes on the companion website www.routledge.com/cw/alevelphilosophy.

See *Philosophy for AS*, DESCARTES ON THE EXISTENCE OF THE EXTERNAL WORLD, p. 111, for Descartes' argument that bodies exist.

See *Philosophy for AS*, CLEAR AND DISTINCT IDEAS, p. 107.

ANTHOLOGY: DESCARTES, *MEDITATION* VI

The conceivability argument

Dualism claims that both minds and bodies – physical objects – exist. It is common in contemporary philosophy of mind to assume that bodies exist, and since we are not discussing idealism, we shall share that assumption. Dualism is more controversial, therefore, in claiming that the mind is an ontologically distinct substance.

In *Meditation* VI, p. 29, Descartes presents the following argument for substance dualism:

1. I have a clear and distinct idea of myself as something that thinks and isn't extended.
2. I have a clear and distinct idea of body as something that is extended and does not think.
3. If I have a clear and distinct thought of something, God can create it in a way that corresponds to my thought.
4. Therefore, God can create mind as something that thinks and isn't extended and body as something that is extended and does not think.
5. Therefore, mind and body can exist independently of one another.
6. Therefore, mind and body are two distinct substances.

In (1) and (2), Descartes appeals to his concepts of mind and body. Earlier in the *Meditations*, he analysed mind as something that thinks and body as something that is extended (has a size and takes up space). We can understand (1) and (2) to entail the claim that it is conceivable that mind can exist without body. Nothing in our concepts rules this out.

In *Meditation* VI, Descartes adds (3). Assuming that God is omnipotent, the only reason for thinking that God cannot make something is that the concept of it is contradictory. The concepts of mind and body aren't self-contradictory. So God can create the mind and the body just as Descartes conceives of them – a thinking thing and an extended thing. We can summarise (3), (4) and (5) in terms that don't refer to God: it is possible that mind can exist without body.

Finally, a quick reminder helps in understanding the inference from (5) to (6). A substance, we said above, is something that does not depend on another thing in order to exist. In other words, a substance can exist independently, on its own.

We now have a simpler form of this argument:

1. It is conceivable that mind can exist without body.
2. Therefore, it is possible that mind can exist without body.
3. Therefore, mind and body are distinct substances.

It is important for Descartes' argument that our clear and distinct ideas of mind and body are *complete* and *exclusive*. The mind is *nothing but* thought; the body is *nothing but* extension. We know this to be true, he says, because the ideas of mind and body are clear and distinct.

> Outline and explain Descartes' conceivability argument.

The divisibility argument

Descartes claims that mind and body have different properties – thought and extension. This provides another argument that they cannot be the same thing: if they were the same thing, they would have the same properties. Leibniz later formalised this claim in his principle of the indiscernibility of identicals: if two things are identical (i.e. are just one thing), then they share all their properties. Why? Because one thing cannot have different properties from itself. So if two things have different properties, that proves that they cannot be one and the same thing.

> Explain Leibniz's principle of the indiscernibility of identicals.

In case we aren't convinced that mind and body really do have different properties, Descartes provides an additional argument (p. 32). The mind does not have any parts and cannot be divided:

> When I consider the mind – i.e. consider myself purely as a thinking thing – I can't detect any parts within myself; I understand myself to be something single and complete ... the faculties of willing, of understanding, of sensory perception and so on, these are not *parts* of the mind, since it is one and the same mind that wills, understands and perceives.

Willing, understanding and perceiving are properties of the mind, different ways of thinking. By contrast, the body does have parts. You can literally lose part of your body, e.g. a hand. So the body (physical substance) is divisible into parts, but the mind (mental substance) is not. So mind and body are entirely distinct types of thing.

Outline and explain Descartes' divisibility argument.

Going further: the unity of mind and body

If the mind and body are two distinct things, how are they related? Descartes says that

> Nature also teaches me, through these sensations of pain, hunger, thirst and so on, that I (a thinking thing) am not merely *in* my body as a sailor is in a ship. Rather, I am *closely joined to it – intermingled* with it, so to speak – so that it and I form a unit.
>
> (p. 30)

Because 'a unit' doesn't sound like 'two separate things', this claim and its implications are puzzling.

Reflecting on perception, sensation and feeling, we notice that we perceive that we have bodies, and that our bodies – this particular physical object that we have a close and unique relationship with – can be affected in many beneficial and harmful ways. This is brought to our attention through our bodily appetites, like hunger and

---

thirst, through emotions, such as anger, sadness, love, and through sensations, like pain, pleasure, colours, sound and so on. All these experiences have their origins in the body.

However, this doesn't mean that mind and body are united as one and the same thing. Descartes carefully considers what the idea of the mind really involves. He argues that we can still conceive of ourselves existing complete without imagination or feeling, i.e. without those ways of thinking that are informed by the body.

Nevertheless, our experiences of our bodies through bodily sensations and emotions show that the connection between the mind and body is very close: 'These sensations are confused mental events that arise from the union – the intermingling, as it were – of the mind with the body' (p. 30). If mind and body were not intermingled, then 'I wouldn't feel pain when the body was hurt but would perceive the damage in an intellectual way, like a sailor seeing that his ship needs repairs' (p. 30).

Furthermore, this union of mind and body is a union between the mind (the whole mind – it doesn't have parts) and the *whole* body. We feel pain in the various parts of our body. The mind does have a privileged link with the brain (a point of causal connection in the pineal gland), but the mind does not feel all pains to be in the brain! So Descartes argues that the mind is joined to all parts of the body – the point about the pineal gland is really just a physiological observation about causal pathways.

> Explain Descartes' claim that he is 'closely joined' to his body so as to form a 'unit' with it.

Going further: beyond dualism?

If you find this talk of 'intermingling' is confusing, you are in good company! Descartes himself found it difficult to understand how it is that the mind and body are distinct substances, yet form a 'unit'. In a letter to Princess Elisabeth, 28 June 1643, he wrote

> it seems to me that the human mind can't conceive the soul's distinctness from the body and its union with the body, conceiving them very clearly and both at the same time. That is because this requires one to conceive them as one single thing and at the same time as two things, which is contradictory.

He offers a suggestion as puzzling as it is illuminating: the idea of the union between mind and body is a third 'basic notion' alongside the ideas of mind and body. The idea of mind is known by the intellect, the idea of body is known by the intellect aided by the imagination, but the union of mind and body is known most clearly through the senses. It is the ordinary experience of life that gives us an understanding of this union, rather than philosophical reflection.

Given that the union of mind and body is a third 'basic notion', is it a notion of a *third* type of *substance*? Is there one new type of thing here, created from the unification of two distinct types of thing? Descartes says, in a letter to Regius, December 1641, that 'since the body has all the dispositions necessary to receive the soul, and without which it is not strictly a human body, it could not come about without a miracle, that a soul should not be joined to it'. The comment that, unless united to a soul, a body is not a *human body*, suggests (but not conclusively) that the 'human body', body and soul together, can be considered as a substance in its own right, a substance created from the union of body and soul. However, philosophers

Correspondence between Descartes and Princess Elisabeth, p. 6, from the Early Modern Texts edition: www.earlymoderntexts.com/pdfs/descartes1643.pdf

don't agree on whether or not this is the implication we should draw from his union theory.

To the question, 'What am I?', Descartes' first answer is 'a thing that thinks', and he repeats in *Meditation* VI that we can imagine ourselves existing 'whole' without feeling or imagination. But is it any less true to say 'I am a human being, a union of mind and body, an *embodied* mind' than 'I am a mind'? The mind takes on the body's experiences as its own, i.e. we refer our sensations, emotions, etc., to our *selves*. We 'own' these states just as much as we 'own' our thoughts. We experience ourselves as embodied minds, not just minds.

Descartes accepts all this, but his argument that minds can exist without bodies leads him to say that to lose the experiences that depend on the body would not be to lose our identities.

> **?**
>
> Is it coherent to think that mind and body are different substances yet can also be united?

Issues with Descartes' arguments

The mental is divisible in some sense

Descartes' claim that we will, think, imagine, with the whole of our minds, not a literal part, is appealing. However, cases of mental illness, e.g. multiple personality syndrome, might be used to suggest that the mind can be divided. In such cases, it seems that some 'parts' of the person's mind are unable to communicate with other 'parts'. Theories of the difference between consciousness and the unconscious suggest something similar: people may believe or desire one thing consciously and the opposite thing unconsciously. So it makes sense to talk about 'parts' of the mind.

> Briefly explain the objection to the divisibility argument that the mental is divisible.

However, Descartes could respond that *the way* in which the mind is 'divisible' is entirely different from the way in which the body is. Bodies are *spatially* divisible, while minds are only *functionally* divisible. The different 'parts' do different things, but they aren't in different spatial locations. So his argument that mind and body are different because they have different properties is still valid.

A different objection is that the argument *assumes* that minds exist as substances. If minds do not exist as substances, then we cannot talk about 'their' properties. A materialist will claim that there are no 'minds', only mental properties, which are properties of persons or brains (physical objects). This also provides a completely different explanation of why 'minds' are not divisible. Minds are not 'things', there are only mental properties – thoughts, desires, pains, etc. It is true that these are not spatially divisible, but most physical properties aren't divisible either. For instance, the property of belonging to a particular species (e.g. being a chicken) isn't spatially divisible. Only spatial properties are spatially divisible, if any properties are – really it is physical *substances* that are divisible. Most properties aren't the right kind of thing to 'take up space'. But a substance that is spatially divisible can nevertheless possess properties that are not divisible. So bodies could possess mental properties.

The divisibility argument, then, depends on the conceivability argument to establish first that the mind is a substance, something with ontological independence. If we know that the mind is a substance, then the divisibility argument shows that the mind is a distinct substance from the body.

> Briefly explain the objection that the divisibility argument only succeeds if we assume that the mind is a substance.

Not everything thought of as physical is divisible

We have just seen that physical *properties* are not always divisible. But what about physical *substances*? Descartes argues that extension is the *essential* property of physical objects. He then argues that what is extended is divisible. But we may question whether this theory of physical objects is correct. It was a matter of some debate in the seventeenth and eighteenth centuries whether physical objects are infinitely divisible. If you cut something up, can you always cut it into smaller pieces? The question is not whether we can actually do this right now, with the technology we have, but whether there are physical things that cannot be divided even in principle. If, for example, the smallest physical particles are best understood as packets of energy or force fields, then we can't further divide these – you can't have half a force field! Or again, perhaps not only force fields but also processes or waves or something else that can't be divided spatially form a fundamental part of the physical universe.

One possible response is that even if these things can't be divided in reality, we can still conceive of them having *half the size*. In that sense, we can still talk of spatial 'parts'. There is no *logical* limit to how small spatial parts can be. However, whether this is true or not may depend on the best physical theory of what space is. If we need to change our concept of space, then perhaps there will be such a limit.

The implication of these reflections is that it may not be an *essential* or *defining* property of every physical substance that it is divisible. In that case, the fact that the mind is not divisible does not entail that it is not physical. It could be a form of non-divisible physical thing. So even if Descartes is right that the mind isn't divisible, this doesn't prove that it isn't physical.

This line of thought does not show *how* the mind could be a non-divisible physical thing. After all, the mind is very different from subatomic particles! The objection only seeks to show that Descartes' divisibility argument, as it is stated, fails.

> Explain how the claim that not everything physical is divisible forms an objection to Descartes' divisibility argument.

Going further: am I a substance?

What does it mean to say 'I exist' or 'I think'? Descartes claims that 'I' am a thinking *thing*. I am the *same* thing from one thought to another. But can Descartes know this? Perhaps there is only *a succession of thoughts*, nothing that persists between thoughts which is a *single* thing. Descartes' response, in an appendix to the *Meditations* called 'Objections and Replies', is to say that thoughts logically require a thinker.

This isn't obviously true. It assumes the traditional metaphysics of substances and properties outlined at the start of this chapter, and is challenged by Hume. Even if we agree that there can't be a thought unless something thinks it, that doesn't entail that the 'thinker' is a subject that persists from one thought to another. Each thinker might exist for just one thought. As soon as Descartes says that to be a thinker is to doubt, will, imagine, and so on, he assumes we can say these activities belong to the *same* subject, that he (the same thinker) does all this. Again, this assumes the traditional metaphysics that substances persist through changes over time. But what is the argument for believing this metaphysical picture is true?

Consider this admission from Descartes: 'I exist - that is certain. But for how long? For as long as I am thinking. But

> See *Philosophy for AS*, HUME ON SUBSTANCE AND SELF, p. 150.

perhaps no longer than that; for it *might* be that if I stopped thinking I would stop existing' (p. 5). In dreamless sleep, we certainly cease to think (at least consciously). If Descartes wishes to establish that he is the same person from one day to the next, he will need the idea of the mind as a substance that persists even through those times when there is no thought. For example, when he comes to say that he can distinguish dreaming from waking, he is presupposing that he - the same mind - has experienced both. But that means he must persist between dreaming and waking, and during some of that time, he will have no thoughts at all.

By the end of the *Meditations*, Descartes could reply that he knows that God exists and is not a deceiver. I remember things from previous days, and many of my mental states (beliefs, hopes, plans) are the same. If these are not memories and continuing properties of me - the same mental substance - then this would be tantamount to God being a deceiver. Hence, I must be the same substance before and after such cessations in thought.

Of course, to grant that thoughts require a thinker who is a substance is not to grant that the substance - the thinker - is a mental substance. We could be physical substances with thoughts.

See *Philosophy for AS*, DESCARTES ON THE EXISTENCE (AND NATURE) OF GOD, p. 109.

Do thoughts require a thinker? Are thinkers substances?

We return to this and the next two issues in ISSUES FOR THE ZOMBIE ARGUMENT, p. 283.

What is conceivable may not be possible

Many philosophers believe that Descartes' conceivability argument doesn't work. Objections to an argument either challenge the truth of one of the premises or they challenge an inference. On the simplified version of the argument (p. 203), there is only one initial premise, namely 'It is conceivable that mind can exist without body'. This is discussed below in MIND WITHOUT BODY IS NOT CONCEIVABLE (p. 213). There are then two inferences. First, Descartes infers possibility from conceivability – because it is conceivable that mind can exist without body, it is possible that mind can exist without body. We shall discuss this inference here. The second inference, from the possibility that mind can exist without body to substance dualism, is discussed in the next section. The thought underlying challenges to both inferences is this: just because Descartes can *conceive* of his mind and body as distinct substances, this doesn't mean that his mind and body really *are* distinct substances. Perhaps there is some metaphysical connection between his mind and body that Descartes doesn't know about.

Is what is conceivable always possible? Not obviously. Suppose I believe that the Masked Man has robbed the bank. I also believe that my father has not robbed the bank. Clearly, I conceive that the Masked Man is not my father. Does this entail that it is possible that the Masked Man is not my father?

In one sense, we might say that the Masked Man could be anyone – nobody knows who he is. But we also rightly think that whoever the Masked Man is can't be someone else. No one can be somebody else. I can't be you, and you can't be me. So if my father is not the Masked Man, it is impossible that my father is the Masked Man. And if my father is the Masked Man, then it is impossible that my father is not the Masked Man.

Now I can conceive that my father is not the Masked Man. But this doesn't show that it is possible that my father is not the Masked Man. I could be mistaken about who the Masked Man is – if he *is* my father, then it is impossible for my father to be a different person from the Masked Man. From my conceiving that 'two' people are distinct, we cannot infer that it is possible that they are distinct.

We can apply this result to Descartes' conceivability argument. Descartes argues that it is possible for the mind to exist independently of the body, because he can conceive of it existing without the body. But this doesn't follow. It is possible that Descartes' conception of the mind (or body) is wrong, such that, unknown to him, the mind is not ontologically independent and it is impossible for it to exist separately from the body.

> Briefly explain the objection that Descartes mistakenly infers what is possible from what is conceivable.

However, Descartes is happy to grant that we cannot *in general* infer what is possible from what we think. But in the case of *clear and distinct ideas*, the inference is justified. If we can clearly and distinctly think of some object, *x*, having a certain property, then not only is it *possible* that *x* has that property, it is true! We may rightly claim that it is impossible for a triangle to have internal angles that don't add up to 180 degrees just because it is inconceivable that they should. Likewise, because he can *clearly and distinctly* conceive that mind and body are distinct substances, Descartes argues, it follows that it is possible that they are.

?

When, if ever, is
what is
conceivable a good
guide to what is
possible?

This provides a contrast with the Masked Man. My conceptions of my father and the Masked Man are not clear and distinct in the way that Descartes requires. It is only while we do not know who we are thinking of when we think of the Masked Man that we can think that the Masked Man could be anyone. And so, Descartes would argue, the Masked Man fallacy cannot be used as an objection to his argument.

What is logically possible tells us nothing about reality

Suppose that it is possible that the mind can exist as a distinct substance. Does it follow that the mind *does* exist as a distinct substance?

Let us assume, for the purposes of argument, that we conceive of mind as something that thinks and of body as something that is extended. From this, it does not follow that we conceive of mind as something that thinks *and isn't extended* or of body as something that is extended *and does not think*. There is nothing in the initial conceptions of mind and body that oppose each other. There is no contradiction or (obvious) unclarity in conceiving of mind as something that is extended and thinks, or again as the thinking part of something that is extended. Likewise, there is no contradiction or (obvious) unclarity in conceiving of body as something that is extended, but which may, in some instances, also think. If this is right, then we can conceive of mind and body as distinct substances, or we can think of thought and extension as properties of the same substance.

Assume that whatever we can clearly and distinctly conceive is logically possible. Therefore, given what we said above, it is logically possible that mind and body are distinct substances. But equally, it is logically possible that thought and extension are two properties of a single substance. What we need to know is *which option is true*. Simply knowing what is logically possible does not tell us which possibility correctly describes reality. So just because it is logically possible for mind and body to be separate substances doesn't show that they are separate substances.

Briefly explain
the objection that
what is logically
possible does not tell
us about reality.

Now, we should accept that what is logically *impossible* does tell us something about reality, because what is logically impossible cannot exist. If Descartes could show that it is logically impossible for mind and body to be the same substance, that would show that they must be separate substances. So he could argue that we cannot clearly and distinctly conceive of mind and body as *anything other* than separate substances – just as we cannot clearly and distinctly conceive of a triangle not having internal angles that add up to 180 degrees. But is this right?

Outline the objection that even if Descartes shows that substance dualism is logically possible, he has not shown that it is true.

Going further: mind without body is not conceivable

We granted above that we can conceive of mind and body as separate substances. But is Descartes right about this? Or more precisely, is he right to claim that we can do so clearly and distinctly? What is it to think? What is thought? Descartes assumes that he can identify this from introspection in the absence of anything else – 'I think'. But what makes it possible for me to think 'I think'? Without answers to these questions, we may object, we may *think* it is conceivable that mind and body are distinct substances when it isn't conceivable. We may be confused or simply lack relevant information.

We will see that LOGICAL BEHAVIOURISM (p. 229) argues that the mind – mental states and events – should be analysed in terms of behaviour. To talk of beliefs, thoughts, desires, choices and so on is to talk of how something behaves. Now, without a body, something can't exhibit behaviour; and without behaviour, there is no mind. If this theory is correct, then once we've understood what we mean when we talk about the mind, we will realise that mind without body is inconceivable.

We will leave the evaluation of logical behaviourism for later. But we can object now that this is a very strong conclusion. For example, if it is right, then disembodied minds, such as God, are inconceivable. And yet for most of the history of humanity, people have claimed to be able to make sense of the idea of God. Isn't it more likely that logical behaviourism is wrong to think that in talking about mental states, we are talking about behaviour? Or even if this is right, perhaps 'behaviour' doesn't require a body.

Logical behaviourism provides just one argument supporting the claim that mind without body is inconceivable.

But there may be others. The general point is that we can make mistakes over what we think is conceivable.

Descartes accepts this. We can make mistakes, which is why we must get our ideas clear and distinct first. His claim is that we can't make mistakes with clear and distinct ideas. So to object, what we actually need to argue is one of two things. Either we cannot *clearly and distinctly* conceive of the mind as separate from the body – as the analysis of logical behaviourism claims. Or we can challenge Descartes' theory of clear and distinct ideas guaranteeing truth. Perhaps we can make mistakes concerning even what we conceive clearly and distinctly.

> **?**
>
> Do Descartes' arguments succeed in establishing substance dualism?

Key points: substance dualism

- One traditional definition of a substance is something that does not depend on any other thing to exist.
- Substance dualism holds that there are two types of substances, mental substances (minds) and material substances (bodies), each capable of existing independently of the other.
- Descartes argues that he has clear and distinct ideas of mind and body as separate substances, and that God can create whatever he has a clear and distinct idea of. Therefore, mind and body can exist as, and therefore are, separate substances.
- Descartes argues that bodies are divisible into spatial parts, but minds have no such parts. Therefore, the mind is a distinct substance from the body.
- Our minds are nevertheless very closely conjoined with our bodies, as demonstrated by our sensory experiences. This idea of union is a third 'basic notion' alongside our concepts of mind and body.
- We can object that Descartes' divisibility argument assumes that minds exist as substances.
- We can object that not everything that is physical is divisible. Therefore, showing that the mind isn't divisible doesn't show that it isn't physical.

- Another objection is that Descartes has not shown he (his mind) exists as a substance, a unitary thing persisting through many thoughts.
- We can object that Descartes is wrong to infer that because he can conceive of the mind existing without the body that it can actually exist without the body. Descartes replies that the inference is justified if our conceptions are clear and distinct.
- We can object that not only can we conceive of mind and body as distinct substances, we can also conceive of them as distinct properties of the same substance. So we cannot infer from how we can conceive of mind and body to how they actually exist.
- Finally, we can question whether it is conceivable that the mind can exist without the body. This thought may be confused or uninformed.

B. Objections to (substance) dualism

Causal interaction

Substance dualism is most often rejected because it cannot give an adequate account of the causal role of the mind. In particular, it can't explain the causation of physical events by mental events. It can't explain how walking, talking and other bodily movements, are caused by thoughts, decisions and feelings. There are a variety of positions dualism can take on the causal role of the mind. We will look at two. The first, interactionist dualism, claims that mental events can cause physical events. The second, epiphenomenalist dualism, claims that the mind has no causal powers at all.

Interactionist dualism

CONCEPTUAL ISSUES

Nothing seems more obvious than that the mind and the body interact with each other, e.g. I decide to phone a friend and move my body to do so. But how is it that a mental substance, which is not in space and has no physical force, can affect a physical substance, which is in space and moved by physical forces?

> PROPERTY DUALISM and objections to it are discussed on pp. 266-302.

ANTHOLOGY: LETTER FROM PRINCESS OF BOHEMIA TO DESCARTES IN MAY 1643

Princess Elisabeth of Bohemia posed this question to Descartes in terms of pushing and movement.

1. Physical things only move if they are pushed.
2. Only something that is extended and can touch the thing that is moved can exert such a force.
3. But the mind has no extension, so it can't touch the body.
4. Therefore, the mind cannot move the body.

> Explain Elisabeth's objection to causal interaction between mind and body.

In fact, as Descartes points out in his reply (letter of 21 May 1643), this isn't an accurate understanding of how things are moved. For example, we might explain why something falls in terms of its weight. But weight doesn't 'push' the object whose weight it is! Weight is the result of the force of gravity on the mass of an object, and gravity is a force of attraction that operates without needing contact between the two physical objects.

But this is all a matter of details. We can generalise from the force of pushing to force more generally. If the mind is just thought, it has no physical force of any kind. In that case, how could it possibly affect the body? (The mind is not very insubstantial matter; we can understand how something very refined, like a gas, can have causal effects.) And the mind is *not in space* at all. If causation is thought to involve any kind of spatial relationship between cause and effect, the problem is particularly pressing. Clearly nothing can come into a spatial relationship with a mind which occupies no space.

1. The movement of a physical object is only initiated by some physical force, exerted at some point in space.
2. If dualism is true, then the mind is not in space and cannot exert any physical force.
3. Therefore, either dualism is false or the mind cannot cause (any part of) the body to move.

In a later letter (1 July 1643), Elisabeth says that she accepts, from her own experience, that the mind *does* cause the body to move. The problem is that experience gives us no indication of *how* this happens. She continues, 'This leads me to think that the soul has properties that we don't know – which might overturn your doctrine … that the soul is not extended …. Although extension is not necessary to thought, it isn't inconsistent with it either'. So, we can continue the argument:

4. The mind can cause the body to move.
5. Therefore, dualism is false.

In his replies to Elisabeth, Descartes indicates two possible lines of response. The first appeals to the third 'basic notion' of the union between mind and body. We can only make sense of mental causation in terms of this notion of union. However, this 'basic notion' is not itself entirely clear, so neither is any solution to Elisabeth's objection regarding mental causation.

See BEYOND DUALISM?, p. 206.

The second is that it is a mistake to try to understand the mind's power to act on physical objects in terms of how physical objects act on each other. This is an important point. We have a tendency to conceive of *all* causation in terms of the causation of physical events by other physical events. But perhaps this is mistaken. Then how *should* we think about mental causation? Certainly, we can reflect on the fact that we can move our bodies at will. But as Elisabeth points out, the question remains *how*, according to dualism, this is possible.

The challenge is just as daunting when thinking about how physical objects could cause changes in the mind. How can something which is *not* thought or consciousness bring about changes in a substance that is entirely thought and consciousness? Physical causation operates, as we said, through the exertion of forces at particular points in space. But it seems impossible to exert a physical force on a mental substance which has no spatial location.

Explain the conceptual problem regarding mental causation that faces interactionist dualism.

EMPIRICAL ISSUES

Interactionist dualism also faces some empirical challenges. The first is very general. The law of the conservation of energy states that in any closed system, the total amount of energy in that system remains unchanged. The energy can only change forms; e.g. movement can produce heat. A 'closed system' is simply one that doesn't interact with anything outside itself. The universe is usually understood as a closed system. So the total amount of energy in the universe can't change. If something in the universe, such as your body, moved without that energy coming from some other physical source, the law of the conservation of energy would not be true of the universe. So:

1. If the mind, as a non-physical substance, could move the body, the total amount of energy in the universe would increase.
2. Therefore, if the mind could move the body, the law of the conservation of energy would not apply to the universe, and the universe is not a closed system.
3. Therefore, because what is changing the physical energy in the universe is not itself physical, physics cannot give us the complete, correct account of physical energy in the universe.

While we may want to say that physics doesn't tell us everything about what exists, interactionist dualism entails that physics isn't even the correct account of what exists *physically*. We can make this more specific to link it to the conceptual issues above: physics is wrong to think that physical movement can only be caused by a physical force.

The second empirical challenge is much more specific. If the mind can move the body, how does it do so? Current science indicates that movements of the body are caused by physical events in the brain. So, if the mind moves the body, it does so by changing what happens in the brain. We may object that we have no evidence of the mind changing what happens in the brain.

That is true, but we have no evidence that the claim is false either. This is because, while neuroscience is making good progress, we still have no clear account of the very complicated causation involved in something like making a choice. But we may think that neuroscience could discover the complete story in time. If interactionist dualism is true, then it seems that what it must discover is that some events in the brain *have no physical cause*, because they are caused by the mind.

It is common, but perhaps a mistake, to think that there is empirical *evidence* against substance dualism. The issues are so complex – how does the brain work? Is the universe a closed system? – that we don't yet have definitive evidence one way or another. So both the objections presented focus instead on the incompatibility between interactionist dualism and empirical science.

Epiphenomenalist dualism

We could accept that the objections above show that mental causation is impossible. But this doesn't undermine substance dualism if we accept epiphenomenalism, the view that the mind has no causal powers. On this view, the mind does not cause any physical events.

Epiphenomenalism also holds that the mind causes no *mental* events either – mental events are all caused by physical events, e.g. in the brain. For this reason, it is very unusual for substance dualists to be epiphenomenalists. Substance dualists generally maintain that mental events cause other mental events since the mind is ontologically independent of the body. It is more common for property dualists to accept epiphenomenalism. But it is worth briefly considering the objections that can be raised against epiphenomenalism at this point. For a fuller evaluation, see the later discussion.

THE CAUSAL REDUNDANCY OF THE MENTAL

The most influential objection to epiphenomenalism is that it is obviously false. It is obvious that, e.g., whether I feel pain makes a difference both to what I think (e.g. that I'm in pain) and to what I do (e.g. jump around shouting). To say that the mind is 'causally redundant' (i.e. does not work as a cause) is highly counter-intuitive.

THE ARGUMENT FROM INTROSPECTION

Suppose I am in pain. How do I know that I am in pain? The obvious answer is that my belief that I am in pain is caused by my pain itself. I can tell that I am in pain just from introspection. But epiphenomenalism must deny this, because, as a mental state, *pain doesn't cause anything*. Likewise, it seems that when I say what I think, what I say is caused by what I think. But epiphenomenalism must deny this. Both my belief that I feel pain and saying what I think are caused by physical processes and *not* pain or thought themselves.

This is bad enough, but it has a more serious implication. It threatens our knowledge of our mental states. If my thoughts and feelings don't cause my beliefs about my mind, then I would have those same beliefs about my mind even if I didn't think or feel as I do! According to

Is interactionist dualism true?

An 'epiphenomenon' is a by-product, something that is an effect of some process, but with no causal influence.

See OBJECTIONS TO (PROPERTY) DUALISM, p. 294.

epiphenomenalism, it is physical processes that cause my beliefs about my mind. So as long as the same physical processes occur in my brain, my beliefs about my own mind will be the same *whatever* mental states I have. My beliefs about my mind, therefore, are unjustified and unreliable. So I can't know my own mind.

FREE WILL AND RESPONSIBILITY

A third objection is that we need mental causation in order to be free and take responsibility for our actions. In order to be free and responsible for what you do, you need to be able to choose what to do, and to do it because you choose to do it. Therefore, we might say, your choice needs to cause what you do. If what you do is not caused by your choice, but by something physical over which you have no influence, then you are not free in what you do, any more than you are free in what you do when you are blown over by a strong wind. Choices are mental events. Epiphenomenalist dualism must therefore say that your choices have no causal powers and do not cause what you do. Instead, your choice is simply an effect of some process in the brain, as is your action. It is hard to see how 'you' have chosen what to do.

See VOLUNTARY AND INVOLUNTARY ACTIONS, p. 90.

Outline and explain two challenges facing epiphenomenalist dualism.

The problem of other minds

The threat of solipsism

The problem of other minds is the question of how we can know that there are minds other than our own. We each experience our own minds *directly*, from 'within'. We can each apprehend our sensations and emotions in a way that is 'felt'. We can know what we want or believe through introspection (at least, if epiphenomenalism is false!). But our knowledge of other people's minds is very different, it seems. We cannot experience other people's mental states. It seems that all we have to go on is other people's *behaviour*, what is expressed through their bodies.

This raises an important challenge for substance dualism. If minds and bodies are entirely independent, then how can I infer from seeing a body that there is a mind 'attached'? Other 'people' – other bodies – could all be machines, programmed to behave as they do, but with no minds. If there are no other minds, then my mind is the only one that exists. This is solipsism. The challenge to substance dualism is, how do we know that other minds exist and solipsism is false?

Explain the threat of solipsism to substance dualism.

The argument from analogy

The argument from analogy claims that we can use the behaviour of other people to infer that they have minds too. It was first presented by John Stuart Mill.

1. I have a mind.
2. I know from experience that my mental states cause my behaviour.
3. Other people have bodies similar to mine and behave similarly to me in similar situations.
4. Therefore, by analogy, their behaviour has the same type of cause as my behaviour, namely mental states.
5. Therefore, other people have minds.

The argument is perhaps the 'common-sense' position on how to solve the problem of other minds. But we can object to its use of induction. The conclusion that other people have minds is based on a single case – mine. This is like saying 'that dog has three legs; therefore, all dogs have three legs'. You can't generalise from one case, because it could be a special case. Perhaps I am the only person to have a mind.

However, instead of talking about the causal relation in the single case of my behaviour and my mind, we can formulate the argument to cite many instances of behaviour which we know to have a mental cause.

1. This behaviour has a mental cause.
2. That behaviour has a mental cause.
3. That third behaviour has a mental cause.
4. Etc.
5. Therefore, many behaviours have a mental cause (I know this from my own experience).
6. Other people exhibit the same types of behaviour as cited above.
7. Therefore, those behaviours also have mental causes.
8. Therefore, other people have minds.

Can we object that the argument still relies on analogy, on the contentious claim that like effects (behaviour) have like causes (mental states)? For example, even if behaviour in *my* case is caused by (my) mental states,

> *An Examination of Sir William Hamilton's Philosophy*, Ch. 12. The first form is often attributed to Mill, but the second form is a better interpretation.

> Explain the argument from analogy for the existence of other minds.

> Explain the differences between the first and second versions of the argument.

that doesn't mean that the behaviour of other people could not be caused by something entirely different (say, brain states without mental states).

This objection misunderstands how the argument is intended to work. First, the behaviour picked out in the first premises of the argument is not picked out as *mine*, but as a *type* of behaviour, e.g. raising an arm, walking to the shops, etc. The claim is that we have experience of many instances of such behaviour being caused by mental states. Now, in science, we generalise from the cases we have observed. 'Water boils at 100 degrees Celsius' (at sea level) – we haven't measured the temperature in every case of boiling water, but each time we do, we get the same result, so we make the general claim. We can do the same with behaviour. On this understanding, the argument is not from *analogy* at all. It is simply a causal inference.

Second, of course the sceptical claim that these instances are exceptional – that the behaviour of other people has a different cause – remains *possible* (just as it is *possible* that water doesn't always boil at 100 degrees Celsius). But the argument is only intended to make belief in other minds justified. We can think of it as an inference to the best explanation.

See HYPOTHETICAL REASONING, p. 9.

The solution still faces difficulties. First, it relies on mental causation, in this case, behaviour being caused by mental states. As we saw above, substance dualism has difficulties in explaining mental causation. But we can respond that we only need the claim *that* behaviour is caused by mental states, not an explanation of how. Second, we can object that the belief that other people have minds is not a *hypothesis*, nor do we *infer*, on the basis of *evidence*, that they have minds. This whole way of understanding the way we think about other minds is mistaken. Some first thoughts on this will take us towards our next theory, logical behaviourism.

? Can substance dualism solve the problem of other minds?

Going further: on ascribing mental states

Descartes and solipsists assume that we can ascribe mental states to ourselves, to say of oneself that one is thinking, or that one wants to understand, or that one is frustrated. But what does this ability require? We can argue that, for instance, a child cannot learn that it is angry, that what it feels is 'anger', without also learning what it means to say, of someone else, that they are angry. After all, it learns that it is angry because its parents (and others) help it understand this. One way in which they do this is for the parents to point out when they or other people are angry, and how this is similar to when the child is angry. So the child also learns how to recognise when other people are angry. The ability to ascribe mental states to oneself is learned, and is interdependent with the ability to ascribe mental states to other people. To learn the meaning of 'anger', 'pain', 'thinking' is to learn their correct application to both oneself and others, simultaneously. In that case, to understand a mental property, I have to be able to attribute it to other people. I have to be able to say 'he is in pain' or 'she is thinking'.

This has a number of important implications.

1. If there can be no knowledge of oneself as a mind without presupposing that there are other minds, the problem of other minds does not arise.

2. Our knowledge of other minds is not inferred from knowledge of our own behaviour and its causes. We don't have one without the other.

3. It raises a distinct challenge to substance dualism (which we can relate back to MIND WITHOUT BODY IS NOT CONCEIVABLE, p. 213). Substance dualism claims that mental properties are attributed to minds, while physical properties are attributed to bodies. But in that case, how can we identify other minds so as to attribute mental properties to them? We have no experience of 'minds' on their own. So we have to attribute mental properties to something that also has physical properties. Mental and physical properties have to be attributed to the *same thing* for us to attribute mental characteristics to anything at all. This threatens the claim that the mind is a separate substance from the body.

> Outline and explain the argument that we don't infer that other people have minds.

1) How do we
know that other
people have minds?
2) Is the mind a
separate substance
from the body?

4. It raises a challenge to the substance dualist's concept of mind. We don't know what a mind is unless we already know what a person – an 'embodied mind' – is. We can only understand the idea of a mind by abstracting from the idea of a person; a mind is a disembodied person. In other words, the concept of the 'union' of mind and body (see Beyond dualism?, p. 206) is a more basic concept than the concept of mind.

Key points: objections to (substance) dualism

- Interactionist dualism claims that the mind can cause physical (and other mental) events. It faces the problem of explaining how the mind can cause physical events, given that it is not in space and exerts no physical force.
- The conceptual problem is understanding how this is possible. The empirical problem is that it conflicts with the presuppositions of empirical science.
- Epiphenomenal dualism claims that the mind has no causal powers. We can object that this is very counter-intuitive.
- We can also object that it entails that we cannot gain knowledge of our minds from introspection, since according to epiphenomenal dualism, our beliefs about our mental states are not caused by those mental states.
- Epiphenomenal dualism also appears to undermine free will and responsibility, as our choices are caused by physical events and do not themselves cause our actions.
- Substance dualism faces a further challenge of showing that we can know other minds exist. If minds are logically independent of bodies, any evidence from someone's bodily behaviour does not prove that they have a mind.
- The (first) argument from analogy claims that I can infer other people have minds, because they behave as I do, and I have a mind.
- We can object that we cannot base an inference on one case. I could be a special case.

- A better form of the argument claims that I know from experience, for many types of behaviour, that they have a mental cause. I can generalise this to the behaviour of other people. So I know they have minds.
- We can object that this solution presupposes that minds cause physical events, and substance dualism has difficulty establishing this claim.
- We can also object that the belief that other people have minds is not a hypothesis based on evidence at all. We learn about our own mental states and those of others in one and the same process of acquiring concepts of mental states.

Summary: substance dualism

In this section on dualism, we have looked at Descartes' two arguments for substance dualism (from conceivability and divisibility), objections to those arguments, and two objections to substance dualism itself. In our discussion and evaluation of these arguments, we have looked at the following issues:

1. What does it mean to claim that the mind is ontologically distinct from the body?
2. Is it conceivable for the mind to exist separately from the body?
3. Is it possible for the mind to exist separately from the body? If so, does this show that mind and body are distinct substances?
4. Is the mind distinguished from the body by not being divisible?
5. If the mind is a distinct substance, can mental states cause bodily movements?
6. Do mental states have any causal powers at all?
7. If substance dualism is true, how can I know that other minds exist?
8. Does the ability to identify my own mental states presuppose the ability to ascribe mental states to other people?

II. Materialism: the mind is not ontologically distinct from the physical

The most common alternative to substance dualism is the view that there is only one kind of substance, which is matter. Thus the mind is not a distinct substance; it is not 'ontologically distinct' from what is material, but dependent upon it for its existence. This view is materialism.

Physicalism

In recent years, materialism has been supplanted by 'physicalism', and so from now on, I shall talk about physicalism, not materialism. The most important reason for this is that physics has shown that 'matter' is too crude an identification of the most basic substance that exists; e.g. matter can be changed into energy.

As a first attempt, we could define physicalism as the view that everything that exists is physical, or depends upon something that is physical. 'Physical' means something that comes under the laws and investigations of physics, and whose essential properties are identified and described by physics.

But we should be more precise. Physicalism claims that what is physical is metaphysically fundamental. It is not enough that the only *substance* is physical. The fundamental *nature* of the universe is physical, and this covers events and properties as well. So physicalism says:

1. the properties identified by physics form the fundamental nature of the universe;
2. physical laws govern all objects and events in space-time;
3. every physical event has a physical cause that brings it about in accordance with the laws of physics. (This is known as the 'completeness of physics' or 'causal closure'.)

It is worth saying more about the first and third claims.

The third claim states that all physical events have sufficient physical causes. Of any event involving a change in physical properties (e.g. every movement of your body), that event can be brought about by something physical alone. No other, non-physical causes are necessary.

So if there are non-physical causes, they don't contribute anything *in addition* to physical causes to the way the physical world changes over time.

The first claim states that the properties identified by physics are ontologically 'basic'. Other properties, in particular mental properties, are ontologically dependent on the properties identified by physics (or more broadly, the natural sciences). Mental properties, therefore, if they exist at all, are not part of the *fundamental* nature of the universe, but ontologically dependent on other properties.

It is worth contrasting three explanations of the previous sentence, though the claims that follow may only become clear when we discuss the theories themselves.

1. Elimination: ELIMINATIVE MATERIALISM (p. 303) claims that there are no mental properties. Our concepts of mental properties are fundamentally mistaken – these concepts don't refer to anything that exists.

2. Reduction (identity): MIND–BRAIN TYPE IDENTITY THEORY (p. 248) claims that mental properties are *identical* to certain physical properties. This is known as 'reductive' physicalism. An 'ontological reduction' involves the claim that the things in one domain (e.g. mental things) are identical with some of the things in another domain (e.g. physical things). Mental properties, type identity theory argues, are a subset of physical properties. The identity claim is a reduction because we have 'reduced' mental properties – which we might have thought were a different kind of thing – to physical properties. I.e. there is *nothing more* to mental properties than being a certain kind of physical property.

3. Non-reductive dependency: LOGICAL BEHAVIOURISM (p. 229) and FUNCTIONALISM (p. 256) are both types of 'non-reductive' physicalism. They both argue that mental properties cannot be reduced to physical properties. However, functionalism claims that mental properties can be reduced to functional properties and some forms of logical behaviourism claim that mental properties can be reduced to behavioural dispositions. So (in some forms) both these theories are reductive, but in a different sense to reductive physicalism (type identity theory). They are both physicalist because functional properties and behavioural dispositions depend upon physical properties.

But what is it to say that mental properties 'depend' upon physical properties, if they are not reducible to them? Philosophers spell this out in terms of the idea of 'supervenience'. The essence of supervenience is this: properties of type *A* supervene on properties of type *B* just in case any two things that are exactly alike in their *B* properties cannot have different *A* properties.

For example, a painting has various aesthetic properties, such as being elegant or balanced. It also has various physical properties, such as the distribution of paint on the canvas. The aesthetic properties supervene on the physical ones. We cannot change the painting's being elegant or balanced without changing the distribution of paint on the canvas. There can be no change in aesthetic properties without a change in physical properties. And two paintings exactly alike in their physical properties (i.e. duplicates) will have the same aesthetic properties. If two paintings are completely identical in terms of how the paint is arranged – if they look exactly the same – then they must also be identical in terms of their aesthetic properties. Of two physically identical paintings, one can't be graceful while the other is awkward. Any differences in their aesthetic properties entail that there is a difference in their physical properties.

We need to notice the strength of this claim. It is not enough to say that if the paintings are physically identical, then they *are* aesthetically identical. Suppose we say simply that in this case, as it happens, they are both graceful. This allows that in another case, one could be graceful and one not. But saying that allows that the physical properties don't *fix* the aesthetic properties. The aesthetic properties would be able to vary even as the physical properties remained the same.

This isn't right. We want to say that if the paintings are physically identical, then they *must be* aesthetically identical. It is not merely false but *impossible* that one is graceful while the other is awkward, if they both look exactly the same. Put another way, once the physical properties of a painting are finalised – when the painting is finished – there is no further work to be done to 'add' the aesthetic properties. They are already part of the painting. To change the aesthetic qualities, you *must* change the physical properties.

According to physicalism, physical properties 'fix' *all* the other properties in such a way that it is *not possible* for the other properties to change without changing the physical properties.

? What is supervenience?

By contrast, PROPERTY DUALISM (p. 266) is a non-physicalist theory because it claims that mental properties are not dependent on physical properties in the way physicalists claim.

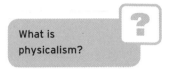

What is physicalism?

A. Logical behaviourism

The theory

Logical behaviourism is a form of physicalism, but it does not attempt to reduce mental properties – states, events and so on – to physical properties directly. Instead, it analyses them in terms of behaviour.

Behaviourism began as a theory of how psychology should conduct itself to achieve the status of a science. Science, it claimed, can only investigate what is publicly accessible. Hence psychology can and must aim only at the explanation and prediction of behaviour, as any talk of or appeal to 'inner', inaccessible mental states cannot be scientific. There is no scientific way to establish their existence or nature. This theory, of how psychology should proceed, is methodological behaviourism. It makes claims about the methods of science and about *how we can know* about mental states.

More interesting to the philosophy of mind is logical behaviourism. This claims that *what* we are talking about when we are talking about the mind and mental states is behaviour. It is a claim about what 'the mind' *is*, not merely how we can know about it, arguing that our psychological concepts and words are actually about behaviour – what people do and how they react.

The simplest form that logical behaviourism can take is to claim that a mental state just is actual behaviour; e.g. to believe something is just to say that you believe it, to be in pain is just to wince, shout, etc. But this is very implausible. First, we can, to some extent, control our behaviour; e.g. I might stop myself from showing that I am in pain. Second, the same mental state could be expressed in different behaviours on different occasions. My belief that there is food in the fridge can be expressed by my stating this, but it could also be expressed by my simply going to the fridge and looking inside when I am hungry. Third, many mental states, such as knowledge, are dispositions, rather than occurrences. They don't occur at a time, like actual behaviour does.

Someone who knows French knows French even when they are talking or reading in English.

So logical behaviourism claims that to talk of mental states and processes is to talk of 'dispositions' to behave in certain ways. On this view, the mind is not a 'thing'. Rather, we can talk about organisms 'having minds', or better, having mental states, on the basis of how they behave.

There are different versions of logical behaviourism. In its strongest form, analytical behaviourism, it is a reductive theory. It claims that we can give a *complete translation* of mental concepts in terms of behavioural concepts. Any sentence using a mental term like 'belief', 'think', 'pain', can be replaced, without changing its meaning, by a sentence that uses terms that refer to behaviour and behavioural dispositions. So mental concepts can be 'reduced' to a series of hypothetical ('if ... then ...') statements about what the person will do in different situations.

However, as the anthology includes Ryle's *The Concept of Mind*, we will focus on his theory, which, we will see, is not reductive in this way. We will draw contrasts between his theory and analytical behaviourism at various points.

> This is explained in
> DISPOSITIONS, p. 233.

> **?** What is logical behaviourism?

ANTHOLOGY: RYLE, *THE CONCEPT OF MIND*, CHS 1, 2, 5

The AQA syllabus doesn't specify which parts of Ryle's *The Concept of Mind* to focus on, but the intention is to understand his main claims and arguments. Ryle is as concerned to attack substance dualism as he is to defend logical behaviourism, and I shall focus primarily on his positive theory, rather than his criticisms. But it is worth beginning with his argument that substance dualism rests on a 'category mistake'.

The category mistake

In Ch. 1, Ryle spells out his understanding of substance dualism, which he calls 'the official doctrine'. It claims

1.   that the mind can exist without the body;

2. that the body exists in space, subject to mechanical (physical) laws, while the mind does not exist in space and is not subject to mechanical laws;

3. that in consciousness and introspection, we are directly aware of our mental states and operations in such a way that we cannot make mistakes; and

4. that we have no direct access to other minds, but can only infer their existence.

Ryle identifies the two main challenges this theory faces as the problem of causal interaction and the problem of other minds. But he goes on to diagnose an implication of the theory that would be even more significant. If substance dualism were right, our mental concepts - a thought, hoping, being imaginative - must all refer to episodes in a secret history of our minds, secret because inaccessible to anyone else. So the only way to know whether a mental description of someone is true or not - whether they hope that there is food in the fridge, or feel cross, or know that penguins are birds - is for the person themselves to check using introspection. The parent, teacher, biographer, friend can never know whether their ascriptions of mental states to others are true. But this, Ryle objects, would make it impossible, in practice, for us to use mental concepts.

Ryle doesn't say much more about why it would make mental concepts impossible to use, partly because his whole book is meant to argue the point. Here is one argument, developing the thoughts in ON ASCRIBING MENTAL STATES (p. 222): to use mental concepts, we must first learn mental concepts. For us to learn mental concepts, the people who teach us these concepts must be able to refer to our mental states and processes for us even to apply them to the episodes we ourselves undergo - our fears, pains, beliefs, etc. But if substance dualism were true, how could they do so? How would they know reliably what episodes we are undergoing, given that we ourselves can't yet confirm or deny them since we haven't learned the concepts?

> Explain the objection that substance dualism would make talk about mental states impossible.

Just this first comment illustrates the very different starting points of substance dualism and logical behaviourism. Descartes starts from his *own* mind, considered in isolation from everything else. Ryle starts from how *we* talk and think about 'the mind' together. Each has strengths and weaknesses. Just as Descartes gets into difficulty when accounting for how we deal with other minds and mental language, we will see in THE CONCEIVABILITY OF MENTAL STATES WITHOUT ASSOCIATED BEHAVIOUR (p. 245) that Ryle gets into difficulty when accounting for our subjective experience of our own minds (first-personal experience).

Ryle argues that substance dualism, 'the dogma of the Ghost in the Machine' (p. 17), rests on a category mistake. Suppose someone is shown around Oxford University – they see the colleges, the buildings with the different faculties and departments, the administrative buildings. But then they ask, 'I've seen the colleges, the faculties, the administration. But where is the university?' They have misunderstood the concept of 'university', thinking that the university is another thing, alongside the colleges, faculties and administration. But the university is not like this; it is how everything that the person has seen is organised. The person has made a category mistake.

Or again, suppose someone is having a game of cricket explained to them. The bowler, batters, wicketkeeper and fielders are all pointed out and their tasks explained. But then the person says, 'I've heard a lot about the importance of team spirit. Who does that?' They have misunderstood the concept and made a category mistake. The exercise of team spirit is not another task like bowling or fielding, nor is someone who is bowling and exercising team spirit doing two separate things. Team spirit is about *how* the players play the game together.

Concepts belong to different logical categories – different ways in which it makes sense to use a concept. A category mistake is to treat a concept as belonging to a different logical category from the one it actually belongs to.

According to Ryle, substance dualism makes the category mistake of thinking that the mind is like the body – another 'thing', a distinct, complex, organised unit subject to distinct relations of cause and effect. The mistake is to think that physical and mental concepts operate in the same way, in the same logical framework of 'things' and 'causes', that talk of mental states and processes understands 'states' and 'processes' along the lines of physical states and processes. But believing something is not a state in the same sense as being solid, and doing mental arithmetic is not a process in the same sense as a log burning.

How is this mistake made? Well, mental concepts don't pick out processes like physical, mechanical ones. Once science reached the stage of plausibly claiming that all physical, spatial processes could be explained in non-rational, mechanical terms, people drew the inference that mental terms must refer to non-spatial, non-mechanical states and processes. Ryle calls this the 'para-mechanical hypothesis' (p. 21).

What is a category mistake?

Dispositions

Ryle opens Ch. 2 by saying that 'when we describe people as exercising qualities of mind, we are not referring to occult episodes of which their overt acts and utterances are effects; we are referring to those overt acts and utterances themselves' (p. 26). In fact, this is too simple, because Ryle does not claim that we refer only to acts and utterances, but also *dispositions* to act and utter.

Central to Ryle's argument is his observation that we often speak of mental states in action, in their expression in behaviour. To know how to play chess is something demonstrated in actually playing chess, and we attribute this knowledge to someone on the basis of what they do. Or again, to do something intelligently or thoughtfully – playing, reading, cooking, arguing, etc. – is to be able to regulate what you do. So some of our mental concepts identify skills. A skill isn't an act – you can't tell from one piece of behaviour whether it is skilful or just lucky or something else again. But a skill isn't some invisible, non-spatial thing either. It is a disposition or complex of dispositions (p. 33).

What is a disposition? A disposition, in its simplest form, is simply how something will or is likely to behave under certain circumstances (p. 43). For instance, sugar is soluble. Solubility is the disposition to dissolve when placed in water. Sugar is soluble even when it isn't actually in water. Solubility is a 'single-track' disposition – it is actualised or manifest in just one way, namely dissolving in water. Other dispositions, such as being hard, have many different ways in which they are actualised. We can infer many different facts from knowing that something is hard; e.g. about whether we can pass other things through it, what sound it will make when hit, whether we can change its shape easily, and so on.

Many mental concepts are also concepts of dispositions, so that when we talk of someone having a certain mental state, like being proud or believing that the earth is round, we are talking of what they would do, could do, or are liable to do, in particular situations or under particular conditions, including conditions that they are not in at the moment. Mental concepts can pick out a whole set of dispositions which are 'indefinitely heterogenous' (p. 44) – think of all the many different and subtle ways in which people can manifest pride (Ryle refers to Jane Austen's novel *Pride and Prejudice*).

Whether someone has a particular disposition is a matter of whether certain statements about what they could or would do are true or not. These are hypothetical statements, conditional statements of the form 'if circumstances *c* occur, the person will do *x*'. They are not 'categorical' statements that say how things actually are; e.g. many of those circumstances may never arise. They don't describe actual states of some mental substance. So 'the mind is not the topic of sets of untestable categorical propositions [as substance dualism must hold], but the topic of sets of testable hypothetical and semi-hypothetical propositions' (p. 46).

Unlike analytical behaviourists (p. 230), Ryle does not think that statements using a mental concept, such as 'he is proud' or 'he knows French', can be 'reduced' to a series of hypothetical

What is a disposition?

Briefly explain the claim that many mental concepts are dispositional concepts.

statements about what the person will do in different situations. The mental concept can be analysed in terms of such statements – this is what it means – but we can never give a complete translation, so that we don't need the mental concept any more. Dispositional statements are 'open'. What they do is 'license' – support and justify – certain inferences, explanations and predictions (p. 119). To say that someone is proud licenses inferences about how he will behave in certain situations, but we cannot draw all possible inferences and replace the concept 'proud' with this set of inferences.

On Ryle's analysis, dispositions are not causes. A disposition isn't something that brings something else about. A cause is something that occurs, something expressed in a categorical statement. So 'He made lunch because *he was hungry*' shouldn't be understood along the lines of 'the glass broke because *a stone hit it*', but along the lines of 'the glass broke when the stone hit it because *it was brittle*' (p. 49). Hunger and brittleness are both dispositions; a stone hitting glass is an event. So when we explain an action by referring to someone's mental state, such as hunger, we aren't referring to a non-physical cause, we are situating the action in relation to a number of hypothetical statements. Making lunch is just the kind of thing someone who is hungry would do, in the right circumstances.

Logical behaviourism is a form of physicalism because it takes what exists to be given by natural science. Categorical facts about substances and causes belong here, in the descriptions of the world that natural science provides. Dispositions depend on such categorical facts – sugar's disposition to dissolve depends on its physical properties, and our dispositions to behave as we do depend on our physical properties.

> Explain why logical behaviourism is a form of physicalism.

Thinking and mental processes

Logical behaviourism is on its strongest ground when talking about the mind in action. But what, we may object, about *just* thinking, without acting (which is where Descartes started)?

Ryle's response is first to note that there isn't just one kind of 'thinking'. Again, thinking is often done in, with and through action. When we act thoughtfully or intelligently, the thinking isn't a separate process from the doing, so that the thinking takes place in the mind and the doing in the physical world. There is one process – behaving (reading, driving, conversing …) intelligently – and what makes it an expression of thinking is that it has a certain manner which can be expressed by dispositional statements about what we can, could and would do in certain situations.

But there is also the matter of thinking quietly 'to oneself'. Ryle's central claim here is that this is *internalised speaking*: 'Much of our ordinary thinking is conducted in internal monologue or silent soliloquy' (p. 28). Speaking is, of course, an overt behaviour, and we only acquire the ability to think – to speak silently to ourselves – with effort. The silence, and the fact that we are speaking only with ourselves, are *inessential* to the nature of thinking. To think through a maths problem, one can do so either with pen and paper, articulating the steps as one goes, or silently, 'in one's head'. Whether a process is public or private is irrelevant to whether it is thinking. 'The phrase "in the mind" can and should always be dispensed with' (p. 40). Mental processes only sometimes and only contingently take place 'in the mind'. Processes that do, as it happens, take place silently don't define thinking any more than those that take place as publicly observable behaviours.

Thinking is something that happens at a time and takes time. It 'occurs', it is a mental 'occurrence'. So we can't say that thinking is *just* a matter of dispositions. The same is true of other mental occurrences, such as being conscious of (paying attention to) what you are doing, feeling or thinking (what Ryle calls 'heeding'). What's the relation between occurrences and dispositions?

To understand this, compare 'it is dissolving'. This states that something is happening, but does so in dispositional terms. From 'it is dissolving', we know that it is soluble, and so dissolves

Explain Ryle's claim that there is nothing essentially 'private' about thinking.

We will say more about consciousness in THE CONCEIVABILITY OF MENTAL STATES WITHOUT ASSOCIATED BEHAVIOUR (p. 245).

in water. So it would do just what it is doing in this situation, given that it has that disposition.

Likewise, to say that someone is paying attention to what they are doing is to attribute dispositions about what they could say if you asked them, but also to add that they are 'in the mood or frame of mind' to do just what it is that they are doing (p. 136). This is what Ryle means by a 'semi-hypothetical' statement – it both explains an actual occurrence and licenses inferences.

The appeal of logical behaviourism

Logical behaviourism avoids the two main objections that face substance dualism. First, it avoids THE PROBLEM OF OTHER MINDS (p. 220). Talking about mental states is just talking about dispositions to behave in certain ways. From how someone behaves, we can infer what behavioural dispositions they have. But from this, we don't then *infer* that they have a mind. The link between behaviour and minds isn't based on evidence, it is logical (conceptual). To say someone has certain behavioural dispositions *just is* to say that they have certain mental states. To understand what others say and do is to understand that they have minds. We can know that other people have minds, because we can know directly that they behave in particular ways.

Second, on Ryle's version at least, it doesn't face the problems raised by CAUSAL INTERACTION (p. 215). There is no mental causation. Mental states aren't causes. This isn't to adopt epiphenomenalism. Rather, mental states aren't the *right kind of thing* to be causes (or fail to be causes). Talk of mental causation is a category mistake. Instead, we explain how people behave in relation to the dispositions they have.

> **How does logical behaviourism solve the problem of other minds?**

Going further: logical behaviourism and mental causation

While logical behaviourism avoids the problem of causal interaction, is its solution really an advantage? We may object that there is mental causation. First, while dispositions may not be causes in the same sense as particular events, we can argue that they are part of the 'causal story'. For example, the stone won't break the glass if the glass *isn't* brittle. So dispositions make a contribution to causal chains, and citing a disposition can be a causal explanation. The same is true of beliefs, desires and other mental states, we may claim. When I say 'I went to the party because I thought you would be there', we are citing something that is causally relevant to my action.

'Actions, Reasons, and Causes'

A famous argument from Donald Davidson supports this. Suppose I have two reasons to do something, but I only act on one of those reasons. For example, I want to see you and believe you'll be at the party, and I believe the party will be fun and I want to have fun. Suppose I go to the party because I want to have fun, not because I want to see you. How can this be true? What makes it the case that the second reason, and not the first, is the reason I act on? 'Central to the relation between a reason and an action it explains is the idea that the agent performed the action *because* he had the reason'. This 'because' must be a causal 'because'. What makes it true that I act on the second reason, and not the first, is that the second reason causes my action. So behaviourism is wrong to think that there is no mental causation.

Should we accept Ryle's claim that there is no mental causation?

Second, there are mental occurrences that may operate as causes like particular events do. For instance, in working through a problem, one thought may 'lead to' the next and this 'leading to' should be understood causally. The whole mental process is a causal chain, with each stage causing the next stage.

Issues

Dualist arguments

The syllabus lists four dualist arguments, two for substance dualism and two for property dualism. We will discuss the implications for logical behaviourism of the arguments for property dualism when we discuss property dualism. What can we say about the objections to logical behaviourism raised by THE CONCEIVABILITY ARGUMENT (p. 202) and THE DIVISIBILITY ARGUMENT (p. 203)?

See THE KNOWLEDGE ARGUMENT, p. 268 and The 'PHILOSOPHICAL ZOMBIES' ARGUMENT, p. 279.

As noted in MIND WITHOUT BODY IS NOT CONCEIVABLE (p. 213), it seems that if logical behaviourism provides the correct analysis of mental concepts, then it is inconceivable for there to be a mind without a body. A mind is not a thing, it does not 'exist' in the same way as bodies exist only with different properties. To think like this is a category mistake, and category mistakes are misconceptions. As dispositions to behave, mental states can only be had by creatures that can behave in certain ways.

Given this, if we can succeed in showing that it *is* conceivable for the mind to exist without the body, then it seems that logical behaviourism must be false. Now, many people have thought that mind without body is conceivable – belief in God and the existence of one's soul in the afterlife demonstrate this. Shouldn't the analysis of our mental concepts make such common thoughts coherent rather than incoherent? Aren't our concepts defined by how we use them?

Ryle argues that such beliefs *don't* actually reflect how we use our concepts in everyday life. The 'official doctrine' conflicts 'with the whole body of what we know about minds *when we are not speculating about them*' (p. 13, my italics). The belief in mind without body is not part of everyday use, but the result of theological and philosophical theorising. We cannot have a clear and distinct idea of ourselves as 'minds' only, and we are mistaken if we think that we can. 'Many people can talk sense with concepts but cannot talk sense about them' (p. 9).

Is a mind without a body conceivable?

The divisibility argument claims that the mind cannot be the body because the mind is not spatially divisible while the body is. But this is no threat to logical behaviourism. The mind is not spatially divisible because it is not a thing at all. Mental states are dispositions. To talk of 'divisibility' and 'non-divisibility' here is a category mistake.

Circularity and multiple realisability of mental states in behaviour

(While discussing this objection, we will ignore mental occurrences, and focus just on the analysis of those mental states that Ryle claims are dispositions.) We can object that logical behaviourism can't supply a successful analysis of mental states in terms of behaviour. If a mental state is a disposition, or set of dispositions, to behave in certain ways in certain conditions, what behaviour is it a disposition towards?

The first difficulty in answering this question is that a mental state might be expressed in quite different behaviours not only in different situations, but even in very similar situations by different people. In fear, I might freeze; you might run. This is known as the multiple realisability of mental states in behaviour. 'Multiple realisability', in this context, just means that there are many ways in which the disposition (the mental state) can be actualised (expressed in behaviour). If different people with the same mental state have dispositions to do different things in similar situations, how can we say that these *different* dispositions are actually the *same* mental state? What is it that makes it the same mental state, given that the dispositions are different?

The second difficulty in analysing mental states in terms of behavioural dispositions is that doing the same thing could, in different instances, be expressions of different mental states. I might run towards something because I'm scared of it, and want to surprise it; or I might run towards it because I'm not scared of it, and want a cuddle.

The logical behaviourist could reply first, that *on the whole* people in the same mental state have very similar dispositions. Many of these similarities hold even when there are some things they do differently (e.g. for fear, there are similarities in how they answer 'are you scared?', their facial expressions, etc.). Second, the objection focuses on individual 'pieces' of behaviour, which misunderstands the theory. Ryle's analysis allows that we can't tell what disposition, if any, is being expressed in a single piece of behaviour. What makes the behaviour the expression of the disposition that it does, in fact, express, depends on whether certain hypothetical statements about *other* situations are true or not. So whether or not I am running towards something because I'm scared of it isn't fixed just by running towards it. It depends on what I would say if you asked me 'Are you scared?', what I do next after running towards it, and so on.

> For a different but related meaning, see THE MULTIPLE REALISABILITY OF MENTAL STATES, p. 251.

> Explain the objection to logical behaviourism from the multiple realisability of mental states in behaviour.

But we can now raise a second objection. We cannot analyse what behaviour a mental state is a disposition for without referring to *other mental states*. Suppose I am afraid of dangerous snakes. Does this dispose me to run when I see one? That depends. Do I *believe* the snake is dangerous? Do I *believe* that this type of dangerous snake is one you shouldn't run away from? Am I able to *recognise* the type of snake? Do I *want* to avoid being bitten? And so on. We can't specify what set of dispositions my fear is without mentioning my beliefs, my knowledge, my desires, and so on. So here's the objection: we can provide a further analysis of these mental states in terms of dispositions as well, but we will face the same problem. What behaviour my belief that the snake is dangerous disposes me towards will depend on other mental states. In fact, it will depend on whether or not I am also afraid of snakes! This is the problem of circularity.

The problem gets worse. A particular mental state could be compatible with a disposition to just about *any* behaviour, depending on a person's other mental states at the time. My fear of dangerous snakes could dispose me to say 'Well, hello there, Mr Muggins' if I also believe that this phrase effectively prevents snake attacks! To conclude the objection: because we can't effectively identify distinct mental states with distinct sets of dispositions, it is a mistake to think that mental states just *are* sets of behavioural dispositions.

1. If mental states are behavioural dispositions, then different mental states are dispositions to different behaviour and the same (type of) mental state is a disposition to the same behaviour.
2. However, there is no fixed set of behaviours that any mental state disposes one towards. The behavioural dispositions that are supposed to 'be' a particular mental state vary depending on what other mental states someone has.
3. Therefore, different mental states may be dispositions to the same behaviour, depending on other mental states. And the same mental state may be dispositions to different behaviour, depending on other mental states.
4. Furthermore, the analysis of one mental state in terms of dispositions may rely on the analysis of a second, while the analysis of the second relies on the analysis of the first.
5. Therefore, mental states cannot be analysed as behavioural dispositions.

Explain the objection that the analysis of mental states as behavioural dispositions cannot avoid circularity.

This objection is particularly forceful against analytical behaviourists who want to 'reduce' concepts of mental states to behaviour and dispositions, who say that we can give a complete translation of mental concepts in terms of behavioural concepts.

However, as we noted above, Ryle rejects this view. First, mental concepts are concepts of 'indefinitely heterogenous' sets of dispositions. Nothing that is 'indefinite' can be exhaustively characterised. Second, disposition statements are 'open', and cannot be replaced by a complete set of hypothetical statements linking particular matters of fact (such as a situation and a behaviour). Therefore, Ryle accepts that it is impossible to *specify* mental states in terms of dispositions, replacing mental concepts with behavioural ones alone in our thought and language. Nevertheless, he argues, a concept of a mental state *is* a concept of a set of dispositions. Ryle's logical behaviourism provides an analysis of the meaning of mental concepts, but it does not justify the claim that we could replace talk of mental concepts with talk of specific behavioural dispositions. Mental concepts work at a higher level of generality that can't be reduced to sets of individual hypothetical statements about behaviour. This makes the point about circularity true but not an objection.

> **Can logical behaviourism reduce talk of mental states to talk of behavioural dispositions?**

The asymmetry between self-knowledge and knowledge of other people's mental states

Ryle observes that it is part of the 'official doctrine' of substance dualism that the ways in which we gain knowledge of our own and others' mental states are very different. We are directly aware of our own mental states, but we can only infer those of others. Our self-knowledge comes from our *consciousness* of our mental states and our *introspection* of that consciousness. We cannot be conscious of anyone else's mental states in the same way. Furthermore, we are aware of our mental states in such a way that we cannot make mistakes, but this is not true of our beliefs about other people's minds.

> See THE CATEGORY MISTAKE, p. 230.

Now if mental states were dispositions to behaviour, all this wouldn't be true. It seems that I would have to infer what mental states I have from how I behave, or how I think I am disposed to behave. But, we can object, this isn't right. I can know what I believe, what I want or fear or hope, directly, without inference. Furthermore, if I am thinking to myself, I know what I am thinking in a way that no one else can.

1. The analysis of mental states in terms of behavioural dispositions seems to rule out an asymmetry between self-knowledge and knowledge of other people's mental states.
2. Yet it seems obvious from experience that there is such an asymmetry.
3. Therefore, logical behaviourism is false.

Ryle's response is to argue that consciousness, understood in this way, is a myth (p. 156). He argues that self-knowledge and our knowledge of other minds is on a par, gained in the same way in each case, by paying attention. This enables us to make reliable dispositional claims about our own or other people's behaviour, whether this is overt or silent. The main difference is simply that we have more evidence available to ourselves.

> Briefly explain the objection to logical behaviourism from an asymmetry between self-knowledge and knowledge of other people's mental states.

ANTHOLOGY: RYLE, *THE CONCEPT OF MIND*, CH. 6

Going further: Ryle on consciousness

Central to Ryle's argument is that being conscious of something is to pay attention to ('heed') it. We can pay attention to what we are doing and to what we have just felt or said silently to ourselves. But we can also pay attention to what someone else is doing and what they say out loud to us. To know what we are thinking or feeling is not to stand in some special, inner private relation to certain mental 'objects' ('thoughts', 'feelings'), but for us to be ready to say what we think or feel and be unsurprised by the occurrence of the thought or feeling.

Compare *not* knowing a process in one's mind: you make a joke spontaneously or come up with a solution to a problem. How did you do it? You can't say – the joke or solution comes as a 'surprise' to you. Knowing what you are thinking or doing is just to be continuously prepared for what comes next in that process.

Hence consciousness provides the same kind of knowledge in cases of knowing our own mental states and knowing the mental states of others. The main difference is that in our own case, we have more to go on, because we are the audience of our silent, inner speech – our thinking – and others are not.

Knowing what you are thinking is not different in *kind* from knowing what someone else is thinking, since I can know just as directly what someone else thinks when they speak, at least when they speak in an 'unstudied', unguarded, unembarrassed and uncalculated way, which is the most natural way to speak. When we talk like this – whether to others, or silently to ourselves – we are directly expressing our mental states. So when we pay attention to what we say, we gain knowledge of the mind of whoever is talking. Introspection is not a form of perception of special mental objects. It is just to pay this kind of attention to ourselves.

Explain Ryle's theory of consciousness.

Objections to Ryle's theory of consciousness

We can make two objections to Ryle's analysis of consciousness and self-knowledge. First, can thinking be adequately understood in terms of inner speech, and can internalised speech form the model for mental processes generally? What about non-linguistic mental processes or changes in feeling and mood?

See QUALIA, p. 260.

Second, Ryle seems to miss out the 'inner', experiential aspect of mental states and processes. There is an element of consciousness that is not about knowledge or paying attention, but 'phenomenology', the distinctive quality of certain experiences; e.g. how a sensation or emotion feels to the person experiencing it.

It may be that these objections don't themselves re-establish a strong asymmetry between self-knowledge and knowledge of others' mental states. But they attack Ryle's rejection of it.

Compare and contrast substance dualism and logical behaviourism on self-knowledge.

The conceivability of mental states without associated behaviour

We can develop the second objection to Ryle's theory of consciousness more generally. It seems that many mental states and processes have an 'inner' aspect that can't be captured by behaviour and behavioural dispositions. We should agree that to be in pain often involves doing certain things, such as wincing, recoiling from the cause of pain, nursing the damaged part of the body, etc. (call all this 'pain behaviour'). But someone stoical might not show their pain (pain without pain behaviour), while an actor might pretend to be in pain (pain behaviour without pain).

There is an easy response to this. The logical behaviourist allows that pain isn't just to do these things, but to have the *disposition* to do them. The logical behaviourist can say that the stoic has certain dispositions that the actor lacks.

But now we can object that this analysis misses an important point. Pain isn't just a disposition to shout or wince; there is also *how pain feels*, 'what it is like' to experience pain. *This* is what distinguishes the stoic from the actor. It is highly counter-intuitive to argue that this aspect of experience is constituted entirely by behavioural dispositions.

Hilary Putnam asks us to imagine a community of 'super-spartans'. (The Spartans were an ancient Greek community who were very tough and discouraged demonstrations of pain.) These are people (or creatures) who so completely disapprove of showing pain that all pain behaviour has been suppressed. They no longer have any disposition to demonstrate pain in their behaviour. Yet, they could still be in pain. Pain is conceivable without any associated pain behaviour. So pain can't be understood just in terms of dispositions to pain behaviour.

The logical behaviourist can reply that Putnam's example isn't coherent. For instance, it is impossible for super-spartans to learn about pain. As argued in ON ASCRIBING MENTAL STATES (p. 222), without behaviour that expresses the mental state, the concept of such a mental state can't be learned or used. Yet they need the concept to know what they are supposed to suppress!

Putnam replies that we can suppose that they are born 'fully enculturated' – with an understanding of their culture. If this is conceivable, then it is conceivable to experience pain, and to know that one is experiencing pain, without any behavioural dispositions at all.

'Brains and Behaviour'

Explain the claim that at least some mental states are conceivable without having any associated behavioural dispositions.

1) Outline logica
beh
one
Doe
beh
a su
of n

Key points: logical behaviourism

- Logical behaviourism is a non-reductive physicalist theory. It argues that mental properties cannot be reduced to physical properties, but can be analysed in terms of behavioural dispositions. Dispositions are how something will or is likely to behave under certain circumstances.
- A category mistake is treating a concept as belonging to a logical category that it doesn't belong to. Ryle argues that substance dualism rests on the category mistake of treating talk about the mind as talk about substances and causes, rather than behavioural dispositions.
- He argues that if substance dualism were true, we could not use mental concepts, since we could never know whether our attributions of mental states to others were true.
- In its strongest, reductive form, logical behaviourism (as analytical behaviourism) claims that talk about the mind and mental states can be reduced to talk about behaviour.
- Ryle defends a non-reductive form of logical behaviourism, arguing that statements attributing mental concepts are 'indefinitely heterogenous' and 'open'. They work at a higher level of generality than individual statements about behaviour. As disposition statements, they 'license' inferences, explanations and predictions of behaviour.
- Ryle argues that thinking is either part of what it is to act thoughtfully or internalised speaking. It is no part of the nature of thinking that it is 'private'.
- Logical behaviourism avoids the problem of other minds. Because mental states are just dispositions to behave, to know how others tend to behave is to know they have minds.
- Ryle argues that dispositions are not causes. Therefore, mental states don't cause behaviour, and our explanations of behaviour are not causal. This avoids the problem of mental causation.
- We can object, however, that this analysis of dispositions is incorrect, and that there are mental occurrences that cause behaviour and other mental occurrences.

- We can object that it is conceivable for minds to exist without bodies. Logical behaviourists can reply that it is inconceivable, and the belief derives from speculation about the mind that rests on a category mistake.
- The multiple realisability of mental states in behaviour indicates that the same mental state in different people can involve different behavioural dispositions, while the same behavioural disposition can involve different mental states. So mental states can't be behavioural dispositions.
- The logical behaviourist can reply that, first, this is not true – the same mental state involves very similar dispositions in different people. Second, when we analyse the whole pattern of behaviour, not just individual instances, we will see that different mental states involve different dispositions.
- The circularity objection argues that we cannot eliminate references to mental states when trying to analyse what behaviour a mental state is a disposition towards. How someone behaves, when they have a particular mental state, depends on the other mental states they have.
- Ryle can reply that his theory does not try to do this. Mental concepts are ineliminable because they work at a higher level of generality.
- We can object that logical behaviourism rejects the asymmetry between self-knowledge and knowledge of other people's minds.
- Ryle defends this rejection by arguing that 'consciousness' and 'introspection' are simply a matter of paying attention to ourselves, especially our internalised speech, just as we can pay attention to others and their speech. So we learn about our mental states and theirs in the same way.
- However, we can object that mental states have an 'inner', qualitative aspect, such as how they feel. This aspect of consciousness cannot be completely analysed in terms of behavioural dispositions.
- Logical behaviourists can respond that these felt aspects of mind must also be linked to behaviour, or we could never have learned to identify and describe them.

B. Mind-brain type identity theory

PHYSICALISM (p. 226) claims that everything that exists is dependent on something physical in order to exist. 'The mind' is not a separate substance, a 'thing'. It is more accurate to talk of mental properties – mental events, states and processes. We can then say that these properties are possessed not by a mind, but by a person or a brain, which are physical objects. While physicalists agree on this, they differ on what mental properties are and how they relate to physical properties.

Type identity theory

A swan is a bird and (usually) white – but what makes it a bird (a biological property) and what makes it white (a colour property) are different properties, though both are physical properties. So there are lots of different kinds of physical properties. We can ask, are mental properties a kind of physical property? For example, can thinking a thought, holding a belief, or feeling an itch be neurophysiological properties?

'Type identity theory' claims that mental properties *just are* physical properties. If we say that these physical properties are properties of a brain, then the theory is the mind–brain type identity theory. So this theory claims that thinking a thought or feeling an itch is *exactly the same thing* as certain neurons firing and having a belief is the same thing as certain neural connections existing. Any particular type of mental state is a particular type of brain state.

Mind–brain type identity theory was developed in the 1960s as neuroscience gathered pace. The evidence is that mental events and states are very closely dependent on the brain, so many people now think that 'the mind' is just 'the brain', and everything mental is actually neurophysiological.

However, this claim needs to be distinguished from the claim that mental states are *correlated* with brain states. For example, having a heart is correlated with having kidneys – every animal that has a heart has kidneys and vice versa. But hearts and kidneys are not the same thing! Or again, having a size and having a shape are correlated – everything that has a size has a shape and vice versa. But size and shape are distinct properties. So simply pointing out that everything that has a particular brain state also has a particular mental state doesn't show that mental states and brain states are the same thing. Correlation is not identity.

What is the difference between correlation and identity?

Neuroscientific evidence can establish correlations between mental and physical properties, but this does not establish the type identity theory. The mind–brain type identity theory doesn't claim that mental properties are correlated with certain physical properties. It says they are identical with them. But to demonstrate identity, we need to think philosophically, not scientifically.

The theory is called 'type' identity, because it claims that mental 'types' of thing (mental properties, states and events) are physical 'types' of thing – physical properties, states and events. Mental 'things'; turn out to be the same type of 'thing' as physical 'things'; i.e. mental properties are actually physical properties of the brain, mental states are brain states. They may not *seem* the same, but that's because we have different ways of knowing about these properties – through experience and through neuroscience. Many things turn out to be something they don't seem to be; e.g. solid objects are mostly empty space, water is just hydrogen and oxygen (who'd have guessed?).

Type identity theory is a form of 'reduction'. As we noted in Physicalism (p. 226), an 'ontological reduction' involves the claim that the things in one domain (e.g. mental things) are identical with some of the things in another domain. For example, we can argue that heat is just mean molecular kinetic energy. They are the same thing. Or again, although they seem different, electricity and magnetism are the same force, electromagnetism. Every mental property, type identity theory argues, is a certain physical property. There is *nothing more* to mental properties than being a certain kind of physical property.

Explain why the mind–brain type identity theory is a reductive theory of the mind.

ANTHOLOGY: SMART, 'SENSATIONS AND BRAIN PROCESSES', PP. 141-8

J. J. C. Smart defends the mind-brain type identity theory for sensations, but the theory can be generalised to other mental states and occurrences. The motivation for the theory, Smart says, is simply Ockham's razor. If there are no overwhelming arguments in favour of dualism, then we should reject the idea of distinct non physical substances or properties. Science indicates that the physical properties of the brain are a good candidate for what mental properties are.

Smart's claim is that '[s]ensations are nothing over and above brain processes' (145) – not correlated, but identical. To understand the theory, it is important to get clear on the identity claim. It is not a claim about language or concepts, but about reality. So the claim is not, for example, that the concept 'pain' *means* 'the firing of nociceptors' (a type of neuron involved in pain). The identity theorist is not offering definitions of the terms that we use. The identity claim is, therefore, not meant to be *analytically* true. 'Pain is the firing of nociceptors' (if it is true) is not true in the same way that 'bachelors are unmarried men' is true. The concepts 'pain' and 'the firing of nociceptors' remain distinct. The claim is that both concepts refer to *the same thing* in the world. The firing of nociceptors is what pain is. Two concepts, one property.

(Smart refers to this as a 'contingent' identity claim. We will discuss an argument that there can be no contingent identities in WHAT IS CONCEIVABLE MAY NOT BE POSSIBLE, p. 285. It is easiest to understand Smart as saying that his claim is a non-analytic, i.e. *synthetic*, identity claim.

Understanding the nature of the identity claim helps deal with objections. In particular, we might object that we can talk about sensations without knowing anything about brains. So they can't be the same thing. But, replies Smart, we can talk about lightning without knowing anything about electrical discharge – because the concepts are distinct. That doesn't show that lightning isn't electrical discharge. The same is true of 'sensation' and 'brain process'.

See *PHILOSOPHY FOR AS*, ANALYTIC SYNTHETIC, p. 97.

Explain the nature of the identity claim in the mind–brain identity theory.

Going further: identity theory and mental causation

We saw, in CAUSAL INTERACTION (p. 215) and LOGICAL BEHAVIOURISM AND MENTAL CAUSATION (p. 238), that both substance dualism and logical behaviourism face difficulties explaining mental causation. On the one hand, if minds and bodies are distinct, it is hard to see how events in one could cause events in the other. On the other hand, we do not want to deny that there is any mental causation.

Type identity theory claims to solve the problem. All mental properties are identical with brain properties. Mental occurrences are identical with neurons firing. Mental states that involve behavioural dispositions are neurological connections. And so all mental causation just becomes a form of physical causation. For my desire for food to cause my searching for food is just for certain physical properties of my brain to cause that behaviour. To say my decision to watch TV is the cause of my picking up the remote control is just to say that some particular event in my brain with certain physical properties is the cause of my picking up the remote control. Mental states and processes cause actions because they are physical states and processes.

Explain the type identity theory's account of mental causation.

Issues

The multiple realisability of mental states

ANTHOLOGY: PUTNAM, 'PSYCHOLOGICAL PREDICATES', §3

The most famous objection to the type identity theory was developed by Putnam. He argues that mental properties are not *identical* to physical properties because the *same* mental

Putnam later renamed this paper 'The Nature of Mental States'.

The term 'realisability' comes from FUNCTIONALISM. See the explanation on p. 258.

Briefly explain Putnam's objection from the multiple realisability of mental states.

Explain the differences between the empirical and a priori forms of the argument from multiple realisability.

property can be related to *different* physical properties. For example, the brain states that relate to pain may well be different in different species, in humans and birds, say, but pain is the same mental state. If this is true, there are creatures who, when they are in pain, have different physical properties from us when we are in pain. Therefore, 'being in pain' cannot be exactly the same thing as having a particular physical property. This is the argument from 'multiple realisability'.

As Putnam presents it, this is an empirical argument, but it is a very plausible one. It becomes yet more plausible when we consider other mental states and non-terrestrial species. If there are aliens, given that they evolved completely separately from us, if they have mental states, it is extremely unlikely that they will have the same physical states as us. But according to type identity theory, to have a particular mental state just is to have a particular physical state. So the theory is making a very implausible prediction.

The argument can also be rephrased as an a priori argument from conceivability:

1. It is conceivable, and therefore possible, for a being with quite a different physical constitution from us to have the same thoughts or sensations.
2. But it is inconceivable, and therefore impossible, for something both to have and not have a certain property.
3. Therefore, mental properties can't be the same as physical properties.

The identity theorist could respond that we should talk about 'human pain'; that this is a different property from 'dog pain'. Or again, if there are intelligent aliens who have thoughts, but different brains, we should talk of 'human thoughts' and 'alien thoughts'. But this doesn't seem plausible – pain is pain because of *how it feels*; thought is thought because of *what is thought*. A dog and a human being in pain share something in common, which we identify as the mental property 'being in pain'. If an alien believes that snow is white, and so do I, we have the same type of thought, whatever our physiology.

(This is not to say that there is *no* relation between mental and physical properties. It is just to argue that the relation is not identity. For instance, we can accept that mental states are correlated with brain states in human beings, while also allowing that in different species, the same type of mental state is correlated with a different type of physical state.)

Dualist arguments

THE CONCEIVABILITY ARGUMENT (P. 202)

We can rephrase the argument from multiple realisability in a different way again. It is conceivable that someone has a particular type of mental state without having the brain state with which, the identity theory claims, it is identical. Therefore, the mental state can exist in the absence of the brain state. Therefore, it cannot be the brain state.

THE DIVISIBILITY ARGUMENT (P. 203)

Descartes' divisibility argument also provides grounds to object to the mind–brain type identity theory. The mind cannot be identical to the brain because the mind is not divisible while the brain is.

However, type identity theorists can present the objection that we considered previously, namely that the divisibility argument assumes that the mind is a 'thing' which can be divisible or not. This assumption begs the question against the type identity theory, which maintains that the 'mind' should be understood in terms of mental properties possessed by the brain. There are many properties that it does not make sense to talk of as literally spatially divisible or not. For instance, the brain has a particular temperature. 'Being 35 degrees Celsius' is not a spatially divisible property, yet it is a physical property. So even if mental properties are not spatially divisible, they could still be identical with physical properties of the brain.

The location problem

We can, however, develop the thought underlying the divisibility argument.

1. If mental states are identical to brain states, then they must share all their properties in common. This is Leibniz's principle of the

> We will discuss the implications for the type identity theory of the arguments for property dualism in THE KNOWLEDGE ARGUMENT, p. 268 and THE 'PHILOSOPHICAL ZOMBIES' ARGUMENT, p. 279.

> Explain the mind–brain type identity theory and one objection to it.

indiscernibility of identicals: if 'two' things are really 'one' thing, then the 'two' things must be indiscernible; i.e. you cannot have quantitative identity without qualitative identity.

2.   Second, a brain state, understood as the firing of particular neurons in the brain or the existence of certain neural connections, has certain spatial properties. In particular, it has a precise location in space, occurring in a certain part of the brain or as a certain pattern or shape across many parts of the brain. We can also talk about the spatial relations (up, down, left, right) between the neurons involved and therefore between 'parts' of the brain state. We can also talk about the spatial relations between one brain state and another. Brain states of the prefrontal and frontal cortices occur a few inches closer to your forehead than brain states of the visual cortex.

3.   However, mental states *do not* have such spatial locations. For example, neuroscientists have associated activity in the prefrontal and frontal cortices with thoughts and activity in the visual cortex with visual experience. But my thoughts are not literally a few inches closer to my forehead than my visual experience! Or again, my hopes are not literally about 18 inches above my heart. Mental states are not spatially located in the same sense that brain states are.

4.   Therefore, mental states cannot be identical with brain states.

Put more briefly,

1.   If mental states are identical to brain states, then they must share all their properties in common.

2.   Brain states have a precise spatial location, and stand in spatial relations to both other spatial locations and other physical objects.

3.   Mental states are not located in space, at least in the same way.

4.   Therefore, mental states are not brain states.

Explain the location problem.

ANTHOLOGY: SMART, 'SENSATIONS AND BRAIN PROCESSES', PP. 150-2

Smart considers a version of this objection. His response is that because we don't currently *say* that experiences have any spatial properties, attributing spatial properties to them sounds odd. But it is an empirical discovery that mental states, in fact, have these properties. If they are brain states, then they do have a spatial location. The objection begs the question.

We can reply, however, that this can't be right, because *it makes no sense* to say that my thoughts are, e.g., closer to my auditory experiences than to my visual experiences, or my fears are 2 feet away from my stomach. It is simply *grammatically incorrect*.

Smart replies that this is just a matter of linguistic convention. We could add to our current grammatical rules to allow us to talk of experiences in spatial terms.

Explain Smart's solution to the location problem.

Ryle would object that Smart's solution involves a CATEGORY MISTAKE (p. 230). It is not 'merely' a linguistic convention that we don't talk about the spatial location of thoughts or visual experiences. We should no more accept such claims than the claim that the number '4' is a green triangle. This can't be a matter of empirical discovery, because numbers are not the kind of thing that can take shape. Likewise, mental states are not the kind of thing that can have precise spatial locations. We might want to say that there is a *correlation* between a particular mental state and a brain state that has a spatial location. But this doesn't show that the mental state itself is spatially located.

The identity theorist can reply that we should change our understanding of what 'makes sense' on the basis of scientific discoveries. For instance, they might argue that the correlation between mental states and brain states is best explained by their identity. If we reject type identity theory, our metaphysics becomes more complicated – we cannot reduce mental properties to physical properties.

1) Can it make sense to talk about the spatial location of mental states? 2) Are mental states nothing over and above brain states?

Key points: mind-brain type identity theory

- The type identity theory claims that not only is there just one kind of substance, that identified by physics, but that mental properties are, in fact, physical properties. This identity claim reduces mental properties to physical ones; i.e. what it is to be a particular mental property is to be a particular physical property.
- The identity claim is not that mental concepts mean the same as physical concepts, but that two distinct mental and physical concepts pick out one and the same property.
- The appeal of the theory is that it is simpler than other theories. It explains the mind without appealing to anything beyond physical properties. It also explains how mental causation is possible – it is simply physical causation.
- However, the argument from multiple realisability says that it is (empirically or conceptually) possible for two creatures to have the same mental property, e.g. 'being in pain', but have different physical properties. Therefore, the mental property is not (or cannot be) identical to any physical property.
- The location problem raises the objection that brain states have specific spatial locations and spatial relationships to other physical states. However, mental states do not. Therefore, by Leibniz's principle of the indiscernibility of identicals, mental states cannot be brain states.
- Smart replies that it begs the question against the type identity theory to assume that mental states have no spatial properties. This is an empirical discovery.
- We can reply that it makes no sense (or it is a category mistake) to say that mental states have spatial properties, but Smart responds that this is just a matter of linguistic convention.

C. Functionalism

The theory

According to functionalism, we can give an analysis of what mental states are in terms of their 'inputs' and 'outputs'. Each mental state consists of a disposition to behave in particular ways and have certain other mental states, given certain inputs from the senses and certain other mental states. In the most popular form of functionalism, causal role functionalism, inputs and outputs are understood causally. Different mental states differ in their typical inputs and outputs; e.g. the typical causes and effects of pain are quite different from the typical causes and effects of a belief that snow is white.

The complete description of the mental state's outputs, for each possible set of inputs, is the description of its *function*. It describes what the mental state does. Functionalism claims that mental states just are functional states. What it is to be a mental state is just to be a state with certain causal relations to stimuli, behaviour and other mental states.

Functionalism is a descendant of LOGICAL BEHAVIOURISM (p. 229). But instead of talking of dispositions to behave in certain ways in certain circumstances, functionalism talks of dispositions to behave *and have other mental states*, given certain sensory inputs *and other mental states*. It explicitly recognises that mental states cannot be understood just in terms of behaviour for two reasons. First, mental states often cause other mental states; e.g. pain normally causes the belief that one is in pain. Second, what behaviour a mental state will cause depends on other mental states. So the definition of one mental state will have to mention other mental states. This avoids the objections to logical behaviourism discussed in CIRCULARITY AND MULTIPLE REALISABILITY OF MENTAL STATES IN BEHAVIOUR (p. 240).

Functionalism also avoids the objection to the mind–brain type identity theory from THE MULTIPLE REALISABILITY OF MENTAL STATES (p. 251). The property of 'having the function x' is a property that can occur in many different physical things with different physical configurations. For example, 'being an eye' is a functional property. There are lots of different types of eyes that work in different ways and have different physical properties. What makes them all eyes is what they do – transduce light waves into neural signals to enable an organism to navigate its environment. 'Being a poison' is also a functional property. There are lots of different sorts of poisons that work in different ways and are made of different chemicals. Or to switch from biology to engineering, 'being a carburettor' is also a functional property.

The functionalist argues that 'being in pain' (and each other mental property) is also a functional property. There may be lots of different

How does
. functionalism
differ from
behaviourism and
from type identity
theory?

states, e.g. different brain states, that have this functional property. This can vary from one species to another. But as long as some state of the creature has the function that defines pain – given certain inputs, it causes certain outputs – then the creature is in pain. Functionalism reduces mental properties to functional properties.

Going further: functionalism and mental causation

What does functionalism say about mental causation? Are mental states causal or not? Causal role functionalism says they are. Functions should be understood in terms of causal inputs and outputs. A mental state has a particular causal role in causing other mental states, and together with other mental states, in causing behaviour. We identify mental states by their causal role. Therefore, causal role functionalism claims that a mental state is a state with a particular causal role. That means that someone can only have a particular mental state if they have some 'inner' state, e.g. some state of their brain, that plays just that causal role.

However, there are other forms of functionalism that understand functions non-causally, in a very similar way to how Ryle understands dispositions. On this view, whether someone has a particular functional property is *just* a matter of whether certain hypothetical statements are true about them or not, and whether we can explain and predict their behaviour using such statements. These forms of functionalism do not usually make any claims about 'inner' states that correspond to the functions we identify with our talk of mental states.

On causal role functionalism, the 'inner' state 'realises' the function – it has that functional property. Using our earlier examples, some arrangement of cells realises the functional property of being an eye; some chemical state or other realises 'being a poison'. In each instance, the causal role is played by some biological or biochemical state or other. This can vary from one case to another. Hence, 'being an eye' is 'multiply realisable'. The occurrence of that arrangement of cells is the

Dennett, *The Intentional Stance*

functional property in that instance – it is the occurrence of a state with the causal role that identifies the property 'being an eye'.

Likewise, mental states such as 'being in pain' are realised by particular states of the creature or person playing a particular causal role. Again, which states these are doesn't tell us anything essential about the mental state, which is understood just in terms of the causal role. Things with very different states – different constitutions or internal organisation – can realise the same mental states as long as they are states with the same causal roles. On each occasion, the occurrence of the state with that functional role is the occurrence of the mental state.

> Explain causal role functionalism.

Functionalism and physicalism

If a mental state is just a state playing a certain kind of function, what is the metaphysical nature of this state? It could be anything, say functionalists. Functionalism analyses mental states in terms of what they *do*, not in terms of the nature of the *substance* that realises those mental states. Mental states could be realised by physical states, e.g. of the brain, or they could be realised by states in a distinct mental substance. Functionalism is logically compatible with both substance dualism and physicalism.

However, most functionalists are physicalists. On causal role functionalism, if physicalism is true, then it is a physical substance and physical states that realise mental states, e.g. brain states. On this view, what it is for a thought to cause behaviour or another thought is for the brain state that realises the functional role of the thought to cause behaviour or another thought.

Functionalism reduces mental properties to functional properties; but it does not reduce them to physical properties. As we've seen, functional properties occur throughout science, e.g. being an eye. These functional properties are not themselves physical properties, because there are lots of different ways in which eyes can be constituted physically. However, functional properties are properties which are realised by physical properties operating in causal relationships. They are not a completely new kind of property. So functionalism is not a form of PROPERTY DUALISM (p. 266).

> Explain how functionalism can be a physicalist theory.

Issues

Objections to functionalism take the form of arguments that we cannot reduce mental properties to functional properties. We will focus on certain distinctive properties of consciousness sometimes called 'qualia'.

Qualia

We ended the last objection to logical behaviourism, THE CONCEIVABILITY OF MENTAL STATES WITHOUT ASSOCIATED BEHAVIOUR (p. 245), by talking about the distinctive qualities of certain conscious experiences. A similar objection applies to functionalism.

read

The idea of 'qualia' (single: 'quale') starts with the idea of 'phenomenal consciousness'. Consciousness, especially the sort of consciousness involved in perception, sensation and emotion, has a 'feel' to it, a distinctive 'experiential quality'. The phrase often used to try to capture this experiential quality is 'what it is like'. There is something it is like to taste beer, to see a red rose, to feel sad.

read

'What it is like' here isn't meant to compare the experience to others, it is meant to pick out how the experience is for the subject. When we make comparisons between experiences (e.g. 'Seeing a red rose is like seeing a ripe tomato'), we do so *in virtue of* what it is like to see a red rose in the sense meant here. It is the experience of redness that allows us to compare roses and tomatoes; and there is something it is like to experience redness.

We can call the properties of an experience which give it its distinctive experiential quality 'phenomenal properties'. We are aware of these properties through consciousness and introspection, by turning our attention to our conscious experiences themselves.

Some people think qualia just are phenomenal properties. But this isn't quite accurate. Phenomenal properties are only qualia if they are *intrinsic, non-representational* properties of experience. What does this mean?

An intrinsic property is one that its possessor (in this case, the experience) has in and of its own, not in virtue of its relations to anything else. Think of the smell of coffee. It is the smell 'of coffee' because of its relation to the substance of coffee. That it is 'of coffee' is not an intrinsic property. However, what makes that smell the smell that it is, is not the

> **?** What are 'phenomenal properties'?

fact that it is caused by coffee. Something else could cause the *same* smell as the smell caused by coffee. How that smell smells is an intrinsic property, because it would be that smell even if it wasn't caused by coffee. The smell can't be analysed just in terms of what causes it. Another example: pain wouldn't be pain if it didn't *feel* painful, whatever it is or isn't caused by. Intrinsic properties of experience, then, fix the *identity* of the experience. So people who believe in qualia argue.

Representational properties are properties of a mental state that enable it to represent what it does. What a mental state represents is what it is 'about' (in a loose sense); e.g. the belief that Paris is the capital of France is about Paris, the desire for chocolate is about chocolate, and the smell of coffee is 'about' coffee, how coffee smells. Representational properties, then, depend on the way the mental state 'hooks up' to the world. So they are relational rather than intrinsic properties. So qualia, because they are intrinsic properties, are non-representational properties.

What are qualia?

But do qualia exist? Are phenomenal properties intrinsic and non-representational, or can they be analysed in terms of their relations to other things? The claim that qualia are the best way to understand phenomenal properties is the main objection facing functionalism (it is also the basis of a number of arguments in favour of PROPERTY DUALISM, p. 266). The objection is this: if phenomenal properties are qualia, then they cannot be completely understood in terms of their causal roles, because causal roles are relational properties, not intrinsic properties. If they can't be understood in terms of their causal roles, they can't be functional states. So functionalism can't explain phenomenal consciousness.

1. Qualia, by definition, are intrinsic, non-representational properties of conscious mental states.
2. Intrinsic, non-representational properties cannot, by definition, be completely analysed in terms of their causal roles.
3. Therefore, if qualia exist, some mental properties cannot be analysed in terms of their causal roles.
4. Functionalism claims that all mental properties are functional properties which can be completely analysed in terms of their causal roles.
5. Therefore, if qualia exist, functionalism is false.
6. Qualia exist.
7. Therefore, functionalism is false.

The controversial premise is (6). This maintains that there is something about consciousness – how pain feels, how red looks, how a rose smells – that can't be analysed in terms of functions. Yes, of course, how pain feels is important to what it causes; e.g. it causes you to cry out or withdraw your hand from the fire. But the feeling of the pain isn't *just* these causal relations. The following two objections try to establish this.

The possibility of a functional duplicate with different qualia

We can show that phenomenal properties cannot be understood just in terms of their functions if we can show that it is possible for two people to have states with identical functions but different phenomenal properties. The most popular version of this objection is known as the case of 'inverted qualia'.

Suppose that you and I are looking at ripe tomatoes and fresh grass. Because we have grown up in the same linguistic community, we have learned to use the word 'red' to describe the tomatoes and 'green' to describe the grass. So we both say that the tomatoes are red, the grass is green. But the particular way that tomatoes seem to me is the way that grass looks to you, and vice versa. Functionally, we are identical, and yet we have different colour experiences. 'The way grass looks to you' and 'the way grass looks to me' are functionally identical; both are caused by the same inputs (grass) and cause the same outputs (e.g. saying 'grass is green'). But they are not identical in terms of their intrinsic properties. They pick out different qualia.

Of course, we might not *know* whether this is true or not. But that is irrelevant. The objection is that inverted qualia are *possible*. If functionalism were true, inverted qualia would be impossible. So functionalism is false.

The functionalist can reply that in the case described, you and I are *not*, in fact, functionally identical. There are going to be small, but very important, differences, because the causal relations of phenomenal properties are very complex. For example, 'red' is a warm colour, 'green' a cool colour. If you see grass the way I see tomatoes, will you describe the colour of the grass as 'warm'? To say there is no functional difference between you and me, yet we see colours differently, we have to change a great deal (you have to think of (what I call) green as a warm colour, and

> **Briefly explain the objection to functionalism from inverted qualia.**

so on). If we specify the functional role of 'red' in enough detail, maybe we'll see that whatever plays that functional role must be the phenomenal property 'red' and can't be 'green'. It seems like we can conceive of inverted qualia, but in fact, what we have described is impossible.

Are inverted qualia possible?

The possibility of a functional duplicate with no qualia

The second objection tries to show that phenomenal properties cannot be understood just in terms of their functions because it is possible for two systems to have states with identical functions but one system (you, say) has phenomenal properties, but the other does not. The most popular version of this objection is Ned Block's 'Chinese mind' scenario.

ANTHOLOGY: BLOCK, 'TROUBLES WITH FUNCTIONALISM', §1.2

Suppose we have a complete functional description of your mental states. For each and every one of your mental states, we have an input–output analysis (Block calls this a 'machine table'). Now imagine that a human body, like yours, is connected up not to a brain but to the whole population of China. Each Chinese person plays the equivalent functional role of a neuron in your brain (Block picks China because, he claims, the population of China is roughly equal to the number of neurons in the brain). The Chinese are linked up to each other by two-way radios, and some of these are linked up to the input and output nerves of the body. Then, for a short time, the Chinese population recreates the functioning of your brain.

According to functionalism, this should create a mind; but it is very difficult to believe that there would be a 'Chinese consciousness'. If the Chinese system replicated the state of my brain when I feel pain, would something be in pain? What? The objection is that the Chinese system, although it duplicates your functioning, can't duplicate your mind, because some mental states are qualia, and the system can't have qualia because they are not functional states.

Functionalists can reply that the 'Chinese mind' won't be functionally identical to you. For instance, the Chinese mind could be disrupted by things that your mind isn't disrupted by,

Briefly explain the 'Chinese mind' objection to functionalism.

e.g. the radios running out of batteries or the system being disrupted by bad weather. True, but irrelevant, says Block. First, although this *could* happen, if it doesn't, then we have functional duplication, and the functionalist must say there is a 'Chinese consciousness'. Second, these don't count as inputs or outputs, any more than having a brain tumour counts as an 'input' to our mental states. It is not part of their functioning, but a disruption of it.

Functionalists can object that the Chinese system is much slower than our brains. But, replies Block, why should this matter for whether it has mental states? Couldn't there be much slower minds than ours? In any case, this is just an objection about what is physically possible. A Chinese system that operated as fast as our brains is still metaphysically possible.

read

? Do qualia exist?

A PHYSICALIST RESPONSE

If Block's objection works, then not *everything* about the mind can be explained in terms of functions. But perhaps we can combine functionalism and the type identity theory to argue as follows.

Functionalism provides an accurate account of all mental states except for phenomenal consciousness, which involves qualia. The reason for this is that the intrinsic properties of qualia depend on the specific *physical* properties of the system that realises the functional states. How pain feels to us isn't (just) a matter of what causes it and what effects it has, it also depends on our physiology and the specific chemicals in our brains. So what mental states something has depend on its functional properties *and* its intrinsic physical properties. Mental states are still nothing more than physical states playing a functional role. A physical, functional duplicate of a person with consciousness will have the same conscious states.

As we discuss next, property dualism challenges this claim.

? Are all mental states functional states?

Key points: functionalism

- Functionalism claims that mental properties are functional properties, defined in terms of their typical inputs and outputs (which may include other mental states). A mental state is just a state with a particular functional property.
- Causal role functionalism interprets 'function' as the role played in a network of causes and effects. A mental state can be 'realised' by any state that plays that causal role. Other types of functionalism understand 'function' non-causally.
- Functionalism avoids the objection to the type identity theory from multiple realisability. A functional property (and so mental properties) can be realised by various physical (or even non-physical) properties. Functionalism is compatible with substance dualism, although most functionalists are physicalists.
- Phenomenal properties are those subjective aspects of experience that we try to capture by saying 'what it is like' to have this or that experience.
- Some philosophers argue that phenomenal properties are qualia, i.e. intrinsic, non-representational properties of experience. If they are, then functionalism cannot be a complete theory of the mind, as qualia are not functional properties.
- The thought experiments of inverted qualia and the Chinese 'mind' are designed to show that phenomenal properties are not functional properties, but qualia.
- Some functionalists reply that if we specify the functional role of experiences of pain or seeing red in enough detail, the thought experiments fail. Others argue that phenomenal properties are fixed by functional *and physical* properties, taken together.

Summary: materialism

In this section on materialism, we have looked at three theories:

1. Logical behaviourism: mental states are dispositions to behave in certain ways under certain circumstances.

2. Mind–brain type identity theory: mental states are identical with brain states.
3. Functionalism: mental states are dispositions to behave in particular ways and have certain other mental states, given certain inputs from the senses and certain other mental states.

In our discussion and evaluation of these theories, we have looked at the following issues:

1. What is physicalism? What is the difference between reductive and non-reductive physicalism?
2. What is a category mistake? Do either substance dualism and/or the mind–brain type identity theory make category mistakes?
3. Can we analyse mental states in terms of dispositions completely and without circularity?
4. Are mental states causes?
5. How do we know our own minds?
6. Are mental states 'multiply realisable'?
7. Could mental states have spatial locations?
8. Is there something about what it is like to have conscious experiences that cannot be analysed in terms of either behaviour or functions?

III. Dualism (again)

A. Property dualism

The theory

Property dualism is the view that, although there is just one kind of substance, physical substance, there are two fundamentally different kinds of property, mental and physical. Mental properties are possessed by physical substances; but at least some mental properties do not depend on physical properties in the way physicalism claims. The form of property dualism that is most discussed defends property dualism for phenomenal properties of consciousness. Property dualism claims that these properties, such as pain, the smell of coffee, the visual experience of a red rose, the feeling of joy, and so on, can't be reduced to physical, behavioural or functional properties. These properties, at least, are a completely new, irreducible type of property.

Property dualism rejects PHYSICALISM (p. 226). First, it argues that the properties identified by physics do not form the *complete* fundamental nature of the universe, because in addition, there are properties of consciousness. Physics misses something fundamental. When all the physical properties of the world are finalised, there is still work to be done – properties of consciousness have not been fixed. Property dualists are happy to allow that there may be correlations, even natural (though not physical) laws that connect particular physical and mental properties. But, they argue, mental properties are nevertheless distinct – an entirely new kind of property in the world. Second, as we will see in INTERACTIONIST (PROPERTY) DUALISM (p. 295), some property dualists argue that these mental properties have their own causal powers, which can affect physical events. This threatens physicalism's claim that non–physical causes do not contribute to the way the physical world changes over time.

> **?** What is property dualism?

ANTHOLOGY: CHALMERS, 'CONSCIOUSNESS AND ITS PLACE IN NATURE', §§2, 3.1

Chalmers' 'Consciousness and Its Place in Nature' provides a very thorough overview of the different theories about consciousness. Much of it is very detailed and complicated, so as usual, I will discuss just those sections and those arguments that are most relevant.

> This article is also reprinted as Chalmers, *The Character of Consciousness*, Ch. 5.

Elsewhere, Chalmers distinguishes between what he calls the 'easy' and the 'hard' problems of consciousness. The 'easy' problem involves analysing and explaining the functions of consciousness, e.g. the facts that we can consciously control our behaviour, report on our mental states, and focus our attention. Chalmers thinks that understanding how the brain works will eventually provide the solutions. So this doesn't threaten physicalism. The 'hard' problem relates to the phenomenal properties of consciousness, what it is like to undergo conscious experiences. How and why are certain physical processes in the brain associated with such experiences?

The physicalist says that these conscious experiences *just are* certain physical processes or certain physical states playing a particular functional role. But, Chalmers argues, a physical account of something can only explain its physical structure and function – how something is constituted and how it works. And this, he objects, is not enough to explain phenomenal consciousness. Such explanations miss out how experiences 'feel', what it is like to undergo them, their subjective or first-personal aspect. There is more to phenomenal consciousness than structure and function.

Outline and explain the differences between the 'easy' and 'hard' problems of consciousness.

The knowledge argument

avoids problem of qualia?

ANTHOLOGY: JACKSON, 'EPIPHENOMENAL QUALIA', §1

Frank Jackson defends property dualism on the basis of his 'knowledge argument'. He describes the following scenario. Suppose there is a neuroscientist, Mary, who has lived all her life in a room in which everything is black and white. She has never seen any colour other than black, white and shades of grey. However, she has specialised in the science of vision, and through textbooks and black-and-white TV, she has come to know every physical fact there is to know about colour vision – everything about the properties of light, everything about the eye, everything about the nerves and the brain related to vision. So, Mary knows all the physical information there is to know about what happens when we see a ripe tomato. She is then let out of the black-and-white room, and comes to see something red for the first time. Does she learn something new?

Jackson claims that 'it seems just obvious' that she will. She will learn about what it is like to see the colour red. And so she learns something new about our visual experience of the world. However, we said that she knew all the physical facts while she was in the room. So not all the facts are physical facts. It is possible to know all about the physical properties of the brain involved in having an experience and yet not know about the qualia.

1. Mary knows all the physical facts about seeing colours before being released from her black-and-white room.
2. On being released, she learns new facts about seeing colours.
3. Therefore, not all facts are physical facts.
4. Therefore, phenomenal properties are non-physical and physicalism is false.

By 'all the physical facts', Jackson means not only what we already know about physics and neurophysiology. Mary knows all the physical facts as discovered by a *completed* physics and neuroscience. Furthermore, she has worked out all the causal and functional facts that are entailed by these facts. Because physicalism claims that the world is entirely physical (if we include causal and functional properties), it must claim that to have complete physical knowledge is to have complete knowledge. But no amount of physical information can enable Mary to know what it is like to see a ripe tomato.

In 'What Mary Didn't Know', Jackson puts the argument in another form, which may help to clarify it. Let's generalise Mary's knowledge to everything physical.

1. Mary (before her release) knows everything physical there is to know about other people.
2. Mary (before her release) does not know everything there is to know about other people (because she *learns* something about them on her release).
3. Therefore, there are truths about other people (and herself) which escape the physicalist story.

Explain Jackson's knowledge argument against physicalism.

We can add:

4. Therefore, phenomenal properties are non-physical and physicalism is false.

The knowledge argument as a dualist argument against other theories

The syllabus indicates that dualist arguments in general should be considered as objections to logical behaviourism and the mind–brain type identity theory, and that we should also consider the knowledge argument as applied to functional facts.

The knowledge argument attacks the mind–brain identity theory directly. The identity theory claims that sensations just are brain processes, so it follows that if Mary knows all about brain processes, she knows everything there is to know about sensations. This is precisely the claim that the knowledge argument attacks.

The argument works against functionalism in the same way. Functionalism claims that phenomenal properties are functional properties (or functional + physical properties). When Jackson says that Mary knows all the physical facts, he includes the functional facts. Mary knows exactly how the brain functions during an experience of seeing red. But the argument is meant to show that Mary doesn't know all there is to know about such an experience, so phenomenal properties are not just functional (+ physical) properties, and functionalism is wrong.

The argument also works the same way against analytical behaviourism, which claims that we can reduce talk of colour experiences to talk of behavioural dispositions. But, the knowledge argument claims, Mary knows all about behavioural dispositions, since these are functional facts, but she doesn't know all about colour experiences, because she doesn't know what it is like to experience colour.

Ryle would probably reject the way that Jackson describes Mary's experience. It is a mistake to talk about 'what it is like' to experience red. Experiencing red is not a 'what'. To experience red is just to pay attention to the colour of something red, and to be conscious of doing this is just to be ready to say what you are thinking or feeling.

See RYLE ON CONSCIOUSNESS p. 243.

We can respond that Mary can know that when someone experiences red, they pay attention to the colour and are ready to express their thoughts, and yet she still won't know, the knowledge argument claims, everything there is to know about experiencing red. So experiencing red can't be fully understood in the terms Ryle proposes.

Issues for the knowledge argument

Mary gains ability knowledge, not new propositional knowledge

A first objection points out that there is more than one meaning of 'to know', more than one kind of knowledge. We can and should accept that Mary gains new knowledge when she sees red for the first time. But this doesn't mean that she gains knowledge of some new *fact*. We can argue that instead of gaining knowledge of a proposition (e.g. 'that red looks like this'), Mary gains *know-how* – the knowledge involved in certain abilities. For instance, to see red for the first time is to gain the ability to know how to imagine or recognise red.

Suppose that seeing red gives us these abilities. Are such abilities *all* that is involved in knowing what it is like to see red, Jackson asks in 'What Mary Didn't Know'? Suppose Mary wonders whether what it is like for others to see red is the same as what it is like for her. She isn't wondering about her abilities to imagine and recognise red. She is wondering about the truth of a proposition. So when Mary first learns what it is like to see red, she *does* gain knowledge of a new fact.

Is the objection even right to think that knowing what it is like to see red involves knowing how to imagine red? Suppose there is someone who (for whatever reason) has no ability to imagine seeing red. Now suppose this person looks attentively at something red. While they look at red, they know what is it like to see red. And yet they cannot imagine seeing red. This shows that the ability to imagine is not necessary for knowing what it is like to see red. Now suppose someone else has the most amazing ability to imagine seeing colours. They are told that there is a shade of red, e.g. burgundy, that is between plum red and tomato red. They are now *able* to imagine burgundy, but as long as they don't *actually* imagine burgundy, they still don't know what it is like to see burgundy. This shows that the ability to imagine a colour is not sufficient

Explain one physicalist account of phenomenal consciousness and how the knowledge argument is an objection to it.

Commentary on the anthology text, Jackson's 'What Mary Didn't Know', is integrated into the discussion.

On types of knowledge, see *Philosophy for AS*, TERMINOLOGY, p. 74.

to know what it is like to see it. (We can make similar arguments for recognising colours.)

If the ability to imagine seeing red is neither necessary nor sufficient for knowing what it is like to see red, then when Mary comes to know what it is like to see red, she learns more than simply knowing how to imagine seeing red. The objection fails to show that Mary does not learn a new fact. It fails to show that the knowledge argument is mistaken.

? Is Mary's learning what it is like to see red just her gaining new abilities?

Mary gains acquaintance knowledge, not new propositional knowledge

A second objection argues that Mary gains a different kind of knowledge again, not propositional knowledge (knowing that), but not ability knowledge (knowing how) either. Instead, she gains 'acquaintance knowledge' – a direct awareness of the thing. To see red is a *direct* apprehension of red, as contrasted with descriptions of seeing red. How does the objection work?

Explain the claim that when Mary leaves her room, she gains acquaintance knowledge but not new propositional knowledge. Explain why this claim defends physicalism against the knowledge argument.

Suppose that what it is like to see red is a physical property of the visual experience, which itself is a physical process. In other words, the phenomenal property of what it is like to see red is some property of the brain (type identity). Mary can then know all about this physical property, about what it is, when it occurs, and so, before she leaves the room. However, she is not *acquainted* with the property – she doesn't have direct knowledge of it because *her brain has never itself had this property.* When she sees red, this property occurs in her brain and she becomes acquainted with it. She gains new knowledge, but she hasn't learned any new fact. She already knew all about this property before she left the room.

There are two possible responses to this. First, we can argue that acquaintance knowledge involves propositional knowledge. What it is to be acquainted with red is to know *that seeing red is like this* (having the experience). Becoming acquainted with red involves learning some new fact. So Mary does learn a new, and therefore non-physical, fact when she becomes acquainted with red. So what it is like to experience red can't simply be a physical property of the brain.

Jackson gives a different response in 'What Mary Didn't Know'. The objection misunderstands the argument. He agrees that, of course,

Mary doesn't have acquaintance knowledge of what it is like to see red. As the objection claims, to have such acquaintance knowledge, she would need to have direct experience of seeing red. But the knowledge argument isn't about *Mary's* experience. The argument is that Mary didn't know everything about *other people's* experiences before she left the room, even though she knew everything physical about their experiences. Mary doesn't know what it is like for anyone to experience red. This is a *fact* about experiences that Mary doesn't know. When Mary leaves the room, she realises how impoverished her conception of people's colour experiences has been. So there are facts about other people's experiences of seeing red that Mary learns.

Does Mary learn more than acquaintance knowledge about what it is like to see red?

There is more than one way of knowing the same physical fact

A third objection to Jackson's argument distinguishes between two ways we might talk about 'facts'. Suppose I know that there is water in the glass. Is that the same as knowing that there is H_2O in the glass? No – because someone may know one of these truths without knowing the other. Someone can have the concept of 'water' without having the concept of 'H_2O'. Or again, someone may have both concepts, but not know that water and H_2O are the same thing. So we can say that to know that there is water in the glass and to know that there is H_2O in the glass is to know two different facts. In this sense of 'fact', we count facts in terms of concepts.

However, in another sense of 'fact', the fact that there is water in the glass *just is* the fact that there is H_2O in the glass. Both of these claims are made true by just one state of affairs in the world. In this sense of 'fact', we count facts in terms of how the world is, not how we think about it.

We can now apply this to the knowledge argument. Before leaving the room, Mary has a concept of red in physical terms – wavelengths of light, neurons firing, and so on. Call this the 'physical' or again a 'theoretical' concept of red. We can contrast this with a 'phenomenal' concept of red. A phenomenal concept of something is the concept by which you recognise something when you experience or perceive it. So we gain the phenomenal concept of red by seeing red.

When Mary comes out the room and sees red, she acquires the phenomenal concept of red for the first time. She is now able to think about red in a new way, in terms of what it is like to see red. She couldn't know what it is like to see red before because she didn't have the phenomenal concept. But, we can claim, the phenomenal concept of red is a concept of *the same thing* that her physical concept is a concept of – they are two different concepts of a physical property of the brain (like 'water' and 'H$_2$O' are two concepts of the same physical substance). Mary gains knowledge of a new fact in one sense (because she gains a new concept) but not in the other sense (since she already knew about the property).

Let us accept that the knowledge argument shows that there are different ways of thinking about physical things, some of which depend on experiencing, rather than describing. To know what it is like to see red, you need to have the phenomenal concept of red, and this you can only gain from experience. So Mary gains knowledge of a new fact, in the sense of fact that relates to concepts.

However, and this is the objection, physicalism and property dualism are claims about what exists. They are claims about *properties*, not about concepts. The knowledge argument does *not* show that Mary gains knowledge of a new property. It doesn't show that Mary gains knowledge of a new fact in the sense of learning about something in the world she didn't know about before. It doesn't show that what it is like to see red cannot be a physical property. So the argument fails to show that there are any non-physical properties. So it fails to show that physicalism is false.

> Explain the claim that Mary learns a new concept when leaving her room, but this is no threat to physicalism.

All physical knowledge would include knowledge of qualia

> We discuss this further in JACKSON, 'POSTSCRIPT ON "WHAT MARY DIDN'T KNOW"', p. 288.

The objections above all accept the claim that Mary learns something when first leaving her room. But a fourth objection denies this. If Mary really did know *everything* about seeing red, she would not learn anything when she first sees red. The experience of seeing red is nothing more than highly detailed knowledge of what it is to see red, and Mary already has this highly detailed knowledge.

This objection is, however, counter-intuitive. It requires that Mary is able to work out what it is like to experience a colour without ever having seen one. But, we might argue, we cannot describe such experiences (seeing red) so fully as to know what it is like to experience them without actually doing so. No one can know what it is like to see red without actually ever having seen something red.

In 'What Mary Didn't Know', Jackson points out that we can even allow that Mary could *imagine* what it is like to see red before she leaves her room. Imagining something is not the same as knowing it. You only have to imagine what something is like if you *don't already know*. If Mary knows all the physical facts, and these were all the facts there are, then she *would* know what it is like to see red, so she wouldn't have to imagine it. So even if Mary can imagine what it is like to see red, she still doesn't *know* what it is like.

Is this right, though? This is our intuition, but is there an argument to support it? We don't really know what knowing *all* the physical facts about seeing colours would involve. Perhaps Mary will be entirely unsurprised at seeing red – she already knew what it would be like. Is it impossible for any amount of information describing the experience to convey it? This objection claims that there is, in principle, a complete analysis of phenomenal properties in physical and functional terms.

> 1) Explain the claim that knowledge of all physical facts would include knowledge of phenomenal properties. 2) Explain the knowledge argument and one objection to it.

ANTHOLOGY: JACKSON, 'POSTSCRIPT ON QUALIA'

Going further: Jackson's change of mind

In 1998, Jackson accepted this objection and so concluded that the knowledge argument doesn't work after all.

His change of mind is as controversial as the original argument. Many philosophers prefer the solution that there is more than one way of knowing the same physical fact. That solution claims that it is impossible to work out what an experience is like from theoretical knowledge about it, because knowing what an experience is like requires a phenomenal concept, and that requires actually having the experience. But Jackson maintains that it is possible, from complete knowledge of the physical facts, to work out what experiences are like.

Jackson's argument is very brief.

1. Assume that INTERACTIONIST DUALISM (pp. 215, 295) is false.
2. Therefore, what causes our conscious experiences is purely physical (either physicalism is true or epiphenomenalist dualism is true).
3. Therefore, when Mary comes to learn what it is like to see red, this process has a purely physical causal explanation.
4. Therefore, *what* Mary learns is also something physical – it can be understood and explained in purely physical (and functional) terms. We shouldn't think that what she learns is something that doesn't feature in the explanation of how she comes to learn it.
5. Therefore, we should reject epiphenomenalist dualism and accept physicalism.

An experience, Jackson claims, is simply highly complex functional information. It doesn't seem like this, which is why we *think* that what Mary learns is non-physical. Usually, to acquire complex functional information, e.g. about the effects of a certain drug, we have to investigate and bring information together from different sources, make inferences, do tests and so on. But sensory experience gives us this kind of information in a highly unusual way – remarkably quickly and easily. So it doesn't seem like functional information, but knowledge of some intrinsic property of the experience – qualia. However, appearances are misleading, and this is knowledge of a physical and functional property.

Having argued that, in principle, complete physical knowledge would give someone knowledge of what experiences are like, Jackson doubts whether it is possible for us to gain such complete physical knowledge. There may be too many things about the world that we will never be able to understand.

Should we be persuaded by Jackson's change of mind just because he put forward the original argument?

Qualia (as defined) don't exist

The knowledge argument claims that phenomenal properties can't be understood in terms of physical and functional properties. Instead, it understands phenomenal properties as QUALIA (p. 260) – intrinsic and non-representational properties of experience. The last objection – the claim that all physical knowledge would include knowledge of 'qualia' – rejects this understanding of phenomenal properties. There are no qualia. Phenomenal properties are, instead, just physical, functional properties.

To defend this view, we must find reasons to reject the arguments in favour of qualia. We looked at some of these in ISSUES with functionalism (p. 260). Is the idea of an inverted spectrum really coherent, once we factor in very detailed functions? Is the idea of a Chinese consciousness coherent? (Or perhaps – what's wrong with accepting that there will be a Chinese consciousness?) When we think through carefully just how much knowledge Mary must have in order to know *everything* about colour experience, is it coherent to say that she won't know what it is like to see red before she leaves her room?

We have a good reason to reject the claim that phenomenal properties are qualia, namely Ockham's razor. Our explanation of the mind, and what exists, is simpler if we can explain phenomenal properties in terms of physical and functional properties. We need a really good reason to think that *everything else* in the world can be explained in physical and functional terms *except consciousness*. Are the arguments that qualia exist really strong enough?

Does the knowledge argument show that qualia exist, and property dualism is true?

These points can be compared with the argument of direct realism against sense-data. See *Philosophy for AS*, Direct realism and common sense, p. 36, and Direct and indirect realism on secondary qualities, p. 49.

Going further: logical behaviourism and qualia

We can press the objection another way. Do the arguments that qualia exist even understand consciousness correctly? Ryle and other logical behaviourists argue that the concept of qualia misunderstands our talk of sensations, feelings, images, and so on. These are not each a 'something' that has peculiar properties of 'what it is like'. The whole metaphysical picture here is wrong. When we express our experiences, we use words that derive their meaning from describing physical objects. To say 'what it is like' to see red is simply to describe what we see when attending to the colour of a red object, or if it is not in front of us, we give a report of our memory of seeing it. The redness that we experience is the redness *of the rose*, not a property of our experience of it.

People don't normally talk about 'sensations' or 'what it is like' in the sense of qualia in everyday language, before being exposed to some theory. If you ask someone 'what it is like' to see a rose, they will usually respond evaluatively, e.g. 'it's wonderful' or 'it's calming'. Of course, experiences differ from each other. But this isn't because what each experience 'is like' differs. We can express the difference in terms of what the experience *is of*, and how we evaluate it; e.g. whether we enjoy it or find it boring. The property dualist has misunderstood our mental concepts.

What would a logical behaviourist say about Mary? Perhaps this. In knowing all the physical facts, Mary can't yet understand our normal way of talking about experiences. She has no experiences of coloured objects that she can express and report, and as a result, she has only a limited understanding of our discussions of them. But none of this has to do with knowledge of facts, either facts about some 'inner' conscious experience or facts about the brain. To think otherwise is a category mistake.

Explain the logical behaviourist's argument that qualia do not exist.

The 'philosophical zombies' argument

It is perhaps worth knowing in advance that the zombie argument and objections to it are probably the most philosophically demanding material on the A level. Understanding the next few pages will require even more careful thought than usual.

To understand the 'zombie' argument, we first need to understand the idea of a possible world.

Possible worlds

A 'possible world' is a way of talking about how things could be. Propositions describe 'states of affairs'. Propositions can be true or false. A proposition that is true describes the actual world, the way things are, a true state of affairs. A proposition that is false describes the way things are not, a false state of affairs. However, false propositions can be necessarily false or just contingently false. A proposition that is necessarily false cannot be true – it is impossible for it to be true. A proposition that is only contingently false describes a state of affairs that is possible, but false, given how the world actually is. For example, 'I was born in Kenya' is false, but could have been true. A contingently false proposition describes a way things could be, if they were different. We can say that in some other 'possible world', a contingently false proposition is true, the state of affairs it describes is part of the way that world is. In some other possible world, I was born in Kenya.

Possible worlds are distinct from one another depending on what we are supposing to be true in that world. So the possible world in which I was born in Kenya is different from the possible world in which I was born in Argentina which is different from the possible world in which I don't exist at all. In different possible worlds, different things exist and the things that exist can have different properties from the properties they have in the actual world. We can also imagine possible worlds in which the laws of nature are different, e.g. in which light travels at a different speed.

What is a possible world?

ANTHOLOGY: CHALMERS, 'CONSCIOUSNESS AND ITS PLACE IN NATURE', §§3.2, 3.4

A 'zombie', in the philosophical sense, is an exact physical duplicate of a person – you, for instance – but without any experiential consciousness. It therefore has identical physical properties to you, but different mental properties – it has no phenomenal consciousness.

Of course, zombies are not possible in the actual world; i.e. given the laws of our universe, any being that has identical physical properties to you will also have consciousness. What we are thinking about when thinking about zombies is a different possible world – a world which has all the physical properties of our world but without consciousness. To talk of different possible worlds is to talk of 'metaphysical possibility' – what could exist, but not in this world.

But is such a world really (metaphysically) possible? To argue that a world with zombies is possible is to argue for property dualism. The argument concludes that the properties of consciousness cannot be physical properties. How does it work?

First, it seems that zombies are at least conceivable. I've just described them, and there isn't an obvious contradiction in the idea. Second, given their conceivability, we may argue that zombies are therefore metaphysically possible. There is a possible world which has all the same physical properties as the actual world, but has no properties of consciousness. Now, if consciousness were *identical* with physical properties, it would be impossible for a creature to have the same physical properties as you but not have consciousness. This is Leibniz's principle of the indiscernibility of identicals. If A is identical to B – if A is B – then you can't have A without B or vice versa; they are the same thing. So if zombies are possible – if a creature could be physically identical to you but not have consciousness – then consciousness is *not* identical to any physical properties. So, if zombies are metaphysically possible, then consciousness is not identical to any physical properties, and property dualism is true.

> **?** What is a philosophical 'zombie'?

1. It is conceivable that there are zombies.
2. If it is conceivable that there are zombies, it is metaphysically possible that there are zombies.
3. If it is metaphysically possible that there are zombies, then phenomenal properties of consciousness are non-physical.
4. Therefore, property dualism is true.

Put another way: According to physicalism, everything that exists is either physical or depends on what is physical. So if physicalism is true, a world that is an exact physical duplicate of our world, with nothing else in addition, will be an exact duplicate of our world *in all respects*. Therefore, if there is a possible world that is an exact physical duplicate of our world but is different in any way (e.g. it has different (or no) psychological properties) physicalism is false. If two physically identical worlds have different properties of consciousness, those properties of consciousness don't depend on physical properties. So if zombies are possible, physicalism is false and property dualism is true.

This objection has similarities to two arguments we have already discussed. It is similar to Descartes' CONCEIVABILITY ARGUMENT (p. 202), but it is about properties not substances. And it is similar to THE POSSIBILITY OF A FUNCTIONAL DUPLICATE WITH NO QUALIA (p. 262), but it applies the argument to physicalism generally instead of objecting to functionalism specifically.

> Outline and explain the zombie argument as an objection to physicalism.

Going further: how arguments for property dualism work

In §3.4, Chalmers discusses how arguments for property dualism work. The zombie and knowledge arguments both start from an *epistemic* claim. In the case of the zombie argument, this is established by reflecting on what is conceivable. The claim is that we can conceive of physical properties existing without the phenomenal properties of consciousness with which they are correlated in the actual world. In the case of the knowledge argument, we reflect on what Mary can know before she leaves her room. The claim is that she cannot figure out, just from her knowledge of all the physical facts, what it is like to experience red.

From the epistemic claim, each argument infers an *ontological* claim – a claim about what exists. The properties of consciousness are distinct from, and cannot be reduced to, physical properties. In the knowledge argument, this inference is made on the basis of Mary learning a new fact about the world when she leaves the room. In the zombie argument, the inference is made through considering possible worlds. The argument claims that what we can coherently conceive of is possible; and if it is possible for one thing to exist without the other, this shows that they are distinct things.

There are different ways in which we may object to such dualist arguments, as we saw in ISSUES WITH DESCARTES' ARGUMENTS (p. 207). First, we may argue that what is being proposed is not conceivable (Chalmers calls this 'type-A materialism'). Second, we may argue that although it is conceivable, what is proposed is not in fact possible (Chalmers calls this 'type-B materialism'). We look at both types of response in ISSUES FOR THE ZOMBIE ARGUMENT, below.

The zombie argument as a dualist argument against other theories

Before looking at objections to the zombie argument, the specification indicates that the argument should be considered as an objection to logical behaviourism and the mind–brain type identity theory.

The zombie argument attacks the mind–brain type identity theory directly. Mind–brain type identity theory claims that phenomenal properties are identical with certain physical properties. If this were correct, then zombies would be metaphysically impossible, as explained above. So if zombies are metaphysically possible, then the mind–brain type identity theory is false.

Analytical behaviourism claims to reduce talk of colour experiences to talk of behavioural dispositions. As a physicalist theory, it claims that these dispositions are based in physical properties. Zombies have the same physical properties as us, and so, according to analytical behaviourism, they would have exactly the same behavioural dispositions. Because they would have the same behavioural dispositions, and colour experiences can be understood in terms of behavioural dispositions, zombies would have the same colour experiences as us. In other words, according to analytical behaviourism, zombies are impossible. The zombie argument claims that zombies are possible, so it attacks analytical behaviourism.

On Ryle's account of consciousness, to experience red is just to pay attention to the colour of something red, and to be conscious of doing this is just to be ready to say what you are thinking or feeling. But, if we understand these activities behaviourally, then it seems that zombies will behave like this, but they won't have conscious experiences of redness. So experiencing red can't be fully understood in this way. If zombies are possible, then Ryle's behaviourism must be false.

> Explain how the zombie argument is an objection to either mind–brain identity theory or logical behaviourism.

Issues for the zombie argument

A 'zombie' world is not conceivable

The first premise of the zombie argument claims that we can conceive of beings that have the same physical properties as us but without consciousness. Why think this is conceivable? Because when we think of physical properties, this doesn't determine what we must think of consciousness. By contrast, when we think of the answer to 3×4, we must – if we are thinking clearly – think of 12. It is inconceivable that 3×4 is anything other than 12. Or again, to use Descartes' example, it is inconceivable that the internal angles of a triangle could add up to

Compare the argument in ALL PHYSICAL KNOWLEDGE WOULD INCLUDE KNOWLEDGE OF QUALIA, p. 274.

anything other than 180 degrees. By contrast, it does not seem inconceivable that there could be a being with identical physical properties to you, but without consciousness.

The first objection to the argument is that, despite appearances, zombies are not conceivable. If we think they are conceivable, we are not thinking clearly or we lack some relevant information. It is difficult to recognise that we are not thinking clearly. But we can spell out where we are going wrong in more detail.

First, if physicalism is true, we should note that something's physical properties determine its functional properties. So a physical duplicate of you is also a functional duplicate of you. (We cannot *assume* that physicalism is false, since that is what the zombie argument is trying to prove. To assume physicalism is false is to beg the question.)

Second, we need to revisit the arguments that phenomenal consciousness can be analysed in terms of physical and functional properties; there are no qualia. What prevents us from being persuaded by this claim is that our analysis of consciousness is still underdeveloped. But if we had a complete analysis, we would see that consciousness can be completely explained in these terms. In that case, a physical, functional duplicate of you would also have consciousness.

So, once we are clear on a being's physical properties, we can, in principle, deduce how it functions, and from this, with a complete analysis of consciousness, we can deduce whether or not it is conscious. So to imagine a being with identical physical properties to you but without consciousness is confused. It is like accepting the premises of a deductive argument but rejecting the conclusion. In conceiving of a 'zombie' as having identical physical properties, you conceive of it as having identical functions. To function in certain (highly complex) ways just is to be conscious. So zombies – physically identical, but non-conscious beings – are inconceivable.

1. A zombie is a physical duplicate of a person with phenomenal consciousness, but without phenomenal consciousness.
2. A physical duplicate is a functional duplicate.
3. Therefore, a zombie is a physical and functional duplicate of a person, but without phenomenal consciousness.
4. Phenomenal properties are physical properties realising particular functional roles.

5. Therefore, a physical and functional duplicate of a person with consciousness has phenomenal consciousness.
6. A physical and functional duplicate of a person with consciousness cannot both have and lack phenomenal consciousness.
7. Therefore, zombies are inconceivable.

This objection to the zombie argument depends on there being a complete physical and functional analysis of consciousness. We can reply that there is no such analysis, because an analysis of consciousness in terms of its physical and functional properties doesn't provide an analysis of how something feels, what it is like to experience something. Phenomenal properties are qualia, they cannot be understood or explained either in terms of physical structure or in terms of functions. And so we can know all about something's physical structure and function without being able to account for its consciousness. And so we can conceive of that same physical thing either with or without phenomenal consciousness.

> Explain the objection that philosophical zombies are inconceivable.

> Are philosophical zombies conceivable?

Going further: what is conceivable may not be possible

The objection

A second objection targets the second premise. Although zombies are conceivable, they aren't in fact possible. What we are able to conceive is not always a reliable guide to what is possible.

For example, the two concepts 'water' and 'H_2O' are quite distinct. It is not an analytic truth that water is H_2O. So it is not a contradiction to think that water is not H_2O. Before it was discovered that water is H_2O, people may have had thoughts such as 'I wonder if water is H_2O', 'I suspect that water is H_2O, but it might not be'. These are perfectly coherent thoughts. In this sense, at least, it is conceivable (even if false) that water is not H_2O.

> Compare the argument in THERE IS MORE THAN ONE WAY OF KNOWING THE SAME PHYSICAL FACT, p. 273.

Given this, it is easy to think that water could have been different; i.e. in some possible world, water is not H_2O. However, given that water *is* H_2O, it's not metaphysically possible that water isn't H_2O. This was an important claim made by Saul Kripke. If *A* is identical to *B*, then *A* and *B* are the same thing. It's not possible for *A* to be *B* and for it not to be *B*. If *A is B*, then *A* is *B in every possible world*.

We said earlier that something can have different properties in different possible worlds. For instance, in a different possible world, I was born in Kenya. I would still be me, but just born somewhere else. This is because where I was born isn't an *essential* property of me – it isn't what makes me me. Instead, where I was born is a *contingent* property of me.

Let's apply this distinction to water. It is possible that the water in the oceans in a different possible world could have been fresh, not salty. The fact that oceans are salty is a contingent property of water in our world. It isn't what makes water what it is. Or again, the fact that water falls as rain is a contingent property of water. If it never rained, this wouldn't change what water is. What does make water what it is? What is the *essential* property of water? Its chemical composition, H_2O. Now, what makes water *what it is* is not a property that water can lack in some possible world. A world without H_2O is a world without water, because water just is H_2O. (In some other possible world, there could be something *just like* water that isn't H_2O (it falls as rain, is transparent, drinkable, etc.). But if it isn't H_2O, it just isn't water.)

Kripke concluded that identity claims – '*A* is identical to *B*' – are necessarily true, if true at all. They are true in all possible worlds.

We said that we can conceive of water not being H_2O. But we have argued that it isn't possible that water is not H_2O. This shows that we cannot always infer metaphysical possibility from conceivability.

We can apply the point to zombies. The fact that we can conceive of zombies doesn't show that zombies are

Naming and Necessity

Explain why water is H_2O in every possible world.

metaphysically possible. If phenomenal properties *just are* certain physical and/or functional properties, then it isn't possible for zombies to exist. Given the physical properties we have, if physicalism is true, it just isn't possible for a being with the same physical properties not to have consciousness as well.

We can relate this argument to Smart's point about concepts and properties. We can have two concepts for one and the same thing – water and H_2O, lightning and electrical discharge, phenomenal consciousness and some neurological description. We might *think* it is possible to have one without the other, but in fact we are thinking about one and the same thing in two different ways.

SMART, 'SENSATIONS AND BRAIN PROCESSES', PP. 141–8, p. 249.

Explain the objection that philosophical zombies, though conceivable, are not metaphysically possible.

Reply

Property dualists reply that the analogy between scientific identities and phenomenal consciousness doesn't work. We can agree that something isn't water if it isn't H_2O, because H_2O is the 'essence' of water. The concept 'water' is a concept of something that has a particular structure and causal role, which science can then discover. Water is precisely the kind of thing that could be – and is! – identical with a chemical property. This is why you can't have water without H_2O or H_2O without water.

By contrast, the essence of phenomenal properties is what it is like to experience them. The essence of pain is *how pain feels*. Its essence isn't some physical or functional property. Likewise, the essence of a physical property is not how it feels, but its physical structure; and the essence of a functional property is what causes it and what it causes. Because phenomenal properties and physical and functional properties have different essences, surely they can exist independently. It is only the essential properties of something that can't change in different possible worlds, the contingent properties can. Because phenomenal properties have a different essence from physical properties, each can exist without the other. So zombies are possible.

ANTHOLOGY: JACKSON, 'POSTSCRIPT ON "WHAT MARY DIDN'T KNOW"'

Going further: does conceivability entail possibility?

Jackson provides a different response, but discusses it in relation to Mary. We will apply it to zombies as well.

In essence, Jackson argues that if zombies are conceivable, then they are possible. Physicalism cannot allow that they are conceivable, but not possible. He claims that if physicalism is true, then from a complete physical description of the world, we would be able to *deduce* facts about water from knowing about H_2O and we would be able to deduce facts about consciousness from knowing about the brain. Until JACKSON'S CHANGE OF MIND (p. 275), he argues that this is an implausible claim, so physicalism is false.

Why does he say that if physicalism is true, we can deduce facts about phenomenal consciousness from physical (and functional) facts?

1. We need to remind ourselves how deductive arguments work. In a valid deductive argument (p. 8), if the premises are true, then the conclusion must be true. Put a different way, there is no possible world in which the premises are true, but the conclusion is false.
2. Let's say that the premises are all the physical truths about the world, and the conclusion is some truth about phenomenal consciousness, e.g. that you are in pain.

3. According to physicalism, if a possible world has the same physical properties as this world, then all its properties are the same. In other words, if all the physical truths are the same in two worlds, then all the truths about phenomenal consciousness are the same. This is why zombie worlds are impossible.

4. This means that, according to physicalism, there is no possible world in which our premises (all the physical truths about the world) are true and the conclusion (some truth about phenomenal consciousness) is false.

5. But that is the definition of a valid deductive argument. So if physicalism is true, the physical facts *entail* facts about phenomenal consciousness.

We can now run a similar argument about what Mary can know.

1. If we know that the premises of a deductive argument are true, and that the argument is valid, then we know the conclusion is true. In fact, if we know that a deductive argument is valid, then we cannot coherently conceive that the premises are true and the conclusion is false.

2. Mary is supposed to know all the physical facts, all the truths about physical properties.

3. If physicalism is true, then because the physical facts entail all the facts about phenomenal consciousness, Mary would be able to deduce from her knowledge of the physical facts what it is like to see red.

In other words, the physicalist *must* claim that there is a complete physical, functional analysis of consciousness, as argued in A 'ZOMBIE' WORLD IS NOT CONCEIVABLE above.

If physicalism is true, must it be possible in principle to completely understand consciousness in physical, functional terms?

With water, of course, we can readily accept such a claim. There is a complete physical, functional analysis of water, and so Mary can figure out truths about water from what she knows about H_2O. We would also accept that this is true of amoebas. What we can say in physical terms about amoebas and how they interact with their environment is everything there is to say about amoebas. Now, according to physicalism, there is no difference *in kind* between us and an amoeba, only a difference in complexity. But if we knew all the physical facts, this difference in complexity shouldn't stop us from knowing everything there is to say about our conscious experiences. If truths about water and amoebas can be deduced from complete physical knowledge, then if physicalism is correct, so can truths about conscious experience. But, until JACKSON'S CHANGE OF MIND (p. 275), he argued that this was highly implausible, and so physicalism is false. Qualia cannot be understood in terms of structure and function.

Going further: what is logically possible tells us nothing about reality

Let us grant that zombies are possible. A third objection targets the inference from the claim that zombies are *possible* to the conclusion that property dualism is *true*. The zombie argument shows, at best, that *in another possible world*, physical properties and phenomenal properties are distinct. But why does this entail in the *actual* world that they are distinct? Couldn't it be the case that physicalism is true in the actual world, but property dualism is true in a different possible world?

We can reply that this objection makes two mistakes. First, the objection misunderstands identity. It suggests that phenomenal properties could *be* physical properties in this world but not in another possible world. But this isn't possible. Nothing can be something else. I can't not be me in another possible world. If 'I' am not me, but you, say, then how is that person me? It isn't. In any possible world, the only person I can be is me. Likewise, water can't be something other than water. Since water *is* H_2O, it can't be something else in another possible world.

The same goes for phenomenal properties. If phenomenal properties *are* physical properties in this world, then they are physical properties in every possible world. And if they are *not* physical properties in another possible world, then they are not physical properties in any possible world, including the actual world. When it comes to identity, possibility does tell us about reality.

Second, if the objection is intended to defend physicalism, it misunderstands what physicalism claims. Physicalism claims that what exists is either physical or depends upon what is physical. We need to be clear what 'depends upon' means. As noted in PHYSICALISM (p. 226), in the example of the painting, we want to say that if the physical properties of two paintings are identical, then the aesthetic properties *cannot* be different. It is not strong enough to simply say that they *aren't* different, since that would allow that the physical properties don't 'fix' the aesthetic properties.

What we said about the aesthetic properties applies to properties of consciousness as well, and what applies to paintings is true of whole worlds. According to physicalism, once the physical properties of a world are finalised, then there is no further work to be done to 'add' consciousness. It is already part of the world. Phenomenal properties *cannot* differ independently of physical properties. So physicalism is a claim about what is possible.

The zombie argument attacks this claim. It argues that there can be two worlds that are physically identical but with different phenomenal properties. Once the physical properties

> Explain the argument that if phenomenal properties are physical properties, they are physical properties in every possible world.

Does the philosophical zombies argument establish that property dualism is true?

of a world are finalised, then there *is* still further work to be done to 'add' consciousness. Thinking about possibility does, in this case, tell us about reality.

Key points: property dualism

- Property dualism claims that at least some mental properties cannot be reduced to or understood in terms of physical (and functional) properties. They are a fundamentally new kind of property. Therefore, physicalism is wrong. The mental properties most often discussed are phenomenal properties.
- Chalmers argues that a physical account of anything can only explain its structure and function. Phenomenal properties are qualia, and cannot be explained in terms of structure and function.
- Jackson's knowledge argument argues that Mary, a neuroscientist who knows everything physical about colour vision, learns something new, namely what it is like to see colour, upon first leaving her black-and-white room. Therefore, what it is like to see colour is not a physical property or fact.
- The argument attacks the mind–brain identity theory, functionalism and logical behaviourism by showing that these theories have a counter-intuitive consequence. It argues that they must claim that Mary knows what it is like to see red before leaving her room.
- Physicalists can reply that while Mary learns something upon leaving her room, she doesn't gain propositional knowledge of a new fact. On one reply, she gains new abilities. We can object that her new knowledge of what it is like to see red can't be reduced to new abilities.
- On another reply, Mary is said to gain acquaintance knowledge, directly apprehending (the brain property which is) what it is like to see red. Jackson objects that this is irrelevant – she learns a new fact about other people's colour experience.
- A third reply claims that Mary gains a new, phenomenal concept of red. However, the concept refers to the same physical property which Mary already knows about by means of theoretical concepts.

So although she learns something new – a new way of thinking about the world – this doesn't threaten physicalism.

- A different approach for physicalism is to defend the 'counter-intuitive' consequence of the argument, and argue that Mary in fact would know what it is like to experience colour before leaving her room.

- Jackson later came to accept this argument. Starting from the premise that interactionist dualism is false, he claims that there must be a complete physical causal story about Mary's coming to learn what it is like to experience colour, and so what Mary learns must itself be physical.

- Ryle would argue that the whole story of Mary rests on a misunderstanding of consciousness. 'What it is like' is not a property of a private inner object, a sensation or experience. This misunderstands what talk about consciousness means. Perhaps what Mary lacks before she leaves her room is simply an understanding of our normal way of talking about colour experiences.

- A possible world is a way things could be. A contingently false proposition describes a state of affairs that is true in some possible world; i.e. that would be true if that world were the actual world. A proposition that is necessarily true is true in all possible worlds.

- A 'zombie' is an exact physical duplicate of a person, but without consciousness.

- The zombie argument for property dualism claims that zombies are conceivable and so metaphysically possible. If consciousness were identical to a physical property, it would not be metaphysically possible for something to have that physical property without consciousness. Therefore, if zombies are metaphysically possible, then consciousness cannot be identical to physical properties.

- The argument attacks the mind–brain identity theory and logical behaviourism by arguing against what they imply. If they were correct, then zombies should be metaphysically impossible. But because zombies are metaphysically possible, these theories are mistaken.

- The knowledge and zombie arguments begin from an epistemological claim and infer a metaphysical claim. Physicalists can object to either the epistemological claim or to the inference of a metaphysical conclusion.

- Against the epistemological claim, physicalists can argue that zombies are not, in fact, conceivable if we correctly understand consciousness. A physical duplicate of you is a functional duplicate of you, and consciousness can be completely analysed in physical and functional terms. Therefore, any physical, functional duplicate of you must also be conscious.
- We can object that consciousness cannot be completely analysed in physical and functional terms, as such an analysis cannot capture the intrinsic quality of what a conscious experience is like.
- Physicalists can also object that zombies are not metaphysically possible, even though they are conceivable. Conceivability is not always a reliable guide to possibility. For example, we can conceive that water is not H_2O, but this is not possible. Likewise, if phenomenal properties are physical properties, zombies are impossible.
- We can reply that H_2O is the essence of water, which is why H_2O without water is impossible. However, the essence of a phenomenal property is how it feels, not some physical property. And so it is metaphysically possible to have the physical property without the phenomenal property.
- Jackson argues that if physicalism is correct, then it must be possible to deduce all the facts about phenomenal properties from the facts about physical properties. According to physicalism, there is no difference in principle, only a difference in complexity, between an amoeba and us. But to know all the physical and functional facts about an amoeba is to know all the facts about an amoeba. Because it is implausible to say the same about us, physicalism is false.
- A final objection is that we cannot infer from what is possible to what is real. However, this objection misunderstands both identity and physicalism, which make claims about what is possible.

B. Objections to (property) dualism

The discussion of this section refers back and develops some of the ideas in the discussion of OBJECTIONS TO (SUBSTANCE) DUALISM (p. 215). It is worth quickly reminding yourself of the points made there.

Causal interaction

Property dualism, we said (THE THEORY, p. 266), claims that at least some mental properties, e.g. phenomenal properties of consciousness, are fundamentally distinct from physical properties. They are not ontologically dependent on physical properties in the way physicalism claims. However, there can be basic or fundamental laws of nature that correlate them.

Interactionist property dualists argue that these distinct mental properties causally affect both other mental states and physical states. Epiphenomenalist property dualists claim that mental properties have no causal powers. While physical properties cause changes in mental properties, mental properties cause nothing at all. Both views face objections.

Interactionist (property) dualism

ANTHOLOGY: CHALMERS, 'CONSCIOUSNESS AND ITS PLACE IN NATURE', §3.9

Substance dualism faced challenging CONCEPTUAL ISSUES (p. 215) in trying to explain how a mental substance not in space could cause physical effects in space. Property dualism doesn't face this particular issue, because mental properties are properties of physical objects. The claim is simply that these mental properties make a difference to how the physical world changes. For instance, having a painful experience makes a difference to what I do next, e.g. jumping up and down - my bodily movements are caused by my being in pain.

We can object that we can give no account of *how* mental properties would cause physical effects. But, Chalmers notes, this is an objection to any *fundamental* causal relationship. For instance, we have no account of *how* gravity works (if we did, then that would simply show that gravity isn't a fundamental force, but something else would be, and the question repeats itself). Property dualism claims that mental properties are fundamental in the same sense as fundamental physical properties. There is no further explanation in other terms available. But there is no *special* conceptual problem of mental causation here.

We can also object that the claim that mental properties cause physical effects faces empirical objections. It is incompatible with physics and with neuroscience. But as discussed in EMPIRICAL ISSUES (p. 217), we don't have strong evidence of this. Chalmers notes that there are interpretations of quantum mechanics that actually *suggest* that consciousness plays a causal role in physical events. (If you are interested in physics: this is the interpretation that maintains that conscious observation of a quantum system collapses its superposed state to a determinate state.) Nor do we know enough neuroscience yet to be able to claim confidently that the causal story of how the brain works is a completely physical story.

These remarks don't show that consciousness has the causal role that we think it has, e.g. in causing the movements of my body. But they do support the claim that empirical challenges to interactionist property dualism may not be very strong.

> **?**
>
> Is interactionist property dualism a plausible theory of mind?

Epiphenomenalist (property) dualism

THE CAUSAL REDUNDANCY OF THE MENTAL

ANTHOLOGY: CHALMERS, 'CONSCIOUSNESS AND ITS PLACE IN NATURE', §3.10; JACKSON, 'EPIPHENOMENAL QUALIA', §4

If the knowledge and zombie arguments work, then property dualism is true, it seems. On the other hand, the claims that physical laws govern all events in space-time and that every physical event has a sufficient physical cause seem appealing in light of the success of empirical science. Epiphenomenal property dualism allows both sets of claims to be true. Some mental properties are ontologically distinct from physical properties, but they don't make any causal difference to the world. They are 'causally redundant'.

We can object, however, that epiphenomenalism is very counter-intuitive. It seems obvious that mental properties (e.g. how pain feels) cause other mental and physical events. But the epiphenomenalist can reply with an alternative explanation of why it seems this way to us. The physical process in the brain causes *both* the mental state, e.g. the painful experience, *and* the behaviour which we think is caused by the mental state, e.g. jumping up and down. So the experience and the behaviour are *correlated* because they are both effects of the same cause. It is this correlation that makes us think that the experience causes the behaviour. But it doesn't.

We can press the objection. Unlike the substance dualist, the property dualist believes that mental properties are properties of physical objects, namely certain living creatures. Suppose that Darwin's theory of evolution by natural selection is true. According to this theory, millions of genetic alterations randomly take place. Most disappear without a trace. But some that coincidentally help a creature to survive and reproduce slowly spread. That creature and its descendants reproduce more than others without those traits, so more and more creatures end up with them. The features enables the creature to reproduce more, so its descendants also have that feature and they reproduce more and so on.

So, according to the theory of evolution, the traits that evolve over time are ones that causally contribute to the survival and reproduction of the creature. We can assume that mental properties evolved. But how, if they make no difference to what creatures do and so whether they survive and reproduce? Epiphenomenalism conflicts with our best account of the origin of consciousness.

Jackson replies that natural selection is more complicated than just described. In fact, there are lots of traits that have evolved that don't contribute to survival or reproduction, but are instead *by-products* of traits that *do* contribute. For instance,

> Explain epiphenomenalism's account of why it seems that mental states cause physical states.

polar bears have thick, warm coats which help them survive in the Arctic. A thick coat is a heavy coat. But having a heavy coat doesn't contribute to the polar bear's survival, because it makes the bear slower. However, it is better to have a thick, warm and heavy coat than a thin, cool and light coat. Having a heavy coat is a by-product of having a thick, warm coat, and having a thick, warm coat contributes to survival.

Likewise, there are brain processes that make a difference to how a creature behaves and which are very conducive to survival. Consciousness, according to epiphenomenalism, is simply a by-product of these brain processes. It just happens to be a fundamental law of nature that these physical properties are correlated with certain properties of consciousness.

We can object that this response presents us with a very divided picture of the world. Consciousness sits entirely outside the rest of the natural world, and has no effect on it. Jackson accepts this: we shouldn't expect to understand the world. Our abilities to understand the world themselves relate to survival. As a result of evolution, we are equipped to learn about and understand what we need to know in order to survive. Consciousness doesn't make any difference to this, so it is no surprise that we can't understand it well.

? Is epiphenomenalism compatible with evolutionary theory?

Going further: the argument from introspection

In our previous discussion of the ARGUMENT FROM INTROSPECTION (p. 219), we gave reasons to think that if mental states don't cause anything, even other mental states, then this threatens our knowledge of our own mental states. For instance, according to epiphenomenalism, my belief that I am in pain is caused not by the pain but by some brain state. So if that brain state occurs, I would have the belief that I am in pain whatever I actually feel.

Epiphenomenalists can reply that knowledge of something doesn't always require that thing to *cause* one's belief. I can know that I am in pain without the painful experience causing this knowledge. For instance, suppose the brain state that causes my pain also causes my belief that I am in pain. In this case, I wouldn't, under normal circumstances, have the belief that I am in pain unless I was in pain - the same brain state causes both. So even though my belief that I am in pain isn't caused by the painful experience, I can know that I am in pain because my belief is caused by a reliable mechanism.

Chalmers gives a different response. Knowledge of my experiences is knowledge by acquaintance. I am directly aware of my experiences, but this is not a causal relation. My belief that I am in pain is partly constituted, not caused, by this direct awareness. My being in pain makes my belief the belief that it is. So my knowledge that I am in pain depends on my being in pain, but is not caused by it.

> See *Philosophy for AS*, RELIABILISM, p. 89.

> **?**
>
> Explain the objection from introspection and one response to it.

FREE WILL AND RESPONSIBILITY

In our previous discussion of FREE WILL AND RESPONSIBILITY (p. 220), we noted that free will and responsibility appear to require you to be able to choose what to do, and then do it because you choose to do it. Epiphenomenalism claims that your 'choice' is simply an effect of a brain process, and not a cause of anything. So is there any sense in which you genuinely choose what to do or do what you do because you choose to?

The problem of free will in philosophy is very complicated, and so we can only give a very brief indication of how epiphenomenalism might respond to this challenge. One option is simply to accept that choice and free will are illusions. It seems like we have free will (perhaps because it seems like mental states cause physical events). But we don't.

However, a second option is to argue that the objection misunderstands what choice and free will are. Epiphenomenalism can argue that my choice is not *just* my being aware of my choice. It is this together with the brain state that causes this and my action. We can say that my choice involves something physical, even if it has a non-physical aspect (my awareness of choosing). Mind–brain type identity theory and functionalism will agree that we should understand choices in physical, functional terms.

This solution does not *oppose* free will to what happens physically. This is known as 'compatibilism'. For example, if I choose to help an old lady across the road, immediately before I do this, my brain is in a particular state – the chemicals and neural connections are all a particular way. The neurons fire, my muscles move. That brain state causes my bodily movements, which are part of my action of helping the old lady. To have free will is simply for one's choice to cause one's action. You act as you do because of what you choose to do. If you had chosen to act differently, then you would have acted differently. But choosing is just a process in the brain, and this process causes your action.

Why is this free will? Our discussions of VOLUNTARY AND INVOLUNTARY ACTIONS (p. 90) and CHOICE AND DELIBERATION (p. 93) help us understand. According to Aristotle, at least, to choose to act is to act voluntarily on the basis of deliberation. Compare voluntary action with involuntary action. An action is involuntary if it is done from force. For example, you trip and fall into someone, knocking them over. Or again, someone puts a gun to your head, and tells you to push someone over. Even some voluntary actions are not chosen, and so are not free. Suppose you are addicted to heroin, and acting on the intense desire for it, you steal from a store to get the money to buy more. You hate your addiction and would choose to be without it if you could.

In all these cases, you don't choose to do what you do. On many other occasions, you do what you choose to do. The fact that your choice is a brain process is irrelevant. If free will is doing what you choose to do, then epiphenomenalism can allow that we have free will.

> Explain the argument that epiphenomenalism does not rule out free will.

The problem of other minds

Property dualism faces similar difficulties to substance dualism when it comes to the problem of other minds (see p. 220). If mental properties are distinct from physical and functional properties, how can we know from how other people behave and how they are physically constituted, whether they have any mental properties at all?

Interactionist property dualism can appeal to the ARGUMENT FROM ANALOGY (p. 221). This argument, however, usually depends on accepting mental causation. So it doesn't seem available to epiphenomenalist property dualism. But Jackson argues that this is a mistake. Mental properties are the effects of brain processes. I can know that other people have minds, because I can know that their behaviour is caused by brain processes and these brain processes cause mental properties.

These responses face the same challenges faced by the argument from analogy that we discussed previously.

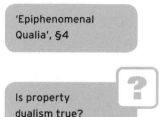

'Epiphenomenal Qualia', §4

Is property dualism true?

Key points: objections to (property) dualism

- Interactionist property dualism claims that mental properties can cause physical (and other mental) events. It faces the problem of explaining how this is possible and empirical objections to whether it occurs.
- Chalmers responds that for *any* fundamental causal relationship, we do not have an account of how it works. There is no special problem here. Furthermore, we have no empirical evidence that mental properties do not affect physical properties, and even some interpretations of quantum theory that support the claim that they do.
- Epiphenomenalist property dualism claims that mental properties have no causal role. To the objection that this is counter-intuitive, it can respond that they appear to have a causal role because what causes them (a brain state) also causes what looks like their effects (bodily movements, other mental states).
- We can object that epiphenomenalism is incompatible with evolutionary theory, because evolution only selects properties that make a difference to the survival and reproductive success of the animal.
- Jackson responds that properties that are selected for can have by-products. And consciousness is a by-product of advantageous brain processes.
- We can object that epiphenomenalism entails that we cannot gain knowledge of our minds. The epiphenomenalist can reply that our beliefs about our mental states are caused by the same brain processes that cause those mental states. As this is a reliable process, we can have knowledge of our mental states. Chalmers responds that our experiences partially constitute our beliefs about them.

- Epiphenomenalism also appears to undermine free will and responsibility, as our choices are caused by physical events and do not themselves cause our actions. Epiphenomenalists can either accept that we have no free will or argue that our choices are physical processes and then defend compatibilism. To be free is simply to have one's actions caused by one's choices.

- Property dualism faces the problem of other minds. If mental properties are logically independent of bodies, any evidence from someone's bodily behaviour does not prove that they have a mind. Property dualists can respond by appealing to the argument from analogy.

Summary: property dualism

In these sections on property dualism and objections to it, we have looked at two arguments for property dualism (the knowledge argument and the zombie argument), objections to these arguments, and objections to property dualism from causal interaction and the problem of other minds. In our discussion and evaluation of these arguments, we have looked at the following issues:

1. What does it mean to claim that phenomenal properties are ontologically distinct from physical properties?
2. Is there, in principle, a complete physical/functional analysis of phenomenal consciousness? Or are phenomenal properties qualia?
3. What, if anything, does Mary learn when she first leaves her black-and-white room?
4. Do we have two different ways – physical and phenomenal – of thinking about just one set of properties in the brain?
5. Are zombies either conceivable or metaphysically possible?
6. Why is identity necessary, not contingent?

IV. Materialism (again)

A. Eliminative materialism

All the views we have discussed in this chapter assume our usual understanding of mental life, in terms of beliefs, desires, emotions, feelings, and so on. By contrast, eliminative materialism (also known as eliminativism) argues that future scientific developments will show that the way we think and talk about the mind is fundamentally flawed. Our mental concepts are so mistaken, in fact, that we should abandon all talk of the mental, and stick to talking about brain processes instead.

This claim is not a form of reductionism; it is a form of *elimination*. Reduction says that there are mental properties, but they are, in fact, physical, or behavioural, or functional properties. Eliminativism says that there are no mental properties – nothing exists that corresponds to mental terms like 'belief', 'desire', and so on.

ANTHOLOGY: CHURCHLAND, 'ELIMINATIVE MATERIALISM AND THE PROPOSITIONAL ATTITUDES', §§1, 2

'Folk psychology'

Churchland's argument for eliminativism goes like this. First, we are able to understand, explain and sometimes predict each other's behaviour very successfully. We do this by referring to each other's beliefs, desires, emotions, intentions and so on. (It is these mental states, rather than phenomenal properties, that Churchland is interested in.) But explanations, claims Churchland, require laws. What is going on is that we tacitly know and use a rich network of common-sense, perhaps rather loose, laws. For example, if someone is thirsty, they will - under normal conditions - look for something to drink. If someone believes it is raining outside, and doesn't want to get wet, they will - under normal conditions - pick up an umbrella or other covering to keep them dry. And so on. Call this body of knowledge 'folk psychology'.

What is 'folk psychology'?

We understand what beliefs, desires, etc., are in terms of their place in this network of laws – in terms of how they relate to other mental states and behaviour. (Desires motivate behaviour, beliefs represent the world, and so on.) There is a similarity here to Ryle's analysis of our understanding of mental concepts in terms of dispositions and hypothetical statements. However, for Churchland, the psychological laws we use aren't a matter of *conceptual* truth. Instead, folk psychology is an *empirical* theory about human behaviour. That we have beliefs, etc., that operate in certain ways is an empirical claim. This is the first premise in the argument for eliminativism.

Second, empirical theories can be tested, and if they turn out not to be accurate, then they should be abandoned in favour of a more accurate theory. If it were shown that our common-sense laws are actually not very good at explaining and predicting people's behaviour, then folk psychology should be rejected. This has an important implication. The concepts of folk psychology gain their meaning from the network of laws. If we reject the laws, then we should abandon our common-sense concepts as well. Why?

Theories seek to explain some aspect of the world. Very often, these explanations hypothesise that certain things exist, and the explanation works by appealing to these things and their properties. For example, Rutherford postulated the existence of atoms in order to explain why tiny particles changed direction when shot through thin gold leaf. Or again, biologists in the nineteenth century postulated the existence of 'germs' (bacteria and viruses) to explain diseases. These are examples of successful theories, and we continue to believe that these things – atoms, germs – exist. But there have also been unsuccessful theories in science. There was a theory that aimed to explain how and why things burn in terms of a substance called 'phlogiston'. But the theory didn't explain burning very well, and ended up having to say that phlogiston had 'negative' weight (it weighed less than nothing). The theory was abandoned, and with it, belief that phlogiston exists, in favour of the correct

See HYPOTHETICAL REASONING, p. 9.

theory in terms of oxygen. Or again, the difference between living and non-living things was explained in terms of a 'vital force'. The rise of modern biological theory in the mid-nineteenth century replaced that theory, and we abandoned belief in a 'vital force'. If folk psychology is an unsuccessful theory, then we should abandon the claim that there are such things as beliefs, desires, etc.

Third, scientific research indicates a strong connection between the mind and brain states and processes; e.g. that behaviour is caused by events in the brain. Therefore, our common-sense theory of the mind needs to be related to a neuroscientific theory. This is the question of reduction. Will the common-sense ontology of states and processes (beliefs, desires, etc.) reduce to the ontology of neuroscience (brain states and processes)? The mind–brain identity theorist thinks it will. The dualist claims it is irreducible, but that neuroscience can't provide a science of the mind. The functionalist thinks that it is irreducible, because neuroscience can only tell us what realises mental states, which must be understood in functional terms. Eliminativism agrees that our common-sense ontology will not reduce, but this is because folk psychology is false. It will (or should) be *replaced* by a neuroscientific theory.

Explain the connection between showing that a theory is false and rejecting its claims about what exists.

Explain the difference between reductionism and eliminativism in philosophy of mind.

Why folk psychology might be false

Churchland supports the claim that folk psychology is false with three reasons.

1. There are many aspects of mental life that folk psychology cannot explain, such as mental illness, the nature of intelligence, sleep, perception and learning.
2. If we look at the history of folk psychology, it reveals no progress since the ancient Greek authors, 2,500 years ago. By contrast, neuroscientific explanations are constantly growing in scope and power.

3. We cannot make folk psychology coherent with other successful scientific theories. In particular, the central idea of 'Intentional content' is highly problematic.

This third objection requires some unpacking. Through most of this chapter, we have focused primarily on consciousness. However, as remarked at the end of the OVERVIEW (p. 197), the other central aspect of the mind is 'thought', broadly understood. 'Thoughts' are 'about' something, objects or events in the world. For example, I might have a belief *about Paris*, a desire *for chocolate*, be angry *at the government*, or intend *to go to the pub*. In all these cases, my state of mind is 'directed' towards an 'object', the thing I'm thinking about (Paris, chocolate, the government, going to the pub). This idea of 'directedness' is known as 'Intentionality'.

From the Latin *intendere*, meaning 'to aim at'.

Intentionality is not about intentions (to mark the difference, I shall use a capital 'I' for 'Intentionality'). If I have an intention, I am 'aiming at' *doing* something. With Intentionality, it is the thought or mental state which 'aims at' its object, what it is about, and no 'doing' needs to be involved. Beliefs, desires, emotions all have Intentionality; they are all 'Intentional mental states'. An Intentional mental state is a mental state with Intentional content. The Intentional content of a mental state is the answer to 'what are you thinking (about)?'

[?]   What is Intentionality?

We can have different mental states with the same Intentional content if we take different 'attitudes' to that content. For example, I can believe I'm arriving late; I can want to be arriving late; I can fear I'm arriving late; I can be pleased I'm arriving late. An Intentional state, then, comprises a particular 'attitude' or 'mode' towards a particular Intentional content. Churchland, following Bertrand Russell, calls these mental states 'propositional attitudes', because the Intentional content is (usually) expressed as a proposition.

To return to Churchland's argument: why is Intentional content a problem for reducing folk psychology to neuroscience? The reason is that it is very puzzling how anything physical could have Intentional content. Physical things are never 'about' anything. A particular molecular structure or physical process, described in physical terms, is not 'about' anything. But the states and processes of your brain are just chemical states and processes. So how could they ever be about anything? So how could Intentional mental states be states of your brain?

Churchland concludes that folk psychology does not fit in with empirically robust theories, such as neuroscience, and so we have reason to abandon it.

> Outline and explain the argument for eliminativism.

Issues

The intuitive certainty of the existence of my mind takes priority over other considerations

We can object that eliminativism is simply very counter-intuitive. What could be more immediately and directly obvious than that we have thoughts, desires, emotions, beliefs and so on? Descartes took 'I think' to be his first certainty, and for good reason. Nothing, it seems, could be more certain to me than the fact that I have mental states. So no argument could be strong enough to justify giving up such a belief.

> Explain the claim that the argument for eliminativism cannot be as certain as my knowledge of my own mind.

But appeals to what is obvious are problematic in the history of ideas. For instance, isn't it just obvious that the sun moves round the Earth? Just look. And yet it is false. Descartes took it as obvious that there can be no thoughts without a thinker, so he was certain that he was a thinking *substance*. And yet there are good reasons to believe that there are no substances whose essence it is to think, and many philosophers have argued, along with Buddhists, that there is no 'self'. So 'my mind' may not be what it seems.

> See THE CONCEIVABILITY ARGUMENT, p. 202, and AM I A SUBSTANCE?, p. 209.

More significantly, the objection misunderstands Churchland's claim. People who argued against phlogiston did not deny that things burnt; biologists who argued against vital force did not deny that things are alive. So Churchland does not deny the existence of psychological phenomena as such. He accepts that the phenomena that we conceptualise as 'thinking' occur; he denies that folk psychology is the correct theory of their nature. He argues that neuroscience will provide the correct account of what these are, and that explanation will have no place for concepts like 'belief', 'desire' or 'Intentional content'.

All we can be 'intuitively certain' of is the existence of the phenomena we want to explain. But appealing to beliefs and desires is not appealing to the phenomena, but to a particular explanation of them. They are theoretical terms that we should reject if folk psychology turns out to be false.

? What does eliminativism eliminate?

Folk psychology has good predictive and explanatory power

Churchland criticises folk psychology for its explanatory failures concerning mental illness, sleep, learning, etc. But we can object that this is unfair. Folk psychology is not *intended* to be a theory of these aspects of mental life, so it is no criticism that it does not explain them. It is only meant to explain human behaviour; or even more specifically, human action. Here, it is incredibly successful. By contrast, neuroscience is almost useless at predicting whether you'll study hard for your exams or explaining why you went to the cinema last night.

Furthermore, folk psychology is the basis of developments in psychology that have extended its predictive and explanatory power. For instance, ideas about unconscious beliefs and desires have become part of folk psychology. The Greeks used an idea of fixed and unchanging 'character', whereas now we tend to appeal more to the situation someone finds themselves in. The importance of situation is a finding in recent empirical psychology, and there are many such findings and theories that use folk psychological concepts and ideas. To eliminate the concepts of beliefs, desires, etc., from psychology would do away with much scientific psychology as well as folk psychology.

Explain the argument defending the explanatory power and importance of folk psychology.

Eliminativism could reply that these points are not very strong. First, we need to know how human action or behaviour relates to the rest of mental life. To have very different *sorts* of theories explaining different aspects of the mind is unsatisfactory. Second, the developments in folk psychology are relatively superficial. Our folk psychological explanations of behaviour are still far less powerful than the kinds of explanations we find elsewhere in the sciences. The only way to address this problem is to look to neuroscience.

Going further: the articulation of eliminative materialism as a theory is self-refuting

Churchland's argument starts from the premise that folk psychology is an empirical theory. This is why we can think about proving that it is false and eliminating its concepts. But there is good reason to suppose that this is a misunderstanding. We can argue for this indirectly.

Eliminativism presents arguments, which are expressions of beliefs and rely on beliefs about what words mean and how reasoning works, in order to change our beliefs about folk psychology. Yet eliminativism claims that *there are no beliefs*. So what does eliminativism express and what is it trying to change? If there are no beliefs, including no beliefs about meaning, no beliefs linked by reasoning, then arguments for eliminativism are meaningless. An argument for eliminativism refutes itself – it concludes that there are no beliefs but it presupposes that there are beliefs.

Eliminativists reply that this objection begs the question. It presupposes that the correct theory of meaning is the one that folk psychology gives. Compare the nineteenth-century argument between people who thought that to be alive required some special energy, a 'vital force', and those who said there was no such force. The vitalists could argue that if what their opponents said was true, they would all be dead! Yet now we know there is no special 'vital force', that life arises from ordinary chemical reactions. Eliminativism simply claims that we need a new theory of what it means to assert a claim or argument.

But we can press the objection. Eliminativism is eliminating Intentional content. The very ideas of meaning, or 'making sense', of 'true' v. 'false' belief, or 'reasoning' itself, are to be rejected, as they all rest on Intentional content. Claims and arguments are all 'about' something. The analogy with vitalism fails. Anti-vitalists accepted that they needed to be alive to make their claims, but offered an alternative account of what 'life' is. Eliminativists claim that they do *not* need Intentional content to make their claims. Without having some *alternative* account of meaning which doesn't use Intentional content, this is what is inconceivable. We *cannot conceive* that folk psychology is false, because that very idea, 'folk psychology is false', presupposes the folk psychological concept of Intentional content. At least until we have another, better theory of meaning, the assertion that eliminativism is true undermines itself.

On this view, folk psychology turns out not to be an empirical theory (which might be wrong), but a condition of intelligibility, a condition for thinking, reasoning, making claims at all. So we can't eliminate it. That means that mental states and properties must exist and be either reducible or irreducible. If Churchland is right that we cannot reduce intentional content to neuroscience, this isn't an objection to Intentional content. It is an argument in favour of the irreducibility of mental properties.

> **?**
> 1) Is eliminative materialism self-refuting? 2) Do beliefs, desires and other such mental states exist?

Key points: eliminative materialism

- Eliminativism argues that 'folk psychology' is an empirical theory of the mind. As empirical, if it is false, it should be replaced by a better theory, e.g. neuroscience.
- We have good reason to think that folk psychology is false. It does not explain many mental phenomena, has not progressed in over 2,500 years, and cannot be made consistent with scientific theories that we know to be true.
- We can object that we can be more certain that we have mental states than that eliminativism is true. Eliminativists can respond that our mental concepts refer to theoretical entities that explain our experience, and we cannot be certain that these explanations are correct.
- We can object that folk psychology does not intend to explain more than people's behaviour and that many developments in psychology use its concepts.

- A more fundamental objection is that eliminativism cannot be true because any arguments for it are self-refuting. One cannot argue that a theory is false without presupposing Intentional content. Eliminativism offers us no alternative way of making sense of the idea of meaning. Folk psychology is therefore not an empirical theory, but a condition of saying anything meaningful at all.

Summary: eliminative materialism

In this section on eliminative materialism, we have looked at Churchland's argument for the theory and objections to it. In our discussion and evaluation of these arguments, we have looked at the following issues:

1. What is the difference between reduction and elimination of mental states and properties?
2. What is folk psychology, and is it an empirical theory?
3. Are there good reasons to think that folk psychology is false?
4. Is eliminative materialism a coherent theory?

4   PREPARING FOR THE EXAM

To get good exam results, you need to have a good sense of what the exam will be like and what the examiners are looking for, and to revise in a way that will help you prepare to answer the questions well. This probably sounds obvious, but in fact, many students do not think about the exam itself, only about what questions might come up. There is a big difference. This chapter will provide you with some guidance on how to approach your exams in a way that will help get you the best results you can.

It is divided into four sections: the examination, understanding the question, revision and exam technique. In the last two sections, I highlight revision points and exam tips. These are collected together at the end of the chapter.

The examination

The structure of the exam

There is one exam, lasting three hours and covering the whole A2. It has two sections: Section A Ethics and Section B Philosophy of Mind. All the questions are compulsory – there is no choice in what you can answer.

Each section has three types of question. First, there are questions that ask you to define or briefly explain an important philosophical concept or theory. On the specimen exam papers, these take the form of one 3-mark and two 5-mark questions, but they may take a different form in the future (always adding up to 13 marks). Second, there is one 12-mark question that asks you to explain something more complex. For instance, you could be asked to explain a complex theory or argument, to apply a theory to an issue (in ethics), to compare or contrast two theories, to explain both a theory and an argument for or against it. There may be other possibilities as well. Third, there is one 25-mark open-ended essay question that asks you to evaluate a philosophical claim.

For each type of question – and especially the essay question – the examiners are expecting more than they did at AS level. The questions or concepts may be a little more demanding, and in some cases, you may need to write more than you did for AS in order to give a full and clear explanation. However, the emphasis is still very much on quality, not quantity.

Here are the questions from the specimen exam paper:

Section A Ethics

1. What does it mean to say that an ethical theory is *deontological*? (3 marks)
2. Briefly explain ethical naturalism. (5 marks)
3. Explain the difference between cognitivist and non-cognitivist theories of ethics. (5 marks)
4. How might a utilitarian attempt to justify preventative imprisonment (imprisoning someone to prevent them from committing a crime, rather than because they have committed a crime)? (12 marks)
5. Is Aristotle's doctrine of the mean useful for making moral decisions? (25 marks)

Section B Philosophy of Mind

1. What are qualia? (3 marks)
2. Briefly explain the philosophical zombie argument for (property) dualism. (5 marks)
3. Briefly outline Descartes' indivisibility argument. (5 marks)
4. What are the similarities and differences between interactionist dualism and epiphenomenalist dualism? (12 marks)
5. Are mental states ontologically reducible to brain states? (25 marks)

If you've been doing the questions in the margin of this textbook, these kinds of questions should be very familiar.

Assessment objectives

The examiners mark your answers according to two principles, known as 'Assessment Objectives' (AOs). They are:

AO1: Demonstrate understanding of the core concepts and methods of philosophy

AO2: Analyse and evaluate philosophical argument to form reasoned judgements

So AO1 requires you to understand how philosophers have argued, and AO2 requires you to be able to argue – to construct and evaluate arguments – yourself. Except for the 25-mark questions, all the marks available are for AO1. For the 25-mark questions, 5 marks are for AO1 and 20 marks are for AO2. How well you write also makes a contribution, so it is important to write clearly and grammatically, so that the examiner can understand what you mean. Don't try to impress using big words or long sentences – it just gets in the way of clarity and precision.

Understanding the question: giving the examiners what they are looking for

More information on this is available in the Mark Schemes that the AQA publish online.

The key to doing well in an exam is understanding the question. I don't just mean understanding the *topic* of the question, like 'utilitarianism' or 'qualia'. Of course, this is very important. But you also need to understand what the question is asking you to *do*. Each type of question tests different kinds of philosophical knowledge and skill.

Short-answer questions

The first questions of each section test the *accuracy* and *precision* of your understanding.

Three-mark questions ask you to define a concept. The examiners want you to be *concise*. State the definition as clearly and precisely as you can and then move on. Don't waffle or talk around the concept. So my answer to 'What are qualia?' is this:

Taken from QUALIA, p. 260.

Qualia are experiential properties of phenomenal consciousness. There is something 'it is like' to experience them. More precisely, if they exist, they are intrinsic, non-representational properties of phenomenal consciousness, properties that an experience has in and of its own, not in virtue of how it represents the world.

Five-mark questions ask you to outline and/or explain an important philosophical concept or claim. Explaining involves not just describing the idea, but giving a sense of the reasoning or thought behind it. Say enough to give a full explanation, but again, stay concise and don't waffle. So, my answer to 'Explain the difference between cognitivist and non-cognitivist theories of ethics' is this:

> Cognitivist theories in metaethics claim that moral judgements are expressions of moral beliefs, which represent how the world is and can be true or false. For example, one cognitivist theory, moral realism, says that whether moral judgements are true or false depends on what properties an action, person or situation actually has.
>
> Non-cognitivist theories claim that moral judgements express some non-cognitive attitude (they disagree on what this attitude is). These are states of mind that do not represent how the world is. As a result, strictly speaking, moral judgements cannot be true or false. For example, one non-cognitivist theory, emotivism, says that moral judgements express our feelings of approval or disapproval.

Taken largely from COGNITIVISM AND NON-COGNITIVISM, p. 144.

It's fine to use numbered arguments, as I have throughout this book. For example, my answer to 'Briefly explain the philosophical zombie argument for (property) dualism' is this:

> Property dualism is the claim that there are two fundamental and distinct types of property – physical properties and (some) mental properties. The zombie argument starts from the claim that we can conceive of physical properties existing without the phenomenal properties of consciousness with which they are correlated in the actual world. It then claims that what we can coherently conceive of is possible; and if it is possible for one thing to exist without the other, this shows that they are distinct things.

Taken from THE 'PHILOSOPHICAL ZOMBIES' ARGUMENT, p. 279.

1. It is conceivable that there are zombies.
2. If it is conceivable that there are zombies, it is metaphysically possible that there are zombies.
3. If it is metaphysically possible that there are zombies, then phenomenal properties of consciousness are non-physical.
4. Therefore, property dualism is true.

It is important not only to state the essential claims but to *order* them and *link* them logically. Without these links ('so', 'because', 'therefore'), you haven't got an explanation.

Twelve-mark questions

Twelve-mark questions ask you to explain more, or more complex, material than 5-mark questions. The marks are still all for AO1, your understanding of the argument or theory, so you should not *evaluate* it. This is very important, because any time spent on evaluation is simply wasted – no marks are available. If you are asked to explain a theory, you should not discuss whether it is convincing or true. If you are asked to explain an argument, this could be an argument supporting a claim or an objection to it. The argument that you are explaining is *itself* an evaluation (a reason to believe or reject a claim). You need to explain the argument or objection and how it works as an argument or objection – but you should not discuss whether it is a *good* argument or objection. If you compare two theories, you should point out the most important differences and/or similarities (whatever is relevant), but you should not try to defend one theory over the other.

On the difference between understanding and evaluation, see UNDERSTANDING ARGUMENTS, p. 10, EVALUATING ARGUMENTS, p. 11 and EVALUATING CLAIMS, p. 12.

As with the 5-mark questions, the examiners are looking for clarity, precision, and an *explanation* that sets out the central claims in a way that demonstrates the logical links between them. The answer needs to work as a single 'whole', rather than a number of disconnected 'bits'. In addition, you will need to stay focused and relevant and use technical philosophical language appropriately (i.e. with clarity, precision and only when it is needed). So my answer to 'What are the similarities and differences between interactionist dualism and epiphenomenalist dualism?' is this:

Taken mostly from INTERACTIONIST DUALISM, p. 215, and EPIPHENOMENALIST DUALISM, p. 219.

Both interactionist and epiphenomenalist dualism are forms of dualism, either substance dualism or property dualism. Substance dualism claims that there are two fundamentally different types of substances: physical substances (bodies) and mental substances (minds). Minds and bodies are ontologically distinct and independent. Property dualism is the view that, although there is just one kind of substance – that identified by physics – there are two fundamentally different kinds of property, mental and physical.

Interactionist dualism claims that mental events can cause physical events and vice versa. There is causation in both 'directions'. By contrast, epiphenomenalist dualism claims that the mind has no causal powers at all, so mental events do not cause physical events. However, it agrees with interactionist dualism that physical events can cause mental events. There is causation in just one 'direction', physical to mental. Interactionist dualism challenges the claim that every physical event has a sufficient physical cause ('causal closure of the physical'), but epiphenomenalist dualism accepts this claim.

You could stop here, or go on to say something more about the implications of these differences:

As a result, the two theories face different objections. In particular, interactionist dualism faces challenges in explaining how it is possible for a non-physical, non-spatial substance to interact with physical objects. Epiphenomenalist dualism is counter-intuitive in denying that our thoughts and feelings cause our actions, a claim that also seems to undermine our freedom and responsibility. It also faces a challenge in explaining how we know our own thoughts, if those thoughts don't cause our knowledge of them.

As forms of dualism, both theories face the challenge of how we can know that other people have minds, since it seems that all we observe is their behaviour.

Because the sample question in ethics is so different, it is worth looking at that as well. My answer to 'How might a utilitarian attempt to justify preventative imprisonment (imprisoning someone to prevent them from committing a crime, rather than because they have committed a crime)?' is this:

Taken mostly from UTILITARIANISM, p. 26, and CRIME AND PUNISHMENT, p. 117.

According to (act) utilitarianism, only three things are relevant when deciding whether an action is right or wrong:

1. Consequences: actions are morally right or wrong depending on their consequences and nothing else. An act is right if it maximises what is good.
2. Happiness: the only thing that is good is happiness.
3. Equality: no one's happiness counts more than anyone else's.

Therefore, an action is right if it *maximises* happiness, i.e. if it leads to the greatest happiness of all those it affects. Otherwise, the action is wrong.

We can apply this claim to punishment. Punishment involves making the person who is punished less happy by depriving them of something good. Therefore, punishment can only be justified if this increase in unhappiness is outweighed by an increase in happiness. The justification for punishing people needs to 'look forwards' to the effects of punishment.

One of the effects of punishment is social protection. Punishment can stop the criminal from harming anyone else, e.g. by locking them in prison. This justification can extend to cases in which someone has not yet committed a crime. A utilitarian could therefore argue that we would be justified in punishing someone *before* they have committed a crime if we think there is a good chance they might. While this will lead to the unhappiness of the person punished, it will lead to greater happiness overall because the crime, which could cause great unhappiness, is prevented.

Twenty-five-mark questions

When you are answering a short-answer question or a 12-mark question, what you need to do is straightforward. There are no choices to make about *what* concepts or arguments to talk about, since that is specified by the question. By contrast, 25-mark questions are much more open-ended. You are asked to evaluate a claim. To do this, you will need to construct and evaluate arguments for and against the claim. Because there are marks available for AO2, if you do not evaluate the philosophical claims, theories and arguments that you discuss, then you cannot get a good mark for the question, no matter how clear and accurate you are in explaining them.

See EVALUATING ARGUMENTS, p. 11 and EVALUATING CLAIMS, p. 12.

In addition to evaluating individual claims and arguments, your answer as a whole needs to work as one long argument. Arguments have a clear conclusion – you need to decide from the very beginning what your conclusion will be. This should never be simply 'there are points against and points in favour'. You need to *weigh up* the pros and cons – this is what evaluation is. For 'Is Aristotle's doctrine of the mean useful for making moral decisions?', your conclusion could be

1. 'yes', that is, you defend the claim that the doctrine of the mean can be appropriately and helpfully used this way
2. 'no', that is, you argue that it fails and this is an objection to the theory
3. something more conditional such as 'no, but ... ', for example, you may argue that it isn't intended to be used for this purpose
4. something sceptical, 'we cannot know because ... ' (this is quite hard to defend for this question! However, it may be possible to take this approach to the sample Philosophy of Mind question, 'Are mental states ontologically reducible to brain states?')

With your conclusion in mind, you need to select which arguments and theories you will discuss. Make sure that you look at arguments both for and against your conclusion. The examiners are more interested in the *quality* of what you write than the quantity. Three points are relevant here:

1. Don't aim for a comprehensive discussion of the question, covering all the angles. Perhaps just discuss two arguments – ones that you think are really strong or important – but discuss them with depth and rigour. One good discussion is worth more than many weak or superficial points.
2. The examiners don't expect you to try to provide a 'balanced' account. They are testing your skill at arguing. So your answer can take the form of a very strong argument in favour of your conclusion and then strong replies to objections that can be raised.
3. To make your answer coherent, what you argue at each point in the answer should make some contribution to your conclusion. It fits into a logical structure.

There is no single right way to do all this (which is one reason I don't give a sample answer here). So you will need to plan your approach and answer to the question carefully. How to do this, and much more on answering essay questions, was discussed in WRITING PHILOSOPHY (p. 16). Once again, it's fine to use numbered arguments. It's also fine to use bullet points, particularly if you are running out of time.

Revision: it's more than memory

There are lots of memory tricks for learning information for exams. This section isn't about those. Revision isn't just about learning information, but also about learning how to use that information well in the exam. If you've been answering the questions throughout this book, then you have been putting into practice the advice I give below.

See THE EXAMINATION, p. 312.

In revising for the exam, you need to bear in mind the structure of the exam and the Assessment Objectives. First, the five questions in each section are all compulsory, and cover different areas of the syllabus, so you'll need to revise the whole syllabus. Second, thinking about the 25-mark questions, structure your revision around the central questions or topics that the syllabus covers. In Ethics, these are the three normative theories (utilitarianism, Kantian deontology and Aristotelian virtue ethics), practical issues, and the cognitivist v. non-cognitivist debate in metaethics. In Philosophy of Mind, they are the six main theories: substance dualism, property dualism, logical behaviourism, mind–brain type identity theory, functionalism and eliminative materialism.

AO1 tests your understanding of central concepts and claims in these areas and how arguments are constructed for or against claims. We can break this down further. For the short-answer questions,

> R1: Learn the concepts and definitions that are central to the philosophical theories studied.

The glossary can help with this. For the 5- and 12-mark questions,

> R2: Learn who said what. What are the most important claims they made? What arguments did they use to defend their claims?

However, AO1 tests your *understanding*, not just your knowledge, of these claims and arguments. So you will need to show how the arguments are supposed to work. What are the premises and conclusion, and how is the conclusion supposed to follow from the premises?

> R3: Spend time identifying the main claims and arguments involved in each issue you have studied, putting arguments in your own words, stating clearly what the conclusion is and what the premises are. Explain how the reasoning is supposed to work.

This is difficult, because philosophical ideas and arguments are abstract and complicated, so it can be hard to know just what they mean. But the examiners also want precision. So it is worth thinking further about whatever you find hardest to understand.

> R4: Revise those concepts, claims and arguments that are hard to understand. Try to identify the differences between different interpretations. Which interpretation is best and why?

The exam questions do not explicitly ask for examples, but examples can prove very helpful when explaining a claim, objection or theory. If you are going to use examples, you want them to be good – clear, relevant and supportive of the point you want to make. You can either remember good examples you have read, or create your own. In either case, you should know precisely what point the example is making. An irrelevant example demonstrates that you don't really know what you are talking about.

> R5: Prepare examples beforehand, rather than trying to invent them in the exam. They must be short and they must make the right point – so try them out on your friends and teachers first.

What about AO2? How do you revise evaluation? Twenty-five-mark questions test you on how well you build an argument, deal with objections, and come to a supported conclusion. *How well you do this is the main skill that distinguishes A2 from AS.* The best way to prepare for it is to spend time *thinking* about the arguments and issues. You might know and even understand Ryle's arguments for logical behaviourism, but you may never have stopped to really work out whether you think they are any good. Get involved!

See EVALUATING
ARGUMENTS, p. 11
and EVALUATING
CLAIMS, p. 12.

So think about the different kinds of objection that can be raised to claims and arguments. Relate a particular argument to other arguments and viewpoints on the issue, and reflect on whether the objections to an argument undermine it. Work through the arguments so that you understand for yourself the pros and cons of each viewpoint.

> R6: Think reflectively about the arguments and issues. Practise arguing for and against a particular view. Think about the place and importance of the arguments for the issue as a whole.

Your answer needs to work as an argument itself, a coherent piece of reasoning. This means that what you write should also take the form of premises and conclusion. The premises will be your judgements as you go along, in response to this view or that objection. These judgements need to add up to a conclusion. You shouldn't end your essay with a totally different point of view than your evaluations in the essay support. In other words, do the judgements you reach reflect the arguments you have presented?

R7: Think about how your judgements on the various arguments you have studied add up. Do they lead to one conclusion, one point of view being right? Or do you think arguments for and against one position are closely balanced?

These first seven revision points relate to taking in and understanding information. There are two more points that will help you organise the information, learn it better, and prepare you for answering exam questions. This is especially important in relation to the 25-mark questions.

Twenty-five-mark questions are open-ended, and so you will need to choose to discuss what is *relevant* to the question being asked. Knowing what is relevant is a special kind of knowledge, which involves thinking carefully about what you know about the theories in relation to the question asked. A good way of organising your information is to create answer outlines or web-diagrams for particular issues.

For example, you could create an outline or web-diagram for mind–brain identity theory. Think about the essential points, and organise them, perhaps like this:

1. What does the claim that mental states are ontologically reducible to brain states mean?
2. Who argued that mental states are reducible to brain states? What are the main arguments?
3. Who argued against this claim, in favour of non-reductivism? What are the most important and powerful arguments?
4. What are the main strengths and weaknesses of the claim that mental states are ontologically reducible to brain states?
5. What is your conclusion on the issue, and why?

With an outline structured like this, you should be able to answer any question that comes up on the mind–brain type identity theory.

> R8. Create structured outlines or web-diagrams for particular issues. Try to cover all the main points.

Finally, once you've organised your notes into an outline or web-diagram, time yourself writing exam answers. Start by using your outline, relying on your memory to fill in the details. Then practise by memorising the outline as well, and doing it as though it were an actual exam. You might be surprised at how quickly the time goes by. You'll find that you need to be very focused – but this is what the examiners are looking for: answers that are thoughtful but to the point.

> R9: Practise writing timed answers. Use your notes at first, but then practise without them.

Exam technique: getting the best result you can

If you've understood the exam structure, and know what to expect, the exam will seem less daunting. You'll have a good idea about how to proceed, and a sense of how the questions are testing different aspects of your knowledge. This section gives you some tips on how to approach the questions when you are actually in the exam.

Exams are very exciting, whether in a good way or a bad way! It can be helpful, therefore, to take your time at the beginning, not to rush into your answers, but to plan your way. The tips I give below are roughly in the order in which you might apply them when taking the exam.

First, how long should you spend on each part? The marks give a rough guide. There are 100 marks available, 50 for Section A and 50 for Section B. You have 3 hours or 180 minutes. That's a little under 2 minutes for each mark. However, this isn't exact – the answer for each 3-mark question will probably take less than 6 minutes, while 50 minutes or a little more is about right for each 25-mark question, especially because these answers require more planning. And because the exam covers five topics, you'll probably find that you know the answer to some of the questions better than others. Give yourself a little extra time for the questions you find difficult. You don't need to answer the questions in the order in which they are set. You might want to answer the ones you are confident about first, to get the best marks you can, and come back to the others later on. Don't lose marks on the questions that you can do, by not giving yourself enough time to answer them well.

> E1. The number of marks available for each part is a rough guide to how long you spend on it. But allow a little extra time for parts you find difficult and perhaps for the 25-mark questions as well. Choose what order to answer the questions in.

Before you start to write your answer to any part, read the question again very closely. There are two things to look out for. First, notice what the question is asking you to do. Remember that you need to display your *understanding*, not just your knowledge, of the philosophical issues. So you'll need to explain claims and arguments, not just state them. Second, notice the *precise* phrasing of the question. For example, the sample question 'What are the similarities and differences between interactionist dualism and epiphenomenalist dualism?' asks you to explain *both* the similarities *and* differences between these theories. Many students have a tendency to notice only what the question is about, e.g. Kantian deontology or mind–brain identity theory. They don't notice the rest of the words in the question. But the question is never 'so tell me everything you know about *x*'! Make sure your conclusion – and your discussion – answers the actual question set.

See UNDERSTANDING
THE QUESTION, p. 314.

> E2. Before starting your answer, read the question again very closely. Take note of every word to make sure you answer the actual question set. Remember to explain, and not just state, claims and arguments.

With 25-mark questions, and for many 12-mark questions as well, before you start writing, it is worth organising your thoughts first. What are you going to say, in what order? Whether you are explaining or evaluating arguments, you need to present ideas in a logical order. Especially for 25-mark answers, if you've memorised an outline or a web-diagram, quickly write it out at the beginning so that you note down all the points. It is very easy to forget something or go off on a tangent once you are stuck into the arguments. Having an outline or web-diagram to work from will help you keep your answer relevant and structured. However, you might discover, as you develop your answer, that parts of the outline or diagram are irrelevant or just don't fit. Don't worry – the outline is only there as a guide. It will also remind you how much you still want to cover, so it can help you pace yourself better. If you do run out of time, you can indicate to the examiners that they should look at your plan – they will give marks for it.

> E3. For longer answers, before you start writing, it can be worth writing out your outline or web-diagram first. This can help remind you of the key points you want to make, and the order in which you want to make them.

Because philosophy is about the logical relationship of ideas, there are a number of rules of thumb about presentation. Here are four important ones.

> E4. Four rules of thumb:
>
> a. Explain 'technical terms', like 'ethical naturalism' or 'ontological independence', unless it is clear from the context that you know what they mean.
> b. Keep related ideas together. If you have a thought later on, add a footnote indicating where in the answer you want it to be read.
> c. Explain a theory before evaluating it.
> d. Don't state the conclusion to an argument before you've discussed the argument, especially if you are going to present objections to that conclusion. You can state what the argument hopes to show, but don't state it *as a* conclusion.

If you use examples, you need to keep them short and relevant, and explain why they support your argument. An example is an illustration, not an argument in itself.

E5. Keep your examples short and make sure they support the point you want to make. Always explain how they support your point.

For 25-mark questions, it is worth noting that evaluation is more than just presenting objections and responses side-by-side. Get the objections and the theory to 'talk' to each other, and come to some conclusion about which side is stronger.

E6. For 25-mark questions, make sure your discussion is not just reporting a sequence of points of view, but presents objections and replies, weighs up the arguments, and reaches a particular conclusion.

Finally, it is very easy to forget something, or say it in an unclear way. Leave time to check your answer at the end. You might find you can add a sentence here or there to connect two ideas together more clearly, or that some word is left undefined. These little things can make a big difference to the mark.

E7. Leave time to check your answer at the end. You may want to add a helpful sentence here and there.

Revision tips

R1: Learn the concepts and definitions that are central to the philosophical theories studied.

R2: Learn who said what. What are the most important claims they made? What arguments did they use to defend their claims?

R3: Spend time identifying the main claims and arguments involved in each issue you have studied, putting arguments in your own words, stating clearly what the conclusion is and what the premises are. Explain how the reasoning is supposed to work.

R4: Revise those concepts, claims and arguments that are hard to understand. Try to identify the differences between different interpretations. Which interpretation is best and why?

R5: Prepare examples beforehand, rather than trying to invent them in the exam. They must be short and they must make the right point – so try them out on your friends and teachers first.

R6: Think reflectively about the arguments and issues. Practise arguing for and against a particular view. Think about the place and importance of the arguments for the issue as a whole.

R7: Think about how your judgements on the various arguments you have studied add up. Do they lead to one conclusion, one point of view being right? Or do you think arguments for and against one position are closely balanced?

R8: Create structured outlines or web-diagrams for particular issues. Try to cover all the main points.

R9: Practise writing timed answers. Use your notes at first, but then practise without them.

Exam tips

E1: The number of marks available for each part is a rough guide to how long you spend on it. But allow a little extra time for the 25-mark questions and parts you find difficult. Choose what order in which to answer the questions.

E2: Before starting your answer, read the question again very closely. Take note of every word to make sure you answer the actual question set. Remember to explain, and not just state, claims and arguments.

E3: For longer answers, before you start writing, it can be worth writing out your outline or web-diagram first. This can help remind you of the key points you want to make, and the order in which you want to make them.

E4: Four rules of thumb:

    a.   Explain 'technical terms', like 'ethical naturalism' or 'ontological independence', unless it is clear from the context that you know what they mean.

    b.   Keep related ideas together. If you have a thought later on, add a footnote indicating where in the answer you want it to be read.

    c.   Explain a theory before evaluating it.

    d.   Don't state the conclusion to an argument before you've discussed the argument, especially if you are going to present objections to that conclusion. You can state what the argument hopes to show, but don't state it *as* a conclusion.

E5: Keep your examples short and make sure they support the point you want to make. Always explain how they support your point.

E6: For 25-mark questions, make sure your discussion is not just reporting a sequence of points of view, but presents objections and replies, weighs up the arguments, and reaches a particular conclusion.

E7: Leave time to check your answer at the end. You may want to add a helpful sentence here and there.

GLOSSARY
(with Joanne Lovesey)

a posteriori – Knowledge of propositions that can only be known to be true or false through sense experience.

a priori – Knowledge of propositions that do not require (sense) experience to be known to be true or false.

abstract – Theoretical (rather than applied or practical) and removed from any concrete objects or instances.

action – Something an agent does intentionally.

actual world – The world as it is. The actual world is a possible world, specifically the one we live in.

ad hoc – A statement or a move in an argument that suits the purpose at hand but has no independent support.

analogy – Similarity in several respects between different things.

analogy, argument from – Mill's argument that we can use the behaviour of other people to infer that they have minds because they behave as I do, and I have a mind.

analysis – Process of breaking up a complex concept or expression in order to reveal its simpler constituents, thereby elucidating its meaning.

analytic – A proposition that is true (or false) in virtue of the meanings of the words. For instance, 'a bachelor is an unmarried man' is analytically true, while 'a square has three sides' is analytically false.

antecedent – The proposition that forms the first part of a conditional statement, usually the part of the sentence that comes after 'if'; e.g. in both 'If it rains then I will get wet' and 'I will get wet if it rains', the antecedent is 'it rains'.

arête – An 'excellence', or more specifically, a 'virtue' – a quality that aids the fulfilment of a thing's ergon (Aristotle).

argument – A reasoned inference from one set of claims – the premises – to another claim, the conclusion.

argument map – Visual diagram of how the premises of an argument relate to one another and to the conclusion.

assertion – The claim that a proposition is true.

assumption – A proposition accepted without proof or evidence as the basis for an inference or argument.

attitude – A mental state regarding how the world is or should be. A cognitive attitude, e.g. belief, has a mind-to-world direction of fit. A non-cognitive attitude, e.g. desire, has a world-to-mind direction of fit.

begging the question – The informal fallacy of (explicitly or implicitly) assuming the truth of the conclusion of an argument as one of the premises employed in an effort to demonstrate its truth.

behaviourism, analytical – A version of logical behaviourism that claims that mental concepts can be reduced to statements about behaviour.

behaviourism, logical – The theory that our talk about the mind can be analysed in terms of talk about behaviour; i.e. that many mental states are behavioural dispositions.

behaviourism, methodological – The theory that claims that because science can only investigate what is publicly accessible, psychology is concerned only with the explanation and prediction of behaviour and not with any 'inner' mental states.

belief – Affirmation of, or conviction regarding, the truth of a proposition; e.g. 'I believe that the grass is green'.

Categorical Imperative – 'Act only on that maxim through which you can at the same time will that it should become a universal law.' (Kant)

category mistake – Treating a concept as belonging to a logical category that it doesn't belong to; e.g. 'this number is heavy' commits a category mistake as numbers are not the sorts of things that can have a weight.

causal interaction, problem of – The problem of explaining how mental states or substance can interact causally with physical states or substance.

In particular, mental causation (the causation of physical events by mental events) is thought to contradict the completeness of physics.

character – A person's habitual dispositions regarding what they feel, how they think, how they react, the choices they make, and the actions they perform, under different circumstances.

character trait – An attribute that is exhibited by an individual as a matter of habit, e.g. honesty or being bad-tempered.

Chinese mind – A thought experiment by Block, presented as an objection to functionalism. If the population of China, using radios, duplicated the functioning of your brain, would this create conscious experiences (just as your brain does)? If not, functionalism (about consciousness) is false.

choice – What we decide upon as a result of deliberation, typically giving rise to voluntary action. Deliberate desire regarding something that is in one's power (Aristotle).

circular – An argument is circular if it employs its own conclusion as a premise.

clear and distinct ideas – A clear idea is 'present and accessible to the attentive mind'; a distinct idea is clear and also sharply separated from other ideas so that every part of it is clear. (Descartes)

cognitivism – A cognitivist account of ethical language argues that moral judgements express beliefs, can be true or false and aim to describe the world. So 'lying is wrong' expresses the belief that lying is wrong, and is either true or false.

coherent – A set of statements is coherent if the statements are consistent and increase each other's probability.

compatibilism – The theory that the causal determination of human conduct is consistent with the freedom required for responsible moral agency.

compatible – Two properties are compatible if it is possible for something to have both of them at once. Two claims are compatible if they are consistent.

completeness of physics – The thesis that every physical event has a sufficient physical cause that brings it about in accordance with the laws of physics.

composition, fallacy of – The informal fallacy of attributing some feature of the members of a collection to the collection itself, or reasoning from part to whole, e.g. sodium and chloride are both dangerous to humans, therefore sodium–chloride (salt) is dangerous to humans.

conceivability argument – Arguments for dualism from the conceivability of mind and body being distinct. Descartes argues that 1) it is conceivable that the mind can exist without the body; 2) conceivability entails possibility; so 3) it is possible that the mind can exist without the body. Therefore the mind and body are distinct substances. The zombie argument is a form of conceivability argument for property dualism.

conceivable – Capable of being imagined or grasped mentally without incoherence or contradiction.

concept – Any abstract notion or idea by virtue of which we apply general terms to things.

conclusion – A proposition whose truth has been inferred from premises.

conditional – A proposition that takes the form of 'if . . ., then . . .'. The conditional asserts that if the first statement (the antecedent) is true, then the second statement (the consequent) is also true; e.g. 'If it is raining then the ground is wet' asserts that if it is true that it is raining, it is true that the ground is wet.

conscience – An inner awareness, faculty, intuition or judgement that assists in distinguishing right from wrong.

consciousness – The subjective phenomenon of awareness of the world and/or of one's mental states.

consciousness, easy problem of – The problem of analysing and explaining the functions of consciousness; e.g. the facts that we can consciously control our behaviour, report on our mental states, and focus our attention. According to some philosophers, it is 'easy' to provide a successful analysis in physical and/or functional terms.

consciousness, hard problem of – The problem of analysing and explaining the phenomenal properties of consciousness, what it is like to undergo conscious experiences. According to some philosophers, it is 'hard' to provide a successful analysis in physical and/or functional terms.

consequent – The proposition that forms the second part of a conditional statement, usually the part of the sentence that occurs after 'then'; e.g. in both 'If it will rain then I will get wet' and 'I will get wet if it will rain', the consequent is 'I will get wet'.

consequentialism, act – The theory that actions are morally right or wrong depending on their consequences and nothing else. An act is right if it maximises what is good.

consistent – Two or more statements are consistent if they can both be true at the same time.

contingent – A proposition that could be either true or false, a state of affairs that may or may not hold, depending on how the world actually is.

contradiction – Two claims that cannot both be true, and cannot both be false; or one claim that both asserts and denies something; e.g. 'It is raining and it is not raining'.

contradiction in conception – In Kantian ethics, the test for whether we can will a maxim to become universal law can be failed if it would somehow be self-contradictory for everyone to act on that maxim.

contradiction in will – In Kantian ethics, the test for whether we can will a maxim to become universal law can be failed if, although the maxim is not self-contradictory, we cannot rationally will it.

correlation – A relationship between two things whereby one always accompanies the other; e.g. the properties of size and shape are correlated. Correlation should be distinguished from identity.

counter-argument – An argument that attempts to establish a conclusion that undermines another argument or the conclusion of another argument.

counterexamples, method of finding – If a theory makes a general claim, such as 'all mental states are functional states', we only need to find a single instance in which this is false (a counterexample) to show that the general claim is false and so something is wrong with the theory.

counter-intuitive – Something that doesn't fit with our intuition.

criterion – A standard by means of which to judge the features of things. If something fulfils the relevant criteria, we are justified in attributing the feature in question; e.g. it is a criterion of an act being virtuous that a virtuous person would do it.

deductive (**deduction**) – An argument whose conclusion is logically entailed by its premises, i.e. if the premises are true, the conclusion cannot be false.

definition – An explanation of the meaning of a word. Philosophical definitions often attempt to give necessary and sufficient conditions for the application of the term being defined.

deontology – The study of what one must do (*deon* (Greek) means 'one must'). Deontology claims that actions are right or wrong in themselves, not depending on their consequences. We have moral duties to do things which it is right to do and moral duties not to do things which it is wrong to do.

desirable – 1) Worthy of being desired. 2) Capable of being desired.

desire – A state of mind that motivates a person to act in such a way as to satisfy the desire; e.g. if a person desires a cup of tea, they are motivated to make and drink a cup of tea.

deterrence, external – External deterrence occurs when punishing a criminal deters other people from committing crimes.

deterrence, internal – Internal deterrence occurs when a punishment deters the person punished from offending again.

dilemma – Two mutually exclusive and exhaustive options (horns), both of which face significant objections.

direction of fit – The direction of the relation between mind and world. In one direction, the mind 'fits' the world, as in belief. We change our beliefs to fit the facts. In the other direction, the world 'fits' the mind, as in desire. We act on our desires to change the world to satisfy our desires.

disanalogy – A point of dissimilarity between two things, something that two things don't have in common.

disjunction – An either/or claim; e.g. 'Either it will rain or it will be sunny'.

disposition – How something or someone will or is likely to behave under certain circumstances: what it or they would do, could do, or are liable to do, in particular situations or under particular conditions, including conditions that they are not in at the moment, e.g. sugar is soluble (It tends to dissolve when placed in water) while someone who has a friendly disposition tends to smile when they are smiled at.

(5 marks)

divisibility argument – Descartes' argument that bodies are divisible into spatial parts, but minds have no such parts. Therefore, the mind is a distinct substance from the body.

dualism, interactionist – The theory that mental and physical events can cause one another even though the mind and body are distinct substances (interactionist substance dualism) or mental and physical properties are distinct fundamental properties (interactionist property dualism).

dualism, property – The theory that there is only one kind of substance, physical substance, but two ontologically basic kinds of property – mental properties and physical properties.

dualism, substance – The theory that two kinds of substance exist, mental and physical substance.

duties, general/specific – Duties are obligations we have towards someone or something. General duties are those we have towards anyone; e.g. do not murder; help people in need. Specific duties are those we have because of our particular personal or social relationships; e.g. to keep one's promises or to provide for one's children.

duties, perfect/imperfect – Perfect duties are those we must always fulfil and have no choice over when or how (e.g. do not kill). Imperfect duties are cases in which we have some choice in how we fulfil the obligation (e.g. giving to charity). No specific person can demand that we fulfil an imperfect duty towards them.

eliminative materialism – The theory that there are no mental properties, so our mental concepts are fundamentally mistaken and should be abandoned, as they don't refer to anything that exists.

emotivism – The theory that claims that moral judgements express a feeling or non-cognitive attitude, typically approval or disapproval, and aim to influence the feelings and actions of others.

empirical – Relating to or deriving from experience, especially sense experience, but also including experimental scientific investigation.

empiricism (**aka 'knowledge empiricism'**) – The theory that there can be no a priori knowledge of synthetic propositions about the world (outside one's mind); i.e. all a priori knowledge is of analytic propositions, while all knowledge of synthetic propositions must be checked against sense experience.

end – What an action seeks to achieve or secure; its aim or purpose.

end, final – An end that we desire for its own sake; we can't give some further purpose for why we seek it.

enumerative induction – The method of reasoning that argues from many instances of something to a general statement about that thing; e.g. 'The sun has risen in the morning every day for x number of days, therefore the sun rises in the morning.'

epiphenomenalism – The theory that mental states and events are epiphenomena, by-products, the effects of some physical process, but with no causal influence of their own.

epistemology – The study (-*ology*) of knowledge (*episteme*) and related concepts, including belief, justification, certainty. It looks at the possibility and sources of knowledge.

equivocation, fallacy of – The use of an ambiguous word or phrase in different senses within a single argument; e.g. 'All banks are next to rivers, I deposit money in a bank, therefore I deposit money next to a river.'

ergon – 'Function' or 'characteristic activity' of something; e.g. the *ergon* of a knife is to cut; the *ergon* of an eye is to see.

error theory – The theory that ethical judgements make claims about objective moral properties, but that no such properties exist. Thus moral judgements are cognitive, but are all false. Ethical language, as we mean to use it, rests on a mistake.

ethics – The branch of philosophy concerned with the evaluation of human conduct, including theories about which actions are right or wrong (normative ethics) and the meaning of moral language (metaethics).

eudaimonia – Often translated as 'happiness', but better understood as 'living well and faring well'. According to Aristotle, eudaimonia is not subjective and is not a psychological state, but an objective quality of someone's life as a whole. It is the final end for human beings.

explanation – An intelligible account; e.g. of why something happens. The thing to be explained (*explanandum*) is usually accepted as a fact, and what is used to explain it (the *explanans*) is usually plausible but less certain.

faculty – A mental capacity or ability, such as sight, the ability to feel fear, and reason.

fallacy/fallacious – An error in reasoning. More exactly, a fallacy is an argument in which the premises do not offer rational support to the conclusion. If the argument is deductive, then it is fallacious if it is not valid. If the argument is inductive, it is fallacious if the premises do not make the conclusion more likely to be true.

felicific calculus – In Bentham's ethics, the means of calculating pleasures and pains caused by an action and adding them up on a single scale. The total amount of happiness produced is the sum total of everyone's pleasures minus the sum total of everyone's pains.

first principles – Basic or foundational propositions in an area of knowledge or theory that are not deducible from other propositions.

folk psychology – A body of knowledge or theory regarding the prediction and explanation of people's behaviour constituted by the platitudes about the mind ordinary people are inclined to endorse; e.g. 'if someone is thirsty, they will normally try to find something to drink'.

formula of humanity – A version of the Categorical Imperative: 'Act in such a way that you always treat humanity, whether in your own person or in the person of any other, never simply as a means, but always at the same time as an end' (Kant).

free will – The capacity of rational agents to choose a course of action from among various alternatives.

function – A mapping from each of the possible inputs to some state to its output. The description of a state's function describes what that state does. (For a distinct term, see the entry on *ergon*.)

function argument – Aristotle's argument that the human good (eudaimonia) will be achieved by performing our characteristic activity (*ergon*) well. Traits that enable us to fulfil our *ergon*, which is rational activity, are virtues (*arête*).

functionalism – The theory that mental states can be reduced to functional states; i.e. what it is to be a mental state is just to be a state with certain input and output relations to stimuli, behaviour and other mental states.

functionalism, causal role – The version of functionalism that interprets the function of mental states in terms of the role they play in a network of causes and effects. A mental state can be 'realised' by any state that plays that causal role.

Ghost in the Machine – Ryle's name for substance dualism.

Golden Rule – The moral guideline that says 'do unto others as you would have them do unto you'.

good – In ethics, what is good provides a standard of evaluation and what we should aim at in our actions and lives.

hedonism – The claim that pleasure is happiness and the only good.

hypothesis – A proposal that needs to be confirmed or rejected by reasoning or experience.

hypothetical reasoning – Working out the best hypothesis that would explain or account for some experience or fact.

idealism – The theory that minds are the only kind of substance. Therefore, all that exists are minds and what depends on them (ideas).

identity (**numerical**) – Being one and the same thing. Everything is identical to itself, and nothing else.

imperative – A command or order. A hypothetical imperative is a statement about what you ought to do, on the assumption of some desire or goal; e.g. if you want to pass your exam, you ought to study hard. A categorical imperative is a statement about what you ought to do, without regard to what you want.

inconsistent – Two statements are inconsistent if they can't both be true at the same time.

indefinitely heterogenous dispositions – Dispositions that can be manifested in many, many different ways. Ryle argued that mental states are indefinitely heterogenous behavioural dispositions, so that while mental concepts can be analysed in terms of behaviour, they cannot be reduced to talk about behaviour.

indiscernibility of identicals – Leibniz's principle that if two things are identical (i.e. are just one thing), then they share all their properties and so are indiscernible; i.e. you cannot have numerical identity without qualitative identity.

inductive (**induction**) – An argument whose conclusion is supported by its premises, but is not logically entailed by them; i.e. if the premises are true, the conclusion may be false, but this is unlikely (relative to the premises).

inference – Accepting a proposition as true on the basis of reasoning from other propositions taken to be true.

inference to the best explanation – An inductive argument form where the conclusion presents the 'best explanation' for why the premises are true.

intention – A mental state that expresses a person's choice. It specifies the action they choose and often their reason or end in acting.

intentionality – The property of mental states whereby they are 'directed' towards an 'object', that is they are 'about' something; e.g. the belief that Paris is the capital of France is about Paris and the desire to eat chocolate is about chocolate.

intrinsic/extrinsic – Distinction in the properties of things. The intrinsic properties of a thing are those which it has in and of itself, e.g. the size of a physical object; its extrinsic features are those which it has only in relation to something else, e.g. the function of a mental state.

introspection – Direct, first-personal awareness of one's own mental states.

introspection, argument from – The argument that epiphenomenalism is incompatible with knowledge gained from introspection. If mental states don't cause anything, even my belief that I have those mental states, then how can I know what mental states I have?

intuition – Direct non-inferential awareness of truths or abstract objects; e.g. the intuition that murder is wrong or that zombies are possible.

intuitionism – The theory that some moral judgements are self-evident; i.e. their truth can be known just by rational reflection upon the judgement itself. Moral intuitions are a type of synthetic a priori knowledge.

invalid – Not valid. A deductive argument is invalid if it is possible for the premises to be true while the conclusion is false.

inverted qualia – The thought experiment that supposes that two people experience subjectively different colours when looking at the same object, but otherwise think and behave in identical ways; e.g. they both call the object 'red'. The argument is presented as an objection to a functionalist account of phenomenal consciousness.

(5 m)

involuntary – According to Aristotle, an act is involuntary if it is either forced or done from ignorance that is not culpable (especially if it is regretted once the ignorance is removed).

jus ad bellum – The justice of resorting to war; e.g. whether it is in a just cause.

jus in bello – Just conduct in war, focusing primarily on how the enemy is engaged and treated; e.g. whether the force used is proportional to the end that the war seeks to achieve.

jus post bellum – Justice at the end of war; e.g. whether the peace settlement is fair.

justice – The principle that each person receives their 'due'. Aristotle distinguishes between wide and narrow senses. In the wide sense, anything legal is just, and anything illegal is unjust. In the narrow sense, justice is fairness.

justice in distribution – Justice concerning who gets which goods and other resources.

justice in rectification – Justice concerning how to correct an injustice.

justification – What is offered as grounds for believing an assertion.

knowledge, acquaintance – Knowledge 'of' something, e.g. knowledge of the colour red.

knowledge argument – Jackson's argument for property dualism, presenting the thought experiment of Mary, a neuroscientist who has lived her entire life in a black-and-white room, but who knows all the physical information there is to know about what happens when we see a ripe tomato. When she first leaves the room and comes to see something red for the first time, does she learn something new? If so, some properties are not physical properties.

knowledge, ability – Knowing 'how' to do something; e.g. knowing how to imagine the colour red.

knowledge, propositional – Knowing 'that' some claim – a proposition – is true or false; e.g. knowing that this is what the colour red looks like.

laws of nature – Fixed regularities that govern the universe; statements that express these regularities.

location problem – The objection to type identity theory that mental states do not have a spatial location, yet type identity theory entails that they do, because they are identical to physical states.

Masked Man fallacy – A fallacious form of argument that uses what one believes about an object to infer whether or not the object is identical with something else; e.g. I believe the Masked Man robbed the bank; I do not believe my father robbed the bank; therefore, the Masked Man is not my father. This is a fallacy, because one's beliefs may be mistaken.

materialism – The theory that the only substance is matter (or physical substance). Everything that exists, including the mind, depends on matter (physical substance) to exist.

materialism, type-A/type-B – Type-A materialism is the theory that philosophical zombies, and the proposal that Jackson's Mary learns something new, are not conceivable. Type-B materialism claims that these thought experiments describe something conceivable, but not metaphysically possible.

matters of fact – States of affairs; how the world is. According to Hume, they are known through experience and induction, especially causal inference.

maxim – A personal principle that guides our decisions; e.g. 'to get a good education'.

mean, doctrine of the – Aristotle's claim that virtue requires us to feel, choose and act in an 'intermediate' way, neither 'too much' nor 'too little', but 'to feel [passions] at the right times, with reference to the right objects, towards the right people, with the right motive, and in the right way'.

meaning, descriptive – The aspect of the meaning of a sentence that asserts something about the world and can be evaluated as true or false.

meaning, emotive – The aspect of the meaning of a sentence that expresses or evokes an emotion.

meaning, prescriptive – The aspect of the meaning of a sentence that acts like a command or imperative. For example, the prescriptive meaning of 'lying is wrong' might be 'do not lie'.

means – What is done to achieve an end. Instrumental means are actions done to achieve some further, independent end; e.g. chopping vegetables in order to eat them. Constitutive means are those which are done as achieving the end; e.g. relaxing on the beach is a way of having a good holiday.

mental causation – See entry on 'causal interaction, problem of'.

mental states – Mental phenomena that can endure over time, such as beliefs and desires. The term is often used more broadly to cover mental phenomena in general (states, processes and events).

metaethics – The philosophical study of what morality is, enquiring into the meaning of ethical language, the metaphysics of moral values, the epistemology of moral judgements, and the nature of moral attitudes.

metaphysics – The branch of philosophy that asks questions about the fundamental nature of reality. *Meta-* means above, beyond, or after; *physics* enquires into the physical structure of reality.

mind-dependent – Depending on a mind for existence or definition; e.g. ideas are mind-dependent.

mind-independent – Not depending on a mind for existence or definition. According to moral realism, good and right are mind-independent properties of actions.

monism – The theory that only one kind of substance exists. Both materialism (physicalism) and idealism are monist theories.

morality – The rules, ideals and expectations governing fundamental aspects of human conduct. It concerns right and wrong, good and bad, in human action and character.

motive – A mental state or consideration that inclines someone to act in a certain way. Someone's motive could be a reason for acting, an end, or a desire.

multiple realisability – 1) The claim that there are many ways in which one and the same mental state can be expressed in behaviour. This is presented as an objection to the claim that mental states are reducible to behavioural dispositions. 2) The claim that one and the same mental state can have its function performed by different physical states. This is presented as an objection to the claim that mental states are identical to physical states.

naturalism, ethical – The theory that claims that moral properties are identical with certain natural (especially psychological) properties; e.g. the claim that goodness is happiness.

naturalistic fallacy – According to Moore, the mistake of identifying moral good with any natural property.

necessary – A proposition that must be true (or if false, it must be false), a state of affairs that must hold.

necessary condition – One proposition is a necessary condition of another when the second cannot be true while the first is false. For example, being a man is a necessary condition of being a bachelor, because if you are not a man you cannot be a bachelor.

nihilism – The view that there are no moral values.

non-cognitivism – The theory that claims that moral judgements express non-cognitive attitudes. Moral judgements do not make claims about reality and are not true or false (they are not fact-stating).

non-naturalism, ethical – The theory that claims that moral properties exist, but they are not natural properties.

non-voluntary – According to Aristotle, an action is non-voluntary if it is done from ignorance and if the ignorance is lifted, the agent does not regret the action.

normative – Relating to 'norms', rules or reasons.

normative ethics – The branch of ethics concerned with developing theories concerning what (e.g. which actions, which character traits, which intentions) is right or wrong, good or bad.

objection – Something that is given as a reason against either an argument or claim.

objective – Independent of what people think or feel. A claim is objectively true if its truth does not depend on people's beliefs.

Ockham's razor – The principle that we should not put forward a hypothesis that says many different things exist when a simpler explanation will do as well. 'Do not multiply entities beyond necessity.' A simpler explanation is a better explanation, as long as it is just as successful.

omnipotent – Having perfect power. Often defined as having the ability to do anything it is possible to do.

ontologically 'basic' – Not dependent on or derivable from some other entity or property; e.g. property dualists claim that mental properties are ontologically basic as they cannot be derived from physical properties.

ontologically 'distinct' – Two things are ontologically distinct if they are not the same thing, neither is able to be reduced to the other, and the existence of one is not determined by the existence of the other; e.g. substance dualists claim that mind and body are ontologically distinct substances.

ontology – The study of (*-ology*) what exists or 'being' (*ont-*).

open question argument – Moore's argument that identifying the property 'good' with any other property is never correct because whether that property is, in fact, good is an open question (logically, it can receive a yes or no answer), whereas whether good is good is not an open question.

pacifism – The view that war is always unjust (and therefore, we should never go to war).

para-mechanical hypothesis – Ryle's name for understanding mental phenomena as non-spatial, non-mechanical states and processes.

passions – In Aristotle, bodily appetites (for food, drink, sex, etc.), emotions, desires, and any feelings accompanied by pleasure or pain.

perception – Awareness of apparently external objects through use of the senses.

permissible – An action that is neither morally forbidden nor required (obligatory).

phenomenal concept – A concept by which you recognise something as of a certain kind when experiencing or perceiving it, e.g. a phenomenal concept of red as 'this' colour. Contrasted with theoretical concepts, which describe something in theoretical terms, e.g. a theoretical concept of red as light with a frequency of 600 nanometres.

phenomenal consciousness – A form of consciousness with a subjective experiential quality, as involved in perception, sensation, and emotion. 'What it is like' to experience such mental phenomena.

phenomenal properties – Properties of an experience that give it its distinctive experiential quality, and which are apprehended in phenomenal consciousness.

physicalism – A modern form of materialism, which claims that everything that exists is physical, or depends upon something that is physical. More precisely, the theory that everything that is ontologically basic is physical, that is comes under the laws and investigations of physics, and every physical event has a sufficient physical cause.

physicalism, non-reductive – A form of physicalism that claims that while mental properties depend upon physical properties, they are not reducible to them. Functionalism and logical behaviourism, in most versions, are forms of non-reductive physicalism.

physicalism, reductive – A form of physicalism that claims that mental properties are physical properties. See entry on 'type identity theory'.

plausible – Fits with what else we already know.

pleasures, higher and lower – One pleasure is higher than another if almost everyone who is 'competently acquainted' with both prefers one over the other. According to Mill, higher pleasures include thought, feeling and imagination, while lower pleasures involve the body and senses.

possible world – A way of talking about how things could be. Saying that something is possible (impossible) is saying that it is true in some (no) possible world.

possible, logically – Something is logically possible if it is conceivable, and doesn't involve a contradiction.

possible, metaphysically – Something is metaphysically possible if there is at least one possible world in which it is true.

possible, physically – Something is physically possible if it could be true given the laws of nature.

practical ethics – The branch of ethics concerned with the application of normative ethical theories to particular issues, such as lying or war.

practical reason – Reasons and reasoning concerned with what we can change and making good choices.

practical wisdom – (*phronesis*) An intellectual virtue of practical reason, 'a true and reasoned state or capacity to act with regard to the things that are good or bad for man' (Aristotle). It involves knowledge of what is good or bad in general and what is good in a particular situation, and the abilities to deliberate well and act on that deliberation.

premise – A proposition that, as part of an argument, provides or contributes to a reason to believe that the conclusion is true.

prescriptivism – The non-cognitive theory that moral judgements are prescriptive; i.e. moral judgements provide commands and recommendations about how to act.

presuppose – To require or assume an antecedent state of affairs; e.g. if Jones has stopped playing basketball, this presupposes that he was playing basketball.

private – Capable of being experienced or known by no one other than the subject themselves.

problem of other minds – The question of how we can know that there are minds other than our own, given that our experience of other minds (if they exist) is through behaviour.

property – An attribute or characteristic of an object, e.g. the property of being green, or being tall. Physical properties are those properties of objects investigated by physics, or more broadly, the natural sciences. Mental properties include mental states, such as beliefs, and mental events, such as having a thought or feeling pain.

property, moral – An attribute or characteristic of an object that is ethically normative, e.g. goodness or being a virtue.

property, natural/non-natural – Natural properties are those that we can identify through sense experience and science. Non-natural properties cannot be analysed in terms of or reduced to natural properties.

property, representational – A property of a mental state that enables it to represent what it does, to be 'about' something. It is an extrinsic or relational property (see entries on 'intrinsic/extrinsic' and 'intentionality').

proposition – A declarative statement (or, more accurately, what is claimed by a declarative statement), e.g. 'Mice are mammals'. Propositions can go after 'that' in 'I believe that . . .' and 'I know that . . .'.

prove – To demonstrate that a proposition is true by giving a sound deductive argument with that proposition as the conclusion.

punishment – An undesirable outcome enforced on an individual in response to that individual having performed a wrong action, e.g. a prison sentence for a crime.

qualia – Phenomenal properties understood as intrinsic and non-representational properties of mental states.

quality, primary – Properties that are 'utterly inseparable' from the object, whatever changes it goes through, even if it is divided into smaller and smaller pieces (Locke). The object has these properties 'in and of itself'. Locke lists extension (size), shape, motion, number and solidity as primary qualities.

quality, secondary – Properties that physical objects have that are 'nothing but powers to produce various sensations in us' (Locke). Locke lists 'colours, sounds, tastes, and so on', later adding smells and temperature.

queerness, argument from – Mackie's argument that moral properties, understood as non-natural properties, are (metaphysically and epistemologically) puzzling and improbable, which is a reason to believe they do not exist.

rationalism – The theory that there can be a priori knowledge of synthetic propositions about the world (outside one's mind). This knowledge is innate or gained by reason rather than derived from sense experience.

realism, moral – The theory that claims that moral judgements are made true or false by objective moral properties that are mind-independent (in some sense).

reason – A statement presented in justification for a claim. A good reason in some way raises the probability that the claim is true.

reasoning – The process of thinking about something in a logical way – in particular, drawing inferences on the basis of reasons.

reducible – A phenomenon or property is reducible to another if the first can be completely explained in terms of, or identified with, the second (which is considered more ontologically basic); e.g. type identity theory claims that mental properties are reducible (identical) to physical properties.

reductio ad absurdum – A form of argument that shows that some claim leads to a contradiction.

reduction – The reducing of one thing to another. An analytic reduction claims that one set of concepts can be translated without loss of meaning into another set of concepts; e.g. analytical behaviourism claims that mental concepts are reducible to behavioural concepts. An ontological reduction claims that the things in one domain are identical with some of the things in another domain; e.g. functionalism claims that mental properties are reducible to functional properties.

reductionism – The belief that statements or properties of one sort (in one domain, e.g. the mental) can be reduced to statements or properties of another, more basic kind (in another domain, e.g. the physical).

redundant – Superfluous, not adding anything.

reflective equilibrium – The end point of a process of reflection in which we revise general moral theories and individual moral judgements in light of each other, justified by intuitive plausibility and coherence.

relations of ideas – Relations of ideas are established by pure thought or reflection and are 'intuitively and demonstratively certain' (Hume). The negation of a relation of ideas is a contradiction.

responsibility, moral – Accountability for the actions one performs and the consequences they bring about, for which a moral agent can be justly praised or blamed. Moral responsibility is commonly held to require the agent's freedom to have done otherwise.

right reason – (*orthos logos*) In Aristotle, the standard for judging whether a character trait or an action conforms to the mean. Virtues and right actions are in accordance with 'right reason'.

rights – Justified moral demands regarding how other people may treat us, especially the freedoms (e.g. from harm) or benefits (e.g. education) they ought to provide. We are entitled to our rights in the sense that others have a moral obligation to respect them.

rule-fetishism – The objection made against rule utilitarianism that it prescribes following the rules even when doing so does not maximise happiness.

sanction, external – Other people's disapproval or punishment for a wrong action (Mill).

sanction, internal – The sense of duty, the pain that we feel when we do not do what we believe we morally should do (Mill).

sceptical – Not easily convinced, or having doubts or reservations. (Not to be confused with scepticism.)

scepticism – The view that our usual justifications for claiming our beliefs amount to knowledge are inadequate, so we do not in fact have knowledge.

secondary principles – In Mill, moral 'rules of thumb' that, if followed, generally produce happiness, e.g. 'tell the truth'. Mill argues that we have learned secondary principles through human history, through trial and error.

self-evident – A proposition that can be known just by rational reflection on that proposition.

sensation – Our experience of objects outside the mind, perceived through the senses. An experience of this kind.

sentience – The ability to feel, perceive, or experience subjectively, in particular the capacity to experience pleasure and pain.

simulated killing – The dramatisation of killing within a fictional context, e.g. in video games, films and plays. It is not merely the description of a killing, as in a novel, but a fictional enactment of killing that the audience or gamer can see and hear.

solipsism – The theory that only oneself, one's mind, exists. There are no other minds and no mind-independent physical objects.

soul – In Aristotle, that part of the person that relates to mind and life. According to Aristotle, the soul has three parts – a part relating to being alive, a part characterised by desires and emotions that are responsive to reason, and rational intellect.

sound A deductive argument is sound if it is valid with true premises

speciesism – Unfair discrimination on the basis of what species something belongs to.

subjective – That which depends upon the subject. In ethics, it relates to the personal or individual, especially where it is supposed to be an arbitrary expression of preference. In philosophy of mind, it relates to the first-personal, conscious experience of the subject.

subjectivism – The theory that moral judgements assert or report approval or disapproval; e.g. 'Murder is wrong' means 'Most people disapprove of murder'.

subjectivism, speaker – The theory that moral judgements assert the approval or disapproval of the speaker; e.g. 'Murder is wrong' means 'I disapprove of murder'. Therefore, whether a moral judgement is true or false depends on the attitudes of the speaker.

substance – Something that does not depend on another thing in order to exist, which possesses properties and persists through changes.

sufficient condition – One proposition is a sufficient condition for another when the first cannot be true while the second is false. For example, being a dog is sufficient for being an animal, because something can't be a dog without also being an animal.

super-spartans – People (or creatures) in Putnam's thought experiment who so completely disapprove of showing pain that all pain behaviour has been suppressed, and they no longer have any disposition to demonstrate pain in their behaviour. The thought experiment is presented as an objection to behaviourism.

supervenience – A relation between two types of property. Properties of type *A* supervene on properties of type *B* just in case any two things that are exactly alike in their *B* properties cannot have different *A* properties; e.g. aesthetic properties supervene on physical properties if two paintings that have identical physical properties cannot have different aesthetic properties.

synthetic – A proposition that is not analytic, but true or false depending on how the world is.

theoretical reason – Reasons and reasoning concerned with what we can't change and what is true.

true – A proposition is true if things are as it states; e.g. the proposition 'The grass is green' is true if the grass is green, and otherwise it is false.

type identity theory – The theory that mental properties are identical (ontologically reducible) to physical properties. Mind-brain type identity theory claims that mental properties are identical to physical properties of the brain.

unanalysable – Not subject to analysis.

unconscious – A mental state is unconscious if the subject is not aware of having that mental state.

union theory – The claim that the 'human body', body and soul together, can be considered as a substance in its own right, a substance created from the union of body and soul (Descartes).

universalise – To apply to everything/everyone.

unsound – A deductive argument is unsound if it is either invalid or has at least one false premise.

utilitarianism – The theory that only happiness is good, and the right act (or rule) is that act (or rule) that maximises happiness.

utilitarianism, act – The theory that only happiness is good, and the right act is that act that maximises happiness. Hedonist act utilitarianism understands happiness in terms of the balance of pleasure over pain.

utilitarianism, preference – The theory that we should maximise happiness, which is understood not in terms of pleasure and pain, but in terms of the satisfaction of people's preferences.

utilitarianism, rule – The theory that only happiness is good, and the right act is that act that complies with those rules which, if everybody followed them, would lead to the greatest happiness (compared to any other set of rules).

utility – The property of an object or action in virtue of which it tends to produce happiness.

utility, principle of – The defining principle of act utilitarianism: 'that principle which approves or disapproves of every action whatsoever, according to the tendency which it appears to have to augment or diminish the happiness of the party whose interest is in question' (Bentham).

valid – If the premises are true, then the conclusion must be true. In this case, we say that the conclusion is entailed by the premises. Only deductive arguments can be valid.

value judgement – A judgement regarding whether something is good or bad in some way.

value theory – Any theory about what is good; e.g. a utilitarian value theory claims that only happiness is good.

verification principle – The principle that all meaningful claims are either analytic or empirically verifiable. A statement is analytic if it is true or false just in virtue of the meanings of the words. A statement is empirically verifiable if empirical evidence would go towards establishing that the statement is true or false.

vice – A trait that is morally bad. Aristotle argues that vices are dispositions to feel or choose not in the mean, but either too much or too little.

virtue – A trait that enables us to live a morally good life. Aristotle argues that virtues are traits in accordance with reason, and distinguishes virtues of intellect and virtues of character.

virtue ethics – The normative theory that starts from the question of what it is to be a good person, then derives an account of morally right action as what a good person would do. Aristotle argues that a good person has the virtues, which enable them to achieve eudaimonia.

voluntary – According to Aristotle, we act voluntarily when we act as we choose. We know what we are doing, and we bring it about ourselves.

will, good – In Kant, the good will is the will that is motivated by duty, which Kant argues means that it chooses in accordance with reason. It is the only thing that is morally good without qualification.

will, the – Our ability to make choices and decisions. Our wills are rational, that is we can make choices on the basis of reasons.

zombie argument – The argument for property dualism that if consciousness were identical to some physical (functional) properties, it would not be metaphysically possible for something to have that physical (functional) property without consciousness. However, 1) philosophical zombies are conceivable, and so 2) metaphysically possible. Therefore, 3) consciousness is non-physical and physicalism is false.

zombie, philosophical – An exact physical duplicate of a person, existing in another possible world, but without any phenomenal consciousness. It therefore has identical physical properties to the person (and identical functional properties, if these are fixed by physical properties), but different mental properties.

INDEX BY
SYLLABUS CONTENT

Philosophy of Mind

The mind-body problem: What is the relationship between the mental and the physical?

INDEX

Page numbers in *italics* refer to figures.